NORTH FACE OF SOHO

CLIVE JAMES
NORTH FACE OF SOHO

UNRELIABLE MEMOIRS VOLUME IV

PICADOR

First published 2006 by Picador
an imprint of Pan Macmillan Ltd
Pan Macmillan, 20 New Wharf Road, London N1 9RR
Basingstoke and Oxford
Associated companies throughout the world
www.panmacmillan.com

ISBN-13: 978-0-330-48128-1
ISBN-10: 0-330-48128-2

3 5 7 9 8 6 4 2

A CIP catalogue record for this book is available from
the British Library.

Typeset by SetSystems Ltd, Saffron Walden, Essex
Printed and bound in Great Britain by
Mackays of Chatham plc, Chatham, Kent

Visit **www.panmacmillan.com** to read more about all our books and to buy
them. You will also find features, author interviews and news of any author
events, and you can sign up for e-newsletters so that you're always first to hear
about our new releases.

To Norman North,
with thanks

I wonder if I am not yet talking again about myself. Shall I be incapable, to the end, of lying on any other subject?

Samuel Beckett, *Malone Dies*

An old man remembers everything, but then he forgets that he told you.

Montaigne

Introduction

A few days ago, in the beautiful city of Valletta, I was helping a two-year-old boy paint a portrait of his equally beautiful mother. As I vainly tried to demonstrate the concept of using only a small amount of pigment on a fingertip at any one time so as not to get blobs and streaks of red paint all over himself, her, me and the floor, I remembered something. I remembered the afternoon when, at the more advanced age of five, I was helping my own mother make extra Christmas decorations. There were some manufactured ones left over from before the war but they needed supplementing. We made paper chains. The interlocked loops of coloured paper were fixed by a blob of paste, applied with the fingertip. She left me unsupervised for about ten minutes and I got paste all over the kitchen table, her chair, my chair and the chest of drawers. When she saw the mess she leaned suddenly against the tall cupboard that held the crockery. I heard some of it rattle. But I remember all that now only because the texture of the red paint on the same finger reminded me of the white paste. The dizzy speed with which the echo of a sense memory kills time continues to astound me. I suppose that one day, not very far away now, I will die of the astonishment. If this fourth volume of my memoirs sometimes plunges back into even earlier times than those evoked in the first, it will be because the beginning of my life draws nearer as the end approaches. Perhaps they are the same thing: a loop of paper that will finally be closed by the paste of silence. Stand by for other perceptions equally cheerful.

Soon it will be forty years since my undergraduate career at

Cambridge finished and my professional career began. It feels like forty minutes. Quite commonly, people who make a splash at university aren't much heard of afterwards. For a long while I looked like being one of those. Overnight success took more time than even I can credit, but when the dust of the effort finally cleared it turned out that I had hit two different kinds of jackpot. I managed to become a small part of the British media landscape, and also to be thought of as part of the Australian expatriate movement. Such a movement never really existed – most of us who sailed away did so in order to foster our individuality, not to gang up – but the myth was a tenacious media standby, and especially in the Australian press, whose more enthusiastic practitioners, a bit hazy in their sense of history, are capable of putting Dame Nellie Melba and Cate Blanchett in the same kitchen, for a cup of tea and a chat. The post-war Australian expatriates were looked at with suspicion by their countrymen early on. Later, they got too much favour. My own view is that, of those among us who sailed away to England in the early 1960s, those who soon sailed back again did best. This especially applied to the theatre. In earlier times, a long and powerfully talented line of Australian theatre people stretching from Robert Helpmann to Michael Blakemore had done the right thing by staying abroad, because there would have been no chance of creating a context for themselves had they gone home: Australia just wasn't ready for them. But in my generation, people like Ken Horler and John Bell – to name only two among the many I knew personally from my days at the University of Sydney – did better for themselves, and far better for Australia, by leaving English theatre to the English and going home to start an Australian equivalent, which they were able to energize by what they had learned, and especially by what they had learned to avoid. Nevertheless, with all that said, I still think that the stay-away Australian expatriates have made a respectable contribution. Posterity will have its own ideas about who ranks where. Sometimes, when I am reading one of the marvellous little novels of

Madeleine St John, part of whose genius was for avoiding all publicity, I think that the only lasting fame for any of the rest of us will reside in the fact that we once knew her. But one way or another we have all made a fist out of our time away. The nice thing is that the Australian literate public largely agrees. So for my share, and more than my fair share, I have lately had their appreciation to add to the welcome I always enjoyed in Britain.

This wealth of acceptance has been a lot better for me than rejection, on which I would have lacked the moral strength to thrive: so it would be churlish to deny that I did all right. On any objective scale, I can't complain of having been ignored. But it's the subjective scale that can haunt your waking hours, and even deprive you of sleep. On that scale, I have only seldom, and never for long, felt that I got my career into focus after I was obliged to make my way in the wider world. I made a living, and I made my name: made it, indeed, in several different fields, first in Grub Street and Fleet Street and then later in television, which only those who just go on and smile would ever call Easy Street. But I still don't feel that I have Made It, in the sense of knowing exactly what I'm doing and being comfortably certain of doing it again tomorrow. This might seem an absurd claim, a counter-claim, a claim to lack of claims. When I look along the shelves of my books and videos, even I can see that I have been quite busy: whatever the quality or lack of it, there is certainly quantity. And there is my name over and over, usually written vertically, so that I have to turn my head sideways. The crick in my neck is evidence that I am not shy about doing so. An onlooker might say that I have Done Something. But I'm still not entirely sure about the 'something', and not at all sure about the 'I'. If I were, I might be less thrilled about seeing my name in print. Ten letters in two groups of five, it still rings a bell of reassurance for its owner. But why does he need the reassurance?

Who is this character? Perhaps, as I write these introductory paragraphs, I am in a trough of uncertainty, but I have a suspicion that the troughs join up in a long line which has always been there and will continue to the end. Always a keen student of other people's careers, I reached the conclusion quite early on that there is often a discrepancy between the outer show of confidence and the inner assurance. In my own case, I think, the discrepancy is about as large as it can be without a fragmentation of the personality. There might even be a possibility that my personality remains intact only because it never fully formed: an embryo disguised as a golf ball. Whatever the truth of that, I can assure the prospective reader of this volume of my unreliable memoirs that the same principle applies as applied in its predecessors: a principle to rely on. Each of those volumes was an instalment in a serial confession of how I learned to do the right thing only by doing all the wrong things first. This volume will work the same way. The only essential difference between my professional career and its long period of preparation is that I have benefited from the opportunity to blunder on a larger scale. The main benefit has been in immediacy. When I told a story in the school playground and my audience didn't laugh, I could always blame them for not getting it. When I screwed up on television with ten million people watching, even I got the message straight away. To be fair to myself, if I had got nothing right at all, there would be no achievements to show, whether good or bad. But the reader can be sure that this will be no parade of self-satisfaction. It may, of course, have self-aggrandisement as an underlying motive, just as conceit almost always underlies a show of modesty. But the conviction that informed the first three volumes will be even stronger in the fourth. The conviction is that, though the desire to entertain is not to be despised – if only because the capacity to do so is rare – it rates quite low on the scale of social importance, a long way behind dentistry and not necessarily very far above the ability to clean lavatories. Most of those who make a living from it are very lucky, and I am even luckier than most.

The best an entertainer can hope to do, when writing about what he does (and nobody asks him to do that: he decides to do it for his own reasons), is to be instructive. As a consequence, this book will be full of homilies about what to avoid. These homilies are sincerely meant, but with one proviso, which I hope is a saving grace: if I myself had avoided all these things, I would probably have got nothing done at all, because the errors were essential. There is hope, therefore, that young people contemplating a career in the arts and the media might find guidance here, and those less young people who have run into difficulties might find consolation. For readers leading normal, and therefore more important, lives, there might also be the consolation of any evidence I can offer that those of us who have been granted a disproportionate ability to express ourselves may not always have the best selves to express. I hope to get all the way to my grave without committing any major crimes, but within the limits of the law there are very few human failings that I have not embodied. Some of them I can't specify without embarrassing other people. But if I did not embarrass myself, this book would be too far short of the truth to repay reading, or to be worth writing. The older I get, the more time I spend wishing I had done things differently. I wish that could be different, but there you go. Or rather there I go, still trying to clean up the paste with the good lace doily from the chest of drawers.

– London, 2006

1. BLOTTO VOCE

In the closing pages of the last volume, I got married. The ceremony marked a rare outbreak of normality in my life. It was symbolized by my personal appearance. I was clean-shaven and had a hairstyle in reasonably close touch with my head. I was wearing a rather good-looking dark grey suit specially purchased in Carnaby Street. For a suit whose price had not been high, it was elegantly understated. There was no excess cloth, and at that time there was still no excess flesh. The suit's drainpipe trousers had drainpipe legs inside them. Posing in front of a full-length mirror, I had to say that the suit was well chosen. Usually people who choose their clothes badly never realize it when, once in a while, they accidentally choose well, but my powers of self-assessment must have been blessed by the felicity of the event. I vowed to look after the suit for a long time, in keeping with its manifest high quality.

After the next occasion on which I wore the suit, I noticed that the cloth had frayed on both legs in the area of the upper thigh. After only a single further occasion, the crotch fell out. Perhaps some mental projection of deep-seated anxiety about my fitness for marriage had eroded the fabric. Freud probably had a word for it: *Trausertraumerei*. But a more likely explanation, I slowly realized, was that the suit had been cheap because its materials were flimsy. By dead of night I dumped the suit into a garbage bin, and it was never mentioned again. I'm not sure that Oxfam, in the late sixties, was as yet accepting discarded clothes, but even if it had been, I still would have hesitated. The thought of some poor tramp wandering around with his balls hanging out would have put me off.

After that sartorial hang-up, as it were, I rejoined the main-stream, in the sense that even when dressed for best I looked like a comedy of errors. If, during the course of this volume, I refer to my mode of dress as if I looked outstanding, the reader should grasp in advance that standing out, in that period, was unusually hard to do. We all looked like that: or, at any rate, the younger men did. The Duke of Edinburgh never dressed to get attention. If he didn't, why did we? It is a very hard thing to evoke an era. Pick up a notebook and a pen right now, stick your head outside the door, and command yourself to evoke your era. How, for example, would you capture your era's atmosphere of squalid menace in public places? Where would you start? As the sixties slithered into the seventies, the streets were still almost incompa-rably safer than they are now, but the post-punk body-piercing hoodies of today look diffident, almost self-effacing, compared to the young males of that time. With few exceptions, we all looked more amazing than anything seen in Britain since the Restoration brought in horned wigs and stilt heels. You can't really tell from photographs how universal the bizarrerie actually was, to the extent that nobody noticed because everybody was doing it. In a photograph there are usually too few people to give you the full impression, or else, if there are a lot of them, they are too far away. At the time, the unaided human eye, with its depth of field greater than any camera, could see, all the way to the horizon, nothing except young men dressed to make a cat laugh.

After the disintegration of the dark grey suit I joined them in their frenzy of bad judgement. The fashion dictated long and thick sideboards to the hair, as if the head had been joined on each side by a small sofa deprived of its covering and tilted on end. There were velvet jackets, flared trousers, zip-sided boots. With the possible exception of the hair, all these elements entailed a lavish use of industrially generated materials, especially polyester. It meant that the average young male was carrying a greater proportion of artificial fabrics than an airliner's interior. My own range of shirts included an electric-blue number that

made the unwary spectator's eyes ache. As its proud owner, I
thought it looked particularly good with a cravat. The cravats I
favoured were of a chemically derived material printed with a
paisley pattern. I had a whole rack of them. Today, my wife still
remembers them as 'those cravatty things you used to wear', so
obviously they were not without impact. They sometimes delivered electric shocks when touched, but so did almost everything
else I was wearing. When charged up by walking for long enough
on the right kind of nylon carpet, I could be seen in the dark,
but that still didn't mean that I looked unusual. Almost everyone
under forty looked something like that. It was the style of the
time. Some of you may remember it. But those who don't will
have to imagine it. For them, the best way I can think of to sum
it up is that it was an era of dandies without taste.

So much for the evocation of the exterior life. The interior
life, as always, was more personal. Even I could see that the first
consequence of getting married was the necessity to earn a living.
Until then I had lived like a student, which is another way of
saying that I had lived like a bum. Such a way of life would still
be my first choice today. When life gets too much for me I have
no trouble identifying with the man dressed in a pile of rags as
he sleeps in another pile of rags somewhere against the concrete
wall of a London underpass, just far enough away from a puddle
of his own urine. Wedded to paucity, he rarely makes the mistake
of trying to improve matters. His Tokyo equivalent is a construction worker from out of town who sets up home in a Shinjuku
underpass, sleeping in a spanking new cardboard carton and
sharing a small stove with his fellows. Somehow or other they all
have access to washing facilities and even a laundry. They sit
around in circles passing bottles of Kirin beer while they tell
stories. They are as neat and cute as a blossom party of junior
accountants in Ueno Park. Too much effort. I prefer my London
guy, but if I succeeded in getting him to swap lives I suppose I
would soon spoil the borrowed simplicity. The rags around my
feet would be an invitation to do a soft-shoe shuffle. I would

write a monologue, pull a crowd, get an agent, and it would all begin again.

After I was married, though, it was still in question just how I would pull the crowd. I was reluctant to let go of Footlights and for a while it looked as if I might not have to. Had I been wise, I would have quit while I was behind. It was a body blow when the most successful Footlights revue I ever directed for the Edinburgh Fringe was not allowed into London. Professional companies would have envied some of the notices we got. There were several commercial bids to bring the show in, but the actors' union, Equity, had recently imposed a strict embargo on university students being granted union membership merely because they'd had their names in the Sunday papers. As some of my cast members were keen to remind me in later years, I chose the worst possible tactics when arguing our case with the Equity tribunal. I pleaded eloquently that all of us were really only on our way to serious professions and wouldn't be in this theatrical caper very long: therefore it would not be a case of denying food to more deserving mouths. My own mouth deserved a kicking. What I should have said, of course, was that we were all dead serious about the theatre and ready to wear greasepaint until the grave. For some of us it would have been true. It might even have been true for me. Even today, I feel most at my ease when I go on stage. Even though I don't do much more than read out my own stuff from memory, the discipline of turning up, waiting around and going on gets me away from everything like nothing else. And some of our people really had a gift to explore. They weren't just looking for a bolt-hole. But my advocacy sank them. Advocacy, if it is to work, usually has to be on behalf of a cause that would win anyway. Our cause was probably lost from the start. But it soon became clear to me that I had done the opposite of helping to win it.

The guilt was compounded by the further realization that it hadn't become clear soon enough. While the case was being heard, over the course of several days at Equity's Lubyanka-like headquarters somewhere in the back-blocks of Bayswater, the revue in question, with its West End offers pending the decision, was running on an edge-of-town semi-amateur basis at Hampstead Theatre Club. In those days, Hampstead Theatre Club was a glorified pre-fab perched in a car park near Swiss Cottage tube station. Boiling with frustration at the uncertainty of our status, I did not adjust easily to the unglamorous conditions. At Lauriston Hall in Edinburgh we had played to a packed house every night, with extra houses twice a week to take the overflow. Edward Heath had attended. Either soon to be, or having recently been, Prime Minister, he came backstage afterwards to declare himself amused. ('Amusing,' he said, shifting his shoulders to indicate amusement. 'Some of the turns were really quite amusing.') At Hampstead the really quite amusing turns went down well enough, but perhaps I should not have included myself in the cast. The second-string critics who came were sufficiently tolerant, but there were none of the hosannas employed by the first-string critics in Edinburgh. Most of the tickets sold but there weren't all that many tickets to sell. From the tiny stage, I couldn't help noticing that the auditorium was not much bigger, and therefore contained few people even when full. The people, in their turn, could not help noticing that the fourth chap from the left, the one with the Australian accent, looked as if he wanted to be somewhere else. The Equity frustration came to a head when I was finally told that not only would the show be denied access to a West End theatre, but that I, if I really wanted that Equity card, would have to change my name, because somewhere in the North of England there was already a Clive James playing tuba for a novelty act called the Wurzel Bashers. Eventually the latter stricture was rescinded, but it was definitely no go on the larger issue. Towards the end of our Hampstead run, I had to tell the cast that the dream was cancelled. Without exception, they took it better than I would have done if one of them had been telling me.

To console myself before we went on stage that night, I had a few beers, and then a few more. The first one would have been fatal, because I can't take even a single drink before I perform or else the words grow fur. Having had half a dozen drinks at least, I went on to stuff up my opening monologue so thoroughly that not even I knew what I was talking about. There is no more dreadful feeling for an actor than a tongue out of control. Some drunken actors can live with it, but only because they feel even more dreadful when they are sober. More dreadful than the feelings of the drunken actor, however, are the feelings of the audience. Not long before that evening, I was in the audience for a late-night symposium at the Traverse Theatre in Edinburgh. The symposium had a panel of featured guests who included Patrick Wymark, at that time a star of stage and screen. A talented actor with a splendidly grating voice, Wymark was well known in the profession for his ability to go on stage at night after spending all day drinking one pint of milk after the other, each pint with a double brandy mixed into it. Most of the legendary British thespian drunks – Trevor Howard, Hugh Griffith, Richard Harris, Richard Burton – tried to make a point of waiting until the show was over before they hit the sauce. There were always a few, however, who were already loaded before the curtain went up, and who went out to the pub to refuel between scenes. In the West End, where some of the theatres are tightly packed together, there were several cases of a pissed actor going on at the right time but in the wrong play. Apparently Wymark was not of their number. A coping toper, he could stay upright in roughly the same spot and say the words in roughly the right order, always with the gravelled timbre that drew all ears to him. But his elocution was the giveaway. In the crowded Traverse on the night in question, speaking on the topic of the social role of the artist, he told an endless story about how people had once laughed at the man working up there in the Sistine ceiling. The audience was held breathless for twenty minutes until he got to his punch line. 'And that man . . . was Leonardo da Vinci.' Even then, nobody laughed. They knew he meant Michelangelo, but they had been reduced long before to the depths of horror and pity by the way the words were coming out. 'Sistine ceiling' came out as 'sixteen Ealing'. I knew exactly what was happening in his mouth: his tongue had turned to a sea cucumber. You would have thought that I would have got the message about myself then. Actually the penny didn't drop until years afterwards, and on that night in the Hampstead Portakabin it simply never occurred to me that life was possible without getting fairly regularly plastered. I was only a few minutes into the evening, however, before I abandoned the notion that a performance was possible. The audience had realized already, and so had my cast. Since I had previously threatened to fire any of them who turned up drunk, I had no choice except to call a meeting after the show and fire myself. Nobody protested.

I should have left it at that, because the evidence was in. Looking after other people, in the sense of working on their behalf, was not my strength. I could work with other people – a glib tongue and a desire to be liked would always easily combine to ensure that – but I couldn't look after them. Really this should have been no surprise, because there is nothing more rare in show business than the talent to handle talent. But I lacked it to a lethal degree. My sense of responsibility was insufficiently developed. I found it hard enough to look after myself. The comparative sloth of my years in the forgiving cloisters had been replaced by a frantic multiple activity of which the theatrical venture was only a part. Except when I was at home in Cambridge, I had no time even to eat properly. So I ate improperly, especially when I was writing. Much of the writing was done in London, in a tiny room high upstairs in a Swiss Cottage house full of my Footlights contemporaries: the very ones I had made a show of leading to universal success, and who had generously decided not to lynch me when I failed to do so. It was a big night when some of us ate together at the Angus Steak House, where the halved tomatoes were notched like automotive spare parts to indicate luxury. More often I stoked myself with fast food while hitting my second-hand Underwood typewriter. I forget now what the fast food was. I was already forgetting it while I ate it. I don't think Kentucky Fried Chicken had yet invaded Britain. It was probably the British version of fried chicken, which had the same relation to the later American version as the Wimpey hamburger had to a McDonald's Big Mac: i.e. it was begging to be superseded by anything that at least tasted of something, if only of sugar. I vaguely remember sinking my teeth through a crust of crumbs to encounter a rubbery nothingness while I hunted and pecked at the typewriter keyboard with my free hand. The warm tissue having been washed down with even warmer beer, I went back to touch-typing flat out as I transcribed the handwritten draft of my latest article or book review. When dawn came I ate cornflakes.

2. GATEWAY TO GRUB STREET

I was in demand for that kind of work, partly because I had established a fatal reputation for getting it done at short notice. Now that I was theoretically free to pursue a career as a journalist, Nicholas Tomalin of the *New Statesman* would send the kind of book my way that nobody in his right mind wanted to review. Could I do it by Tuesday? When I proved that I could, Richard Boston of *New Society* recognized a potentially useful candidate for reviewing another book in the same doomed category. Could I do it by Thursday? The evidence rapidly mounted that there was a new contender in town for the post that every literary editor needs to fill: the trick pony who can work like a draught-horse. In no time at all I had become a denizen of Grub Street. Naive American scholars sometimes go looking for Grub Street but it has never existed as a geographical entity. Grub Street is a collection of periodicals that deal with literature and of newspapers that have literary pages: a collection of those, and of the people who edit and write for them. Grub Street is like a small Great Rift whose favoured watering holes continually change position. In the times of Swift and Dr Johnson, the gathering places were the coffee houses. In my time, they were the pubs.

In Fleet Street, the pubs were near the newspaper offices: sometimes so near that the drinkers could feel the vibration through the pub wall when the presses started rolling. But a Grub Street pub could be anywhere. The most important one was in Soho. At the Pillars of Hercules in Greek Street, Ian Hamilton set up the drinks while he persuaded me that I was ideal not only

for providing unpaid articles for his acerbic little magazine, the
Review, but paid articles for the *Times Literary Supplement*, of
which, wearing his other hat, he was the literary editor. Though
the contributor would see his name on a cheque, he would not
see it in print: the *TLS* still had its policy of anonymity in those
days. The news, however, would soon get around if you could
review a whole batch of new poetry books in a thousand words
and make the piece more readable than most of the poetry. That
part of the challenge wasn't hard: then as now, most of the poets
were writing verse only because they lacked the sense of structure
to write prose. The hard part was to get it done. The work would
have been easier if Hamilton had been less scrupulous. Right
there in the Pillars, he would blue-pencil your copy while
everybody else watched. Everybody else included his other reviewers and sometimes, hovering dangerously at the rim of the scrum,
one or two of the poets whose slim collections I was presuming
to hose on. Hamilton wouldn't kill a phrase on that account –
often he would show you how to sharpen it up – but he never let
a slack sentence go by. It was invaluable training. I should say
at this point that I was smart enough at the start to spot the
difference between curatorial editing and blithering interference.
Curatorial editing I could benefit from, and to some extent still
need even today. My style, if such it is, works by packing stuff in,
not stretching it out, and there is always a danger of trying to say
too much at once. Hamilton, his own prose a model of sardonic
limpidity, had an unerring eye for the slipshod simile and the
overblown cadence. The final work of excision and emendation
done, I would go on drinking with Hamilton and the others,
buying my round along with them but getting drunk much faster.
At that time, the Pillars still closed after lunch along with all the
other pubs, but there was an upstairs club a few doors away
where the diehards would go on soaking until the Pillars opened
again for the evening. My light head and frequent visits to the
toilet soon became notorious.

The light head would prove to be my salvation in the long

run, but I was foolish enough to be ashamed of it then. If I didn't exactly fall over, I certainly bounced off the walls on the way to and from the can. Come to think of it, I did fall over, but not exactly. I fell in various directions. Once, on the last train to Cambridge, I slept all the way to King's Lynn and had to come back in a cab, at a price that the payment for the latest piece would barely cover. My wife, who had been unaware that I had ambitions to recreate the leading role in *The Lost Weekend*, was not impressed. But the piece was safe in Hamilton's pocket. Now suitably shaved, sponged free of its indignities, it would go into the *TLS*, where I would read it with satisfaction. Other people must have done so too, because the invitations kept on coming in. Charles Monteith, the revered senior editor at Faber and Faber, sent a written request that I should call by to see him. I had better sense than to think he was after my poetry, which I knew he had never seen, because a collection of it had been sitting for more than a year on the desk of an editor in a less illustrious house – one of those editors who are so enthusiastic about your manuscript that they will do everything they can to persuade the board of directors to take a chance on an unknown, and are reasonably certain that the green light will be given just as soon as there is an economic upturn on Wall Street and a general withdrawal of Soviet troops from Eastern Europe. (Such skills for procrastination should be cherished, because they have saved many a young poet from sending out to die a slim volume that was never fit to live.)

But I could scarcely hope that Monteith was after a whole book of prose. He was, however. Sweetly pretending not to be disconcerted by my appearance – I still suffered from the delusion that a satinized polyester tie looked good with a fake Viyella shirt – he suggested that I might consider taking a crack at writing a biography of Louis MacNeice, a Faber poet, not long dead, whose reputation was already cooling in the shadow of W. H. Auden's. In one of my poetry reviews for the *TLS* I had invoked Mac-Neice's precision of imagery while condemning some respectable windbag's vagueness in the same department, and Monteith had been so taken with my choice of paragon that he foresaw a whole monograph fuelled by the same admiration. Foolishly, so did I, although I already knew that I was short of spare time, and that none could be made available at the price Monteith was suggesting. There were no big advances in those days, but the sum he proposed was more like a retreat. I would practically be paying him. The offer, however, was too flattering to resist. So I didn't resist, and thus once again made a commitment that I couldn't come through on without removing other commitments from my diary. The offence was made easier by the fact that I had no diary. For several years I had kept a journal and would go on keeping it for several more, but a journal dealt with the past. A pocket diary for noting future appointments had never been part of my equipment. I was still under the impression that I could trust my memory. How I had ever got that impression was a bit of a mystery, because there had been evidence since my schooldays that any fixture more than a few hours ahead would disappear from my mind, especially if it entailed an inconvenience. People with that characteristic should above all get out of the habit of saying 'yes' when asked to do things. Since I invariably said 'yes' in order not to disappoint, I was effectively mixing malleability and fecklessness – binary ingredients of a powerful explosive. Eventually I was to learn some measure of reliability, but only because the explosions accounted for so many innocent civilians. For the moment, however, the MacNeice biography joined the list of things I would do soon, once I had dealt with the things I must do that day, because they had been promised for yesterday.

Perhaps the idea that I might have a place in literary life had scrambled my brains. Scrambled them even further, one might say. Back there in Sydney I had loved my evenings in the King's Cross coffee bars. One of them was called the Platypus Room, Another, Vadim's, was named after its New Australian proprietor, a poet manqué. It should hardly need saying that he was no relation to the Vadim who, back in faraway Europe, would not long later seduce a long line of beautiful young actresses culminating in Jane Fonda. Our Vadim had shortened his name from something like Vadimskapolonskiewicz. Still working hard on his English, Vadim would strain valiantly through the hiss of his Gaggia espresso machine to eavesdrop on the conversation of the half-dozen literary journalists who counted as the city's intelligentsia in those torpid days before the arts boom. But as the new boy I was sitting below the salt, and forced to do much more listening than talking. The London scene was on a grander scale, and although I was a new boy all over again, I could do all the talking that my tongue allowed before the beer and wine numbed it at the root. The Pillars of Hercules was the focal point, but there was a glittering periphery. At Nicholas Tomalin's house in Gloucester Crescent, Camden Town, there were big guns to be seen. The area had already been colonized by some of the people who would make it as famous as the old Bloomsbury. Alan Bennett and Jonathan Miller were both in the area, working on the new careers that would take them beyond *Beyond the Fringe*. But the chief attraction was Nick himself. Unplaceable in the usual social order, he had limitless charm to go with the three qualities that he had notoriously said every journalist must have: a certain amount of literary ability, a plausible manner and rat-like cunning. His charm was the first quality you noticed. Well-connected and beautifully constructed young women fell for him, which made life all too interesting for his wife Claire, but obviously she adored him. It was impossible not to. Young men felt the same, partly because he was a good enough listener to make them feel that they might be almost as fascinating as he was. When you spoke, he had a way of looking sideways and downwards through his heavy black horn-rims that convinced you he was doing so only in order to favour his good ear, not wanting to miss a word. (In fact he had a bad neck, but typically he turned the affliction into a point of style.) What impressed me most was the way he had come to terms with what he saw as his lack of originality. If he couldn't make things up, like a proper writer, he would find the best way of writing down what happened in front of him: corporate fraud, voyages by mad yachtsmen, wars. Actually, of course, this determination was deeply original in itself: he was in at the start of what would later be called the New Journalism. Headed by his famous piece about Vietnam – he had made the notes for it while looking sideways through the open doorway of an American gunship at vibrating miles of jungle stiff with armed men in black pyjamas – his collection of journalism still reads well today, and at the time he seemed to some of us the embodiment of a possibility: permanent work in an ephemeral medium.

Not that he didn't enjoy the passing moment for itself. I made myself popular with him one summer evening when I got the time wrong and turned up an hour early for dinner, bearing a dubious gift of two bottles of cheap white wine. It wasn't Piat d'Or, which hadn't yet established itself as the would-be sophisticate's cut-price bring-along. It was some variety of Lieb-fraumuck with a label full of gothic lettering. Nick saluted it gravely as if it were a prize-winning vintage that I had bank-rupted myself buying, and actually smiled when I put both bottles in the garden fountain to cool. 'In Australia,' I explained, 'we used to sink the stuff in the river and fish it out later. Sometimes we got more bottles out than we put in.' He guessed immediately that there had been a party in the same spot previously. He loved the idea and told people the story later on as something typical of me, the boy from the bush who could quote Wittgenstein. He was creating a role for me, as he did for everyone. As roles go it wasn't bad, and when I realized I was stuck with it anyway I tried to make the most of it. Not fitting a category: it was a category in itself. Nick, a dazzling example, was one of the first to see it as a social trend. The media meritocracy would be the next Estab-lishment. Most of this I would figure out only gradually and much later, but I could tell straight away that Nick was something new. It meant a lot to me that he seemed to think the same of me. He nodded assent, instead of snorting, when I declared that a literary career could and should draw sustenance from involvement in show business and popular music. My theory that any genre could be practised as if it were a field of poetry prompted some gratifyingly thoughtful puffs on one of his black cigarillos – from both of us, because I was helping myself to his supply. When we fished the first bottle of wine out of the fountain he even pretended to enjoy it as much as the champagne that Claire had been serving us previously, although at the first sniff of my stuff he must have known that it was battery acid. The man who broke the story on the European junk-wine scandal wasn't going to be fooled by a label that looked like a page from Martin Luther's Bible. But he didn't even flinch.

Yes, the literary world should have been enough. But I had already noticed that it was full of casualties. Even the byline journalists tended to die poor after the salary was switched off, and among the poets it had never been switched on. There would have been good reason to think that a more abundant source of income might be worth seeking. Hitting four deadlines a week, I was earning scraps that added up to a pittance. Also I often had to stay up all night to hit them. When I tried doing that at home in Cambridge, the woman who had already realized she had married a maniac was kept awake by a typewriter yammering away like a rivet-gun. (It's one of the ways that a writer's life has most profoundly changed since computers came in: writing used to be noisy.) In Swiss Cottage the noise didn't matter so much: I was just somebody having one essay crisis after another. But I could tell by the way the boys brought me the occasional cup of instant coffee that I must have looked like someone on the road to ruin. It was instinct, however, and not reason, that led me to keep the theatre thing going. Like a broken love affair, it was begging to be fixed. Eventually, I was convinced, the songs I was still writing with Pete Atkin – in his own small room off the next landing, he was bent over his guitar as he set my latest lyrics about death and destruction – would make us both big money.

Meanwhile, the current Footlights bunch, still at university, asked me to direct their Edinburgh Fringe revue on a professional basis.

I did the job with passable results, but there was a bigger job on the near horizon. Still the dominant powers on the Fringe, Oxford and Cambridge teamed up to mount a production of *A Midsummer Night's Dream* to tour the American colleges. The play was to be directed by a professional, Richard Cottrell, who was excellently qualified: his production of *Richard II* had been a huge hit at the official Edinburgh Festival and later in the West End, with the young Ian McKellen making himself famous in the leading role. I had seen McKellen's performance in Edinburgh and been suitably stunned by how his Olivier-like athleticism was compounded with the ability to float a line like Gielgud. I had seen both Gielgud and Olivier on stage earlier in the decade, but they were in separate plays. McKellen was both of them, made young again and sharing the same body. Cottrell had provided McKellen with a set in which the furiously posturing boy monarch could descend from the upper levels in a series of leaps to appear suddenly on the forestage like Spiderman arriving in a gay nightclub. The future knight was still years away from outing himself but his performance left little room for doubt, just as the production left nothing to be desired for its verve and grace. If all theatre had been like that I would have spent much less time at the movies. The Oxbridge bunch were lucky to have Cottrell aboard, because in normal circumstances a director of his calibre is wasting his time marshalling the limited abilities of amateur players: it's like hiring Michael Schumacher to drive a minicab. But Cottrell, still manfully scraping the money together for his Prospect Theatre Company, agreed to take the Shakespeare job on. Since the Oxbridge bunch also wanted an accompanying revue as part of the tour package, however, he specified that he would direct that only if he could be provided with an assistant director, script doctor and dogsbody – someone steeped in the revue business, about which, he was honest enough to say, he knew little and cared less. Headed by my old friend Jonathan

James-Moore, the Oxbridge people approached me. I wasn't hard to find. The whole deal was going to be rehearsed in the Footlights clubroom in Cambridge and I just happened to be standing outside in Petty Cury with my hands in my pockets, whistling. The fee was more than I could earn by reviewing ten different hopeless books so I said yes, reflecting that if I reviewed the books anyway, I would double my money.

Scarcely an hour of rehearsal had elapsed before I realized I should have said no. Though Cottrell was large-hearted in saying that humour was not his forte, he was also definite about having the last word. There was a power struggle right from the jump, which I was bound to lose. I didn't much like his ideas, he positively hated mine, and the helpless cast were caught in the middle. For them, what should have been a joyous conjunction of two separate undergraduate revue traditions turned into the most miserable time of their young lives. Most of them were also in the *Dream* production and the difference must have been startling. Cottrell did a dazzling job with the play. In an opalized Athenian forest designed by Hugh Durrant, he deployed the student actors almost as if they could act. The cruel truth about university actors is that although they often go far, they rarely do so as actors, mainly because even the most gifted of them have chewed up essential years that they should have spent at RADA learning to speak, move, and fence, or even at Raymond's Revue Bar learning to stand in a spotlight as if they belonged there. Apart from Julie Covington, who made an enchanting Peas-blossom, only a few of the *Dream* cast went any distance in the professional theatre later on. Some showed up on the small screen, but as presenters and newsreaders rather than actors. (An exception was Mark Wing-Davey, who eventually grew an extra head to play Zaphod Beeblebrox in *The Hitchhiker's Guide to the Galaxy*.) Michael Wood, now one of the most prominent historians on television, deployed a fine leg as Oberon but would spend his future in tight jeans, not loose tights. Others became bank managers and academics. But they all had bliss to look back on. In that pixillated forest, they had been touched with a magic wand.

When they came back to the Footlights clubroom to rehearse the revue, the contrast was brutal. At the end of the rehearsal period, the revue was ready to go on in the Arts Theatre, and it even held the stage, but the critic for *Varsity* was not the only member of the audience to note that the cast looked as if they had all spent the previous week beside the death-bed of a loved one. Three nights into the run, after three days of re-rehearsing some of the sketches in the attempt to make them funnier than a mock execution, I spat the dummy. One of my last memories of the resulting shambles was of James-Moore, called Jo-Jo for short, throwing up in the washbasin of his dressing room. Many years later he was a power in the land, in charge of comedy at BBC radio, but I bet he didn't forget how his own lunch looked when it was staring back at him. It took me almost as long to get a realistic perspective on what I had helped to let them all in for. Too much of it had been my fault, a truth that I wasn't then equipped to consider. When it mattered, I had spent too much time taking umbrage and not enough taking pains. I should have settled for my subordinate position, done what was required, and, above all, put the welfare of the troops first. But I threw a tantrum instead, right there in the Green Room of the Arts Theatre, the gift of John Maynard Keynes to civilization. I foamed at the mouth and smashed my fist into a mirror. It was the right target, I now realize, because the true culprit was on the other side of it. The fact of the matter was that I was nowhere near as good at dreaming up sketch material for an ensemble as I had thought. My only reliable ability was to dream up material for myself. The tantrum was an excellent example. Bugsy Siegel would have recognized a gifted imitator, especially when I climaxed the routine by threatening to kill Cottrell. Luckily he was elsewhere at the time, but when he heard about it he put his foot down. Either I was removed from the picture or else the American expedition would not include him. Since the production of the *Dream* was what really mattered, Jo-Jo and his colleagues had no choice. Effectively, I had already fired myself, by converting my tantrum into a nervous breakdown.

I owe my wife the courtesy of leaving her as a background figure in this book, along with my daughters, who would combine to lynch me if I went into detail about their virtues. All three women in my immediate family are united in the belief that private life and publicity are incompatible, and I agree with them. One of the dire consequences of the celebrity culture is that this belief has come to seem perverse. So much for the celebrity culture. But I can say this much: over the next two weeks, my wife got into training for her first baby. I went to bed and stayed there, like Stalin when he got the news that the German army had invaded his country after all, despite his express instructions that it should not. The shock of reality had reduced me to immobility. I sent long groans towards the ceiling while doing nothing except grow a beard. I groaned louder at the effort of turning my pillow to the dry side. I could just about make it to the bathroom on my own. Otherwise I didn't go anywhere, even to the kitchen, where the refrigerator lived which in normal circumstances I could never pass without stopping to look in. But I was indifferent to what I put in my mouth. As long as it was a cigarette, it would do. As soon as I could raise myself on one elbow, I got busy starting small fires in the bedding. For a while I couldn't even read a book: the first time since World War II that I had been unable to do so. The *Guardian* took me all day and the *Observer* took me all Sunday. Finally, from one of these papers, I noticed that there was a four-volume collection of George Orwell's journalism due to come out. I must have grunted at the right moment, because the complete set was brought to me as a gift, ready-wrapped in its jackets of deep Socialist red.

From the first page of the first volume, I was on the road to recovery. Many years and a much bigger bank balance later, at just the moment when she felt the walls of the house were closing in, I bought my wife a 3 Series BMW, and suddenly she was out

and about like Emma Peel in *The Avengers*. It was only a partial
return for the perfect timing of that Orwell set. Most of the essays
I knew by heart already, but here they were in the weekly context
of his indefatigable toil. Here was the proof that it took effort to
write plain prose but, if you could do so, the results might have
the effect of poetry. A simple-seeming sentence could have a
cadence to remember. There was also the matter of Orwell's
political sagacity. He could be batty on the side issues but on
the big issue he was right. It was the main reason he remained
relevant, because those who had been wrong had spread a
pervasive influence, and some of them remained in business even
in old age. While sticking his head above the parapet in the
Spanish Civil War, Orwell had said that it wasn't enough to be
against the Nazis, you had to be anti-totalitarian, which meant
being against the Communists as well. The latter part of this
message continued, after more than thirty years, to be a pill hard
to swallow for thinkers on the Left. Even if they were ready to
accept that Stalin had been conducting a massacre of the inno-
cents, they still wanted to believe that there might be a vegetarian
version of absolute state control. Orwell's central belief was thus
enduringly unpopular even among those who shared his detesta-
tion of capitalism.

No fan of capitalism myself – there had to be something easier
than working for a living – I had nevertheless been raised in a
house where that central belief of his didn't need to be stated, so
when I read him at length it was like a long verification of what
I had always felt. My mother and father, both of them prime
examples of the suffering proletariat in the 1930s, would have left
me a Communist heritage if they had thought that there was
anything to it. My father's copy of Bellamy's anti-capitalist classic
Looking Backward was in the hall cupboard waiting for him while
I was growing up. He never came home to read it again, but its
presence was a reminder of his championship of workers' rights.
Yet my mother assured me that he would have detested the idea
of giving the state unbridled power over the individual. Like my

father, she had met the Communists before the war when she was working on the production lines, and remembered their tone of voice. But when Prime Minister Menzies staged a referendum to outlaw the Australian Communist Party in 1952, my mother, during a single dinner of beef, potatoes and cabbage, gave me a political education that has lasted me a lifetime. She told me how she had voted in the referendum earlier that day. She had voted against Ming's move to outlaw the Commos. (In Australia, Menzies was Ming and the Communists were the Commos for linguistic reasons we won't go into here.) She thought the state should not be given so much power to repress opinion, even if the opinion was wrong. That, she said, was the principle my father had fought and died for, and the only reason why his death had meaning.

Still in short pants at the time, I struggled to comprehend, but I was so fascinated that I ate the cabbage. Since the right not to eat cabbage was one of my own most jealously guarded political tenets, this was a large concession, and a tribute to my mother's quiet passion. At the time she spoke, George Orwell had only recently published *Nineteen Eighty-Four*, so my mother was up there with him at the heroic forefront of intellectual adventure. I remembered that moment as I lay there in my smouldering bed, at last telling myself to get up, get out and get going. Above all, the collection was a persuasive demonstration that periodical journalism could be built to last. Much of it had been written for publications of restricted, or no, circulation. I resolved to despise no outlet that would print my work. I also resolved that the theatre thing could still be fixed, if I could just avoid my previous mistakes. With these two resolutions – the first questionable, the second suicidal – firmly in mind, I cast the charred coverlet aside and went back to work. If my wife could go on functioning as a conscientious don while nursing her mental wreck of a husband, the least I could do was persevere. One thing I can tell myself, from this distance, is that I was always pretty good at getting busy again after a catastrophe. I was just bad at realizing that being too busy had got me into the catastrophe in the first place. Hamlet had said it to the corpse of Polonius: 'You find that to be too busy is some danger.' But Polonius wasn't listening, and it turned out that Hamlet wasn't either.

The idea that periodical journalism could be built to last was never likely to apply to *Oz* magazine, but I deluded myself into believing that it could. A new wave of hungry young Australians had hit London, having the immediate effect of making the young Australians who were already there feel that they were getting old. Perhaps that was what drove me to say yes when they asked me to contribute to *Oz*. Richard Neville, the editor, was dedicated to the belief that Play Power could transform politics. I never believed that – I had enough trouble believing in his hairstyle, which he had apparently copied from Bette Davis in *All About Eve* – but I did think that this new emphasis on youth, music, soft drugs and less uptight sex might have an ameliorating effect. My stance, however, was to contend that all thoughts of actual revolution were the kind of nonsense that could be excused only through ignorance. I soon found that Neville and his confrères had plenty of ignorance to excuse themselves with. They seemed to have read nothing but *The Naked Lunch*. But my counter-revolutionary polemics were printed anyway. Usually they were printed in white type on pink paper with an oil-slick overlay, so that there was no danger of the stoned readership actually reading them. Germaine Greer's contributions, by contrast, were printed clearly, often accompanied by startling photographs of their author. One photograph showed her with her legs behind her neck: an advanced position even for a swami. In a previous volume of this memoir I gave Germaine the name Romaine Rand, on the principle that if I was going to attribute foul language to her it would be ungentlemanly to use her real name. In the context of *Oz*, however, it would be ungentlemanly not to, because by that time her habitual and madly entertaining subversion of linguistic decorum stood fully revealed as a big component in a political attitude that was transforming the speech of the country. I admired her boldness, and still do. Though she sometimes seemed to harbour the impression that ordinary young women could liberate themselves if they became groupies for the sort of American rock band that looked like a pack of rapists in search of a fresh victim, she was undoubtedly striking a blow for freedom from stifling conventions. Her weak point, obvious to everyone but her, lay in her generous confidence that women, if they could be released from bondage, would all prove to be as creative as she was. Girls, you don't have to spend all that time wiping the poop off the back end of your child. Hand it to your grandmother while you write a symphony.

My own view, that the shattered conventions might one day become objects of nostalgia, sounded pretty stifling even to me. Luckily nobody could decipher what I said. There was quite a lot of it, and later on I was careful to reprint none of it. Long before the *Oz* trial at the Old Bailey I had tacitly opted out of the Youth Culture: my hair, as it were, didn't make the cut. Even when accompanied by the soft music and pastel swirling smoke of psychedelia, propaganda for a consensus of individual rebellion had no appeal to me as a genre, and it was clear that protesting against rebellion in a rebel publication made no sense at all. When Richard Neville and Felix Dennis appeared in court, it became obvious that this was a mere prelude to their appearance on television. In other words, the trial was a stage: a stage on the road to institutionalized protest, although nobody at the time could guess that Dennis would one day be a publishing tycoon on the scale of Robert Maxwell and Conrad Black, if a bit more careful with the petty cash. The judge, confidently mistaken as English judges so often are, informed the court that Dennis was clearly of low intelligence. The judge lived long enough to find out that he had been wrong by many millions of pounds, but it was never a case of two worlds colliding. It was the one world, hiccuping on a breath of fresh air. The fresh air turned stale later on, as it was bound to do. Social changes get nowhere if they are not needed, and when they succeed they soon cease to be news.

Not having been really a part of it, I was easily out of it, with no regrets except that I no longer had an excuse to gaze at the angelic face of a young woman who rejoiced in the name of Caroline Coon. She was billed as the scene's expert on drugs. I suppose she knew a lot about them for the usual reason – that she had taken a lot of them – but although I had no idea of what she was talking about I loved watching her delicately sculpted mouth when she spoke. No expert about clothing at that stage (certainly I was no expert about my own) I could nevertheless not help noticing that her revolutionary outfits were composed of cashmere, suede and silk, all hanging on the lissom figure of a debutante by Boldini. She was draped across two-page spreads in the colour supplements and the glossies almost as often as Germaine herself. Here was a revolution for men to die for, but strictly in the spiritual sense.

Orwell had said that you could see what was wrong with radical movements by the kind of women they attracted. By that test, the Youth Culture had a lot right with it. There was a great deal of glamour about. One of the spin-offs of *Oz* was an Alternative Newspaper called *Ink*. If anything, it had even less editorial judgement than *Oz* – the itinerant Australian journalist Leon Selkirk even managed to sell it his standard scoop about the missing uranium, a story that he had been carrying around for years – but the office was full of Biba-clad lovelies from the shires wondering what keys to press down on the electric typewriters, which like all the other equipment had been bought instead of hired, thus guaranteeing almost immediate insolvency. None of the girls was more beautiful than the paper's cultural editor Sonny Mehta, whom I had known at Cambridge. (In *May Week Was in June* he appeared as Buddy Rajgupta, so that I might cover myself against the potentially libellous implication that he had done no academic work at all.) Though Sonny was much more focused as a newspaper executive than he had been as a student, the newspaper was doomed from its inception. But I enjoyed his company as always, and later on the connection was to pay off in a big way, as I shall relate.

At the time, my whole activity as a writer for the Alternative Press added up to a no-no. Lest I doubt the fact, Karl Miller of the *Listener* pointed it out firmly, although 'no-no' was not the kind of word he would have used, either then or later. A classically educated Scot, a rebel angel from Dr Leavis's dour Empyrean who gave the impression that he had found its irascible ruler insufficiently serious, Miller had no time for the light-minded. The *Listener* was still the printed voice of the BBC as Lord Reith had once conceived it, and Karl Miller was universally acknowledged as a worthy successor to the paper's founding editor, J. R. Ackerley. Miller had all of Ackerley's discerning attributes and none of the frailties. Miller, you could be sure, would never have a love affair with an Alsatian dog. (Ackerley did, and recorded his emotional commitment in a book whose sex passages take some swallowing even today.) Such was Miller's reputation that to be invited to write for the *Listener* was a sure mark that one had arrived at the point where Grub Street's reeking gutters turned to polished marble. I entered his office at Langham Place with roughly the feelings I had once had when asked to call on the Deputy Headmaster of Sydney Technical High School. Miller had a similar reputation for severity, although it was fairly certain that he did not keep a cane. But at our first meeting he throttled back on the withering impatience and confined himself to the laconically sarcastic. He made it clear that my involvement in the Alternative Press was a waste of what in a less barbaric context might almost be mistaken for a certain effectiveness in English prose. According to him, there was no such thing as an Alternative Press, there was only the press, which was either responsible or frivolous; just as there was no such thing as Experimental Writing, there was only writing, which was either competent or worthless. Some of what I had done for the *New Statesman* and the *TLS*, he told me, could have been

regarded as competent if I had curbed my exuberance. He had
already printed a radio script that I had written and delivered for
Philip French, BBC radio's omniscient arts editor. (The *Listener*
was contractually obliged to reprint a quota of radio scripts,
an obligation which sometimes weighed heavily on Miller, but he
carried out the duty faithfully, quietly subtracting the solecisms
from some eminent professor's would-be mandarin diction.) My
script, however, he informed me, had been marred by deficiencies
of coherence, which he had felt bound to expunge. I could have
said that there had been plenty of other deficiencies of coherence
that Philip French had expunged first, but for once I had the
sense to shut up and take the compliment. Proof that it had
actually been a compliment, even if expressed like a rebuke from
Captain Bligh, was provided by what happened next. Miller
asked me to try my hand at writing a critical column about radio
once every four weeks. There were three other radio critics, he
explained, who each also wrote a column every four weeks, the
collective thus furnishing the paper with a column every week.
While he searched my face for signs that I might not have grasped
the mathematics, he further explained that the work had to be
taken seriously: I must listen to all the important programmes,
analyse their qualities, point out their shortcomings, and provide
a concise summary with no deficiencies of coherence. It was easy
to assume that the critic I was replacing had died under the
strain.

Philip French had a gentler nature but he was just as punishing on the facts and details, partly because he already knew more
about everything than all his contributors put together. Both men
were models of conscientiousness, and I could have learned even
more from them had I been as good as they were at concentrating
on one task at a time. As it happened, I added their deadlines to
all my other deadlines, in the belief, sadly correct, that a freelance
writer could accumulate his piece-rate fees into a living wage only
by working until the night sky paled. My typewriter squeaked
as it ran out of oil, its ribbons frayed as they ran out of ink. In

order to make marks through a dry ribbon I hit the keys extra hard, thus gradually turning the platen into a cylindrical Rosetta Stone. (How many people are left who know what a platen was? And where did all the typewriters go? In what vast quarry do their rusting frames coagulate?) In those days you needed carbon paper to keep a copy and I can remember choking back a sob when I discovered that I had put the carbon paper in backwards. (In childhood, I had sobbed the same way when I spilled flavoured milk into my box of crayons. In the course of time we cry for different things, but we always cry the same way.) As the plaintive note of these parentheses suggests, there was thus some reason for dreaming of a big score that might get me into another financial league, and so buy me some time to finish that book on Louis MacNeice, or anyway start it.

The big score didn't have to be in the theatre. It could be in the movies. Part of the Oxford and Cambridge Theatre Company disaster had included a proposed film of the revue, to be supervised by me because Richard Cottrell, after taking one look at its proposed financial backers, sensibly didn't want to know. The backers, or at any rate the people who said they could get the backing, were a bunch of grandees from the Lord's Taverners, one of those charitable outfits that do good things for the deprived. Along with a sprinkling of dedicated and efficient philanthropists, such organizations are invariably haunted by a shambling squad of superannuated burghers in continual search of some pointless event that they can have meetings about. It was just such a bunch of blazer-wearing drones who had put them-selves in charge of immortalizing our revue on celluloid, thus to benefit their charity from the inevitable worldwide sales. Nor-mally they would have had no means of advancing such a project beyond the stage of getting all of You Young People (that was us) packed together in the Arts Theatre boardroom so that we could admire their Hush Puppies and silk cravats while they told us how diverting Prince Philip had been at their last annual lunch. But they had an ace in the hole: one of their new members was

Jack Cardiff, the veteran cinematographer who had been responsible for the look of *Black Narcissus* and *The Red Shoes*. Perhaps
in the hope of meeting Prince Philip at next year's lunch, Cardiff
had come over from Switzerland to make the film. Success was
therefore assured.

3. ENTER THE MASTER SWORDSMAN

What happened next is quickly told: almost nothing. After half a century of dealing with maniacs in the film industry, Cardiff soon spotted that his fellow Lord's Taverners had no idea of what they were doing. A stocky, self-contained figure in his suede car-coat and leather hat, he was not one for any signs of disgust beyond a wry smile and a raised eyebrow, but only the men who had got him into this balls-up could have believed that he was pleased. The camera they had hired for him had last been used by Alfred Hitchcock before he left England in the early 1930s. It took three men to lift it. Nobody had realized that extra lighting would be necessary to film the show inside the Arts Theatre. The Lord's Taverner who went off to hire some lights never returned. The only revue number we got on film was an exterior action sequence. Our jocund young company ran spontaneously along the riverbank above the Mill while a couple of us fell spontaneously out of a punt. Off to one side, a thin crowd of townspeople spontaneously yelled abuse. We would have been better off capturing the abuse, but the camera needed a locomotive to turn it around. Despite the manifest hopelessness of all this, Cardiff was sufficiently impressed with my verbal skills to suggest that I might help him with a screenplay he had in mind. His long career as a cinematographer, for which he had won two Oscars and countless other awards, had eventually earned him the chance to become a director. His first film as a director, *Sons and Lovers*, had done well: the script had already been prepared before he was brought on board, but he was justly praised for the thoughtful handling of actors in a lustrous black and white ambience. More recently, however, and from a script developed by his own hand, he had directed *Girl on a Motorcycle*, which had been a critical disaster. With a big heart to go with his experienced head, Cardiff was slow to blame the young Marian Faithfull's difficulties in staying on the motorcycle, although the filming had taken place during a phase of her life when she was having difficulties staying on a chair. The phrase he used was 'script problems'. Eager to avoid script problems on his next project, he thought I might be just the man he needed.

How wrong he was, but there was no reason for either of us to think that at first. I, indeed, had every reason to believe my family finances would be transformed. For the preliminary script conference in Switzerland, not only would an airline ticket be provided each way, but I would live at Cardiff's expense for a whole week as a guest in his apartment, with an actual fee on top of the largesse. Beyond that, there was the prospect of big rewards when the film went into production. My wife, who could have been an agent in another incarnation, pointed out that the initial fee specified amounted to no more than what I would have received for journalism in the same period, and that I was meanwhile, with winter coming on, running myself ragged hitting the deadlines before I caught the plane. I assured her that my ashen face would benefit from the change of air. The implication that Switzerland had a Caribbean climate was not very convincing, but I was already in the sky and heading for Zurich.

Cardiff picked me up at the airport in his big Mercedes and drove me to his apartment in Vevey, at that time a redoubt for film-world tax exiles: Charlie Chaplin lived on the same hill. Cardiff's apartment occupied the top floor of an ordinary-looking block of offices. Opening out endlessly from a modest vestibule, the apartment was lavishly appointed, especially when it came to works of art. The first thing you saw when you entered the enormous living room was an astonishing pair of Renoirs. One of them, however, though sensitive and accomplished, was patently an exact copy of the other, and not by Renoir himself. When Cardiff challenged me to pick the original, I instantly realized that he himself had painted the copy. Diplomatically, or perhaps hypocritically, I pretended to dither, but finally I summoned up enough integrity to point to the right one. Only mildly disappointed, he explained to me that painting had become the passion of his later years. From further evidence – every Monet and Corot had its eerie twin – I deduced that his concept of painting consisted entirely of reproducing masterpieces already in existence. For him, the look of the thing was everything. Individual expression was not among his motives. He had left school at the age of about twelve and had been hard at work with practicalities ever since. As one of the first colour cinematographers – in the days when the Technicolor camera exposed three separate strips of film and was as big as a small house – he had personally helped to invent the look of modern movies. Female film stars had fallen in love with him one after the other because he not only had the guardianship of their beauty, he was a nice bloke: a cuddly bear in a business populated mainly by hyenas. But he was an interpretative artist, not a creative one, and the raw stuff of movies – the script – depended on a mystery he was not equipped to penetrate. An intelligent man denied a higher education, he was a living demonstration, by negative example, of what a higher education can do even for the stupid: put them at their ease with the written word. For Jack (I should call him by his first name from now on, because he became dear to me and I owe him a lot) the written word was magic. Sometimes the written word is indeed magic, but only when written by a magician. Jack thought words, any words, had a numinous status simply because they had been written down. Reverently he produced for me the cherished book that he wanted to adapt. Stuck together with Sellotape after being read to pieces, it was *The Jade of Destiny*, by Jeffrey Farnol.

I dimly recognized Farnol's name as one that could be seen on the spines of countless historical novels helping to form the warped and dusty stock of the kind of second-hand bookshop that will soon go out of business. But Jack handled the faded volume as if it were a sacred text. He asked me to open it at any page and recite to him a random sample of what he called 'the marvellous dialogue'. The first word of the marvellous dialogue I saw was 'Gadzooks!' It was followed by the sentence: 'Fain would I not face thy glittering blade, Dinwiddie.' I told Jack, with some truth, that I was not enough of an actor to do it justice. So Jack took over. He didn't need the text to tell the story. Over the course of the next hour, he acted the story out. It concerned Dinwiddie, master swordsman of Elizabethan England, a sort of anglicized version of d'Artagnan, with overtones of the Scarlet Pimpernel. Jack moved energetically about, repelling with his phantom rapier a swarm of attackers. As he did so, he described what the camera would see: the close-ups of Dinwiddie's face, the dolly shots as his opponents were driven backward to the balcony and fell into the garden, the ecstatic cry of Lady Rosalind Wedgwood Fitzcastle ('Touché, Dinwiddie, for it is my heart, too, that you have pierced') as she swooned into his arms. It was obvious that Jack had the whole visual aspect of the thing already worked out. What he needed, he said, in order to persuade Richard Burton to play Dinwiddie, was a ten-page treatment that would outline the story while including plenty of the marvellous dialogue. I thought my heart was already in my boots, but actually it must have been only at about the level of my knees, because I felt it sink further when I began to suspect that Jack thought Jeffrey Farnol had not been an over-productive early twentieth-century hack, but an actual Elizabethan writer. (I should hasten to say that I could have been wrong about what Jack thought. He was not without knowledge of the period. After all, his opinion that Shakespeare's plays had been written by Queen Elizabeth herself had no lack of learned endorsement, although the scholars who supported that thesis tended to gibber and run in small circles when aroused.)

I could do the actual writing, Jack told me, when I got back to England. While I was there in Vevey he wanted me to come along and visit various people who might be interested in having a stake in the movie or even appearing in it. Next day we went to visit the one-time leading man Brian Aherne, who lived about a hundred yards away in a magnificent house full of art and books. At his place, the Monets and Gaugins appeared one at a time. Possessed of features so finely chiselled that he appeared to be in profile even when viewed from front on, Aherne was very well preserved. Wealth can do that for you. In the Hollywood of the late 1930s and early 1940s he had put most of his large salary into citrus groves, some of which turned out to have oil under them, and his share of the take had never stopped flowing, because he put the earnings into downtown real estate on the principle that one day there would be no such thing as cheap land in Los Angeles. There had never been such a thing as cheap land beside Lake Geneva, but he could afford the tab. I had read *The Jade of Destiny* during the night and was able to supply some of the storyline verbally while Jack, employing me as full-time commentator and occasional stand-in for the minor roles, showed Aherne how the sword fights worked and what Dinwiddie looked like when swirling his cape. I was surprised that Aherne seemed quite interested. Then, during a pause, I noticed, because of its unusually vivid green and white jacket, that one of the books on his well-stocked shelves was Julian Maclaren-Ross's recently published *Memoirs of the Forties*. A literary drifter who lived on reviewing books, writing for radio and taking small advances for projects never completed and rarely even begun, Maclaren-Ross, though a notorious bore in real life, had yet wielded a gift for evoking his era in pungent vignettes. I told Aherne, because I thought he might not know, that my friend Charles Osborne, working at the time for the *London Magazine*, had extracted the book's manuscript from Maclaren-Ross by advancing him, after the delivery of each chapter, enough to live on while he wrote the next. Instantly the panic in Aherne's eyes told me that he not only did not know this, he knew nothing about the book at all, or about any other book on his crowded shelves. They had all been supplied by a sophisticated dealership as an extension of the facade that began with his brushed silver hair and strangely perfect teeth. I have to say, though, that his manners were immaculate. A long friendship with Jack was not enough to account for his failure to pick up the phone and have the both of us arrested. He even waved goodbye as we backed away up the drive, still thrusting and parrying as we faded into the distance.

It went on like that for several days: a total fantasy. We visited old stars whom I had thought dead, and after being with them for a while I realized I had been right. They had time available because nothing else was going on. I suppose that in Los Angeles the same sort of thing happens, only worse, because everybody involved is still on this side of the hill, with real money at stake. Our evenings, however, were the real education, and I still recall them with gratitude. Jack was going through a rough patch in his marriage at the time, and tended towards melancholy. To suit the mood, he played me his cherished collection of Shirley Bassey records while he told me stories of old Hollywood. He was fascinating about why it was ten times harder to light a beautiful woman's face in colour than in black and white. There weren't many of the great beauties that he hadn't seen through his viewfinder. He didn't talk out of school. It was from other sources that I later learned how Ava Gardner, Marilyn Monroe, Leslie Caron and Sophia Loren had all adored him. But I needed no secondary source to tell me how he had adored them. He spoke of them all with a respect verging on reverence, even when he was telling me how difficult some of them could be. He was the cameraman on *The Prince and the Showgirl*, by which time Marilyn Monroe was becoming harder to handle than plutonium. But he called her ill, not insane, and it was easy to deduce that she must have found his fond patience a valuable refuge. (Jack told me something about Marilyn Monroe and Arthur Miller that I have never seen written anywhere: according to her, it was at Miller's insistence that she wore those low-cut dresses to the premieres – the playwright wanted to show off his prize.)

Without giving anything away, Jack said that there was always an emotional relationship between the actress and the cameraman, even if they didn't sleep together. It was like a troubled patient falling for her psychiatrist. When I asked him whether it was because the power was in his hands to make her look lovely or otherwise, he said it wasn't just that: it was the intimacy. The cameraman can see a long way into her face. He can tell from the whites of her eyes whether she is having a period. And she knows he can tell. It was clear that he was grateful for his wealth of experience, and I was grateful for the way he told me of it. The way he spoke about those women was a lesson for me. He had seen them subjected to punishing regimes of dominance and rejection, and on their behalf he had hated every minute of it. He pronounced the name of one famous director with something as close to loathing as his soft voice could manage. It was because the director had ruled his leading lady by playing on her fears. I could see then one of the key reasons why Jack had wanted to become a director himself: so that he would never again have to be complicit in such conduct. When I said that the life of an actress must be hard, he paused before saying: 'The life of any woman.' We rarely know, at the time, that a casual conversation will become something we will remember all our lives, but I think I knew right then that I wouldn't soon forget what he said. I wouldn't want to claim for myself too much sensitivity on the subject. Marriage to a beauty had done nothing to blind me to the beauty of all the women I had not married: far from it. If my libido could have been given a face, it would have been the face of Robbie Williams singing a one-night date at a training camp for cheerleaders. All the more reason, however, for registering how Jack's mellow flow of reminiscence got to me. I had rarely been impressed so much by a man's range and depth of sympathy. But the mature example he had set was daunting, because it demanded that I have sympathy for him as I grappled with the question of what on earth I was going to do about Dinwiddie, master swordsman of the Elizabethan age. At the airport, when I looked back to catch my trusting employer's eye, he dropped into a crouch and lunged. I clutched my stomach and threw him a reassuring smile.

Back in London, I drafted and typed a monthly radio column for the *Listener* that managed to disguise how at least a week's programmes had not been listened to. Then I went to ground in Cambridge while I plunged into the world of the master swords-man. There was a baby on the way whose future might partly depend on the viability of this project. Winter was setting in by now. In those days we were still living in the first-floor flat of an annexe to New Hall, my wife's college, so if I wanted to pace about I had to go downstairs into the garden. The garden wasn't big enough for the kind of pacing I needed to do, so I went down the lane, turned left and right, and paced along the Backs of the colleges. One of the courtyards of Trinity was especially good for pacing, because it looked like an appropriate setting for Dinwiddie in action. I could see him leaping through an archway in the cloisters, rapier extended.

What I couldn't do was hear him saying, 'Gadzooks!' I couldn't quote that marvellous dialogue. I knew just enough about how to write a screen treatment to know that it should have a few sample scenes in it, complete with speech. I could have learned a lot more about how to write a screen treatment, and it was arrogant of me not to do so. There were already several handbooks that laid out the principles. (Nowadays there are hundreds of such handbooks, because so many writers who have failed at writing screenplays have compensated by telling others how to succeed.) But even if I had known what I was doing, I would still not have known what to do about the speeches. I knew Jack wanted the marvellous dialogue put in, but I kept on finding ways of leaving it out. I gave paraphrases of speeches: a sure-fire formula for boredom. Today, a few decades too late, I realize that I missed an opportunity. I should have told Jack that the story was cobblers as a drama, but that it might have stood a chance as a lampoon. Like *The Crimson Pirate*, the tale of Dinwiddie could have gone for the laughs. Taking that course, I could have tried putting in a bit of marvellous dialogue of my own. Much later on, William Goldman wrote a screenplay for *The Princess Bride* that was a heady cocktail of camp sword-play and real romance. But I wasn't William Goldman, there was no studio executive to weigh the possibilities, and Jack, jealous owner of a dramatic project, would scarcely have been likely to see the virtues of converting it into a comedy. That, I would like to think, was the real reason why it didn't occur to me to try persuading him.

But I'm afraid the truth is that it just didn't occur to me. Deficient both in imagination and in candour, I had put myself, and my mentor along with me, in the worst possible position: a slave to the material, with no authority over its purpose, I was engaged in dressing the corpse of a dead duck. The text of Emperor Hirohito's surrender broadcast had been composed with a lighter heart. After about a fortnight's slow work, with little attention paid to the radio, I had a fistful of manuscript to be taken to London and put through the typewriter. There I paid no attention to the radio at all while I glumly typed away, fitfully embellishing paragraphs already stiff beyond redemption, each new page feeling like a fresh betrayal. I ended up with twenty typed quarto pages of pertly phrased dross. It sounded better than Jeffrey Farnol, but only because there was no 'Gadzooks!' It lacked, in other words, the very thing that Jack had most urgently specified. Or rather, it had that thing, but in other words. Instead of merely quoting Dinwiddie as saying 'Gadzooks!' I would say that he uttered a contemporary Elizabethan expletive. Try filming that. I mailed the finished treatment to Switzerland and heard nothing. A few weeks later Jack came to London on other business, met me in the bar of Claridge's and handed me two hundred pounds as a quitting fee. The two hundred was in ten-pound notes: the first such things I had ever handled more than one at a time. Jack looked more puzzled than angry. He said: 'You didn't put in any of the marvellous dialogue.'

4. EARLY STEPS IN OPPOSITE DIRECTIONS

So ended another fiasco, but I could tell myself that it was a sideshow compared with the interview I had only recently endured with Karl Miller at the *Listener* office. While wrestling day and night with the screen treatment of *The Jade of Destiny*, I had contrived to miss almost everything that mattered on radio, and this time the shortfall showed up unmistakably in my column. Miller carpeted me for a dressing-down that felt like the worst moment of my professional life to date. He did not look beautiful when he was angry. 'If you don't want to do this job properly then for God's sake move aside for someone who does.' Though he was immobile behind his desk, the effect of his words was of Rob Roy McGregor running towards me swinging the broadest of swords. None of Dinwiddie's rapier thrusts: at this rate my head would be coming right off. Caving in immediately, I offered feeble apologies along with a moist-eyed goodbye, backed out of his office and scuttled down the corridor, with the intention of drowning myself in the nearest pub. I had not reached the stairwell, however, before I was overtaken by Miller's secretary. As I recall the scene, she was holding one of her shoes in each hand, but I admit that my memory tends to dress the picture. Probably she just had the gift of sprinting in high heels. I was requested to return to Miller's office immediately. 'His bark,' she said, 'is far worse than his bite, you know.' No doubt Vlad the Impaler's secretary said the same about him.

Back on the carpet in Miller's sanctum, and blowing my nose on the Kleenex his secretary had supplied, I detected a slight shift in the editor's anger, although his words were no more mollifying than before. 'If you can't take a cross word, you shouldn't be doing this sort of thing.' He was right, of course. Even today I will do a lot to get out of a face-to-face disagreement. I could ascribe this debilitating characteristic to a desire to be perfect, and a concomitant disinclination to hear any evidence that I am not, but a simpler explanation could be moral cowardice. When I hear the characters in *The West Wing* reading each other the bad news about themselves in that typical American way, they strike me as being braver than samurai. Please, leave me to my illusions. Convicted of dereliction and touchiness in two rapidly succeeding rockets from the magisterial Miller, I was ready for the scrapheap. But then the message changed along with the mood. 'It's obvious that you don't listen to radio as a matter of course. I expect it's because you're too busy watching the television.' He called it 'the' television, as if it had only recently been invented. 'Perhaps,' he said tentatively, 'you might consider writing about that instead.' Instantly I saw a path into the clear. I did indeed watch television the way I smoked and drank. In Swiss Cottage I would channel-hop throughout the evening before I settled down to hit deadlines until dawn. In Cambridge there had been a television set in the Footlights clubroom and I had watched everything, even *Match of the Day*, until transmission shut down for the night and our barman went home. Only then would Atkin and I go up onto the little stage and start working on a new song. I was a pioneer couch potato. I had even been on television a few times: not as often as I had been on radio, but often enough to get the bug.

    In Australia, television had not arrived until the late 1950s. It made a primitive start. The first television news announcer prepared himself with two weeks in Hawaii to acquire an American accent. 'I'm Chuck Faulkner. Here is the nooze.' In that context of discovery, I had been a panellist on a dire discussion programme about the arts, chaired by a woman in a beret who billed herself as 'a Left Bank bohemian from way back'.

Actually she was from the outback, where she must have got a lot of practice at talking to herself. The few words I managed to get in uninterrupted were not very well chosen, but I was enchanted by the whole idea of my mouth moving in vision. In England, a couple of my Footlights shows had reached the small screen. My monologue was cut from one of them, to my petulant grief, and in the other I had not been a member of the cast, but in my role as director I was allowed to sit in the control gallery, where the technical palaver enchanted me. As in a hospital, it doesn't matter whether the person giving the orders is competent or not: the jargon sounds great. 'Ready with the close-up on camera two. Show me the wide shot, three.' It was like watching a movie about submarines. Torpedoes away! And now here I was in Karl's headquarters, being asked to register my interest. I knew instantly that I could bring an almost insane enthusiasm to the task. Knowing also that Miller might be afraid of exactly that, I managed to make my cry of assent sound suitably judicious. Incipient tears helped. I was well aware that I had barely escaped professional injury.

It was a reminder of how often, and how unjustifiably, I had been spared physical injury in my childhood. As I recorded in *Unreliable Memoirs*, it was the merest fluke I landed flat on my back, instead of at a damaging angle, after I jumped off the roof of an unfinished council house while dressed as the Flash of Lightning. There were other narrow squeaks that I failed to include in that book because I had forgotten them. For some reason they come back to me now with ever-increasing vividness. Many a time, after instructions from my mother that I should check the bottom of the muddy river before diving into it, I dived in without checking. It was the boy from the next street who became the quadriplegic, not me. When, late one evening, I rode my bicycle flat out over the bridge across the creek in the park – I was crouched for speed, my legs a blur – I had no idea that the park ranger had closed the bridge by putting a heavy wooden bar across it until next morning. I found out the hard way, but it could have been harder. The wooden bar hit me exactly in the centre of the forehead instead of converting my skull into a head-hunter's ornamental ashtray. I came to with nothing more serious than a bruised brain. Nor has the same capacity to flirt with doom been sufficiently absent from my adult years. Not long ago I stepped idly in front of a turning London bus whose Sikh driver must have had the reflexes of a fighter pilot. When I looked up and saw his turbaned head bent over the wheel I thought he was praying, until I noticed all the upstairs passengers gathered together at the front window. I should have prayed myself, giving thanks. Similarly, the number of times in my life when inattention should have led to professional ruin, or, more mercifully, to professional death, is too embarrassing to recount in full at this point. Enough to say that when I backed out of Miller's presence, like Anna from an audience with the King of Siam, I was all too conscious of having once again been spared. I had no idea, however, that it was a turning point in my career. You realize these things only later, and I am a bit impatient with memoirists who claim to have foreseen their destiny. I have never been able to foresee very far beyond tomorrow. Even when I lay a long plan, it is never in the expectation that I will live to see it fulfilled. I remember too well the day that the Flash of Lightning lay winded in the sandpit of the building site, breathlessly wondering if he dared to lift a finger.

Call no man happy if he has never been ordered to go home and watch television. Watching habitually yet writing only one column per month, I would have all too much to talk about, rather than, as with radio, all too little. Had I been doing nothing else, I might have choked on the abundance of stimulus, but luckily there were plenty of other things to distract me, quite apart from the ghost of Louis MacNeice, who would visit me during my afternoons of sleep to tell me that everyone else in his part of the underworld had a biography and they were all wondering what had happened to his. The ghost wore a trench coat, like Humphrey Bogart. Soon I would get started, but first there were all these articles and reviews to attend to, and a request from BBC radio to interview C. P Snow. It was kind of them to ask, because not long before I had turned up a week late to interview the ballet pundit Richard Buckle. The producer, normally a very decorous woman, had called me a stupid bastard. Tacitly conceding that she might have hit on the explanation, I bought my first pocket diary, into which C. P. Snow's name was duly entered, with the date, time and place. Humming with efficiency, I even made time to reacquaint myself with the dizzy excitement of one of Snow's novels. 'Part Two: A Decision is Taken. Chapter One: The Lighting of a Cigarette.' There was also a request from Stella Richman of London Weekend International that I should call in at her office off Savile Row. London Weekend Television, or LWT, was one of the two London franchises: I knew that much. But I had no idea of what London Weekend International did. The name sounded enticing, however, and the office was promisingly placed, opposite a tailoring firm called James & James. It turned out that Stella Richman, on behalf of the parent franchise, was charged with the discovery and development of new and unconventional talent. Elegantly groomed, she was very nice about not minding that I knew so little about her. Actually any aspiring television critic, no matter how green, should have known that she had a distinguished track record as a producer. She, on the other hand, knew a daunting amount about me. She had been keeping cuttings on our recent Footlights adventures and had even attended one of the few evenings at Hampstead Theatre Club when I had not looked like a rat packing its tiny bags on the deck of a sinking ship. She declared that my proved ability to marshal the talents of young writers and performers could prove valuable for television. Clearly she had either not heard of the Oxford and Cambridge Revue imbroglio or else chosen to ignore it. Even more cheering from the viewpoint of my twitching ego, she had decided that I myself might have 'presence' on screen. 'Nobody would call you handsome, but you have a face.' Though the same could have been said with equal justice to Lyndon Johnson, I still liked the sound of that.

I would have liked it even better if I could have appreciated the leap of imagination it must have taken on her part, because I had put on my best front for the visit – brown velvet jacket, fawn corduroy trousers, zipped boots, tartan tie with the paisley shirt and new beard quite recently washed – and thus could have been auditioning only for the kind of role that required the wearing of a rubber suit, like the Creature from the Black Lagoon. But Stella (first-name terms were mandatory from the jump) was engaged in the search for potential, which is almost always a matter of discounting the visible actuality. She wanted me to suggest some small programmes that I and my closest colleagues might like to do. I had two ideas right there on the spot. One was for a kind of miscellaneous arts programme done as a two-handed exchange between me and Russell Davies, widely acclaimed as the most gifted all-round writer–performer that the Footlights had hatched since World War II, or possibly since World War I. Stella said that I didn't have to sell him to her: she had seen him in action and thought he was the goods. 'Yes, we could do that with two cameras. Get the pilot right and we can make a set of six for a half-hour slot.' Clueless as I was, I had no inkling that Santa Claus had just run me over with his sleigh and left me buried under a heap of toys, so I forged on with another idea, meant to be more attractive because I wasn't asking to appear in it. How about a song show with Julie Covington and Pete Atkin singing the songs that Atkin and I had written? I explained that not all of our songs had been featured in the stage shows, but Stella was ahead of me. 'Yes, I've got the records that you made in Cambridge.' Before I had time to apologize for their low-budget production values – they had been made on a single tape with hung blankets to adjust the sound balance – she was saying: 'Three cameras. We could do half a dozen of those as well.' She proposed contracts for both shows, with another contract for an option on my further services. I had no agent at the time, but who haggles with the Fairy Godmother? I guessed that she would look after me well: a guess that was to prove correct. I have sometimes been wrong about a father figure, but at sizing up a mother figure I have been right almost every time. Qualified mother figures have the knack of getting you to eat the cabbage, if only by forbidding you to touch it. You can see it in their eyes: they see through to the boy and make a man of him. So there I was once again, happily committing myself to more work than I could possibly handle. But I was also committing myself to something like a salary. For a moment I wondered whether I should be bothering with literary journalism at all.

But only for a moment. Back downstairs in the street, I was already considering the possibility of plunging forward into the new dream without letting go of my previous gains. A double career, that was the ticket. James & James: it was up there on a sign. Though a chance at television stardom was too good to pass up, my instinct – for once functioning helpfully – told me that in show business I would never enjoy the precious freedom to be alone. I had already noticed that television worked like an army, with fifty people pushing paper for every soldier holding a rifle. In journalism, it was just me, the blank sheet of paper, and the cigarette dangling romantically from the lower lip. The attraction, I think, wasn't so much that nobody else could share the glory, as that nobody else could get hurt. In a solo activity I might be disappointed, but in a group effort I might be disappointing: a much more unsettling prospect. So back I went to the typewriter, first to knock out an outline for the programmes as Stella had requested, but then to review other people's programmes for my *Listener* column. I flattered myself that to be engaged in the first activity made me more of an expert on the second. Actually I was fooling myself. As yet I knew very little about the practicalities of making television, and it probably would have acted against me as a reviewer if I had known more. In any field of criticism, there is nothing more damaging than knowing a little bit about how the art you criticize actually gets made. If you don't know everything, it is better to know nothing. What you do have to know is how to register your response, and your first response should be naive, not sophisticated. Was I repelled by what I saw, or was I pleased? Was I interested or not? Was I interested in what was supposed to be interesting, or was I more interested in what was supposed to be trivial? It was a matter of judgement, but the judgement had to be emotional before it was intellectual. My first breakthrough came when I realized that the most fascinating thing about the supposedly realistic police series *Softly, Softly* was the unreal frequency with which the powerfully built Inspector Harry Hawkins (played by Norman Bowler) opened and closed doors. In any given episode, he would open or close every door in the police station. Sometimes he would open and close the same door in rapid succession. He would leave the room just so that he could open the door, close it behind him, open it again, and come back in. He gritted his powerfully built teeth while opening and closing doors, as if opening and closing doors were a feat not just of physical strength, but of mental concentration. I wrote all this down in my column, giving him the nickname Harry the Hawk.

Taking this approach, I found myself writing with a compulsive flow uninhibited even by the thought that Karl Miller might react as John Calvin would have done to a copy of *Playboy*. But I was having too much fun to stop writing, and I soon discovered, when I took the finished pieces to his office, that he was having too much fun to stop reading. I can't exactly say that he laughed aloud, but there were small rearrangements of his tight lips that were almost certainly the indication of a repressed smile, as the armour of some ancient Norse warrior might gleam within a glacier. No doubt there were calculations being made. He had three other television critics of unassailable solemnity. There was perhaps room for a fourth critic to wear a putty nose and a revolving bow tie. Meanwhile I was making calculations of my own. If I put in enough straight-faced stuff about the programmes that mattered, I could do some lampooning of the programmes that didn't. On the *Guardian*, the excellent Nancy Banks-Smith had been striking just such a balance for some time, so the approach was not without precedent. What was without precedent was my next breakthrough. I started writing about television phenomena that couldn't really be classified as programmes at all. Sports commentators, for example, were a rich source of absurdity that often had only to be quoted in order to uncover the remarkable. At Cambridge I had written a Footlights routine, brilliantly delivered by Jonathan James-Moore, about a sports commentator called Alexander Palace: one of the old school, with RAF moustache taking off vibrantly from his top lip and Olympic rings on his white crew-neck pullover. But now a new breed, harder to place by class origin yet even more patriotic, was colonizing the glass tube. David Coleman spoke in a new voice, almost in a new language. This new language was already highly developed, but nobody had yet made it a subject of study. There were social changes going on all over the screen, signalled by speech patterns, hairstyles, gestures. I tried to get some of that in. Miller, whose range of cultural reference was much wider than his strict education might have dictated (the man who printed some of Philip Larkin's poems for the first time had also been one of the first serious critics to write about John Lennon), clearly thought I was on to something. If he hadn't thought that, he would have lowered the boom right across my fingers. So I pushed on with the approach, even if the occasional reader's letter might complain that untamed colonials were destroying the last values of the old Empire. There were other letters that approved. More importantly, the editor didn't disapprove. When the piece was set up in galley, he would move his metal rule down the column line by line, still on the lookout for blemishes. Even at that late stage, a cherished sentence might be struck out. But most of what I had written stayed in place. Making him fight back a smile became a goal in life. The world was too much with him. Once when I entered his office he was in his chair but

holding an open umbrella, 'to ward off my troubles'. I was glad
to see that he lowered the umbrella somewhere during my second
paragraph.

   Though a fresh idea usually happens quite quickly, to make it
a reality invariably takes more time than we care to remember.
My *Listener* TV column felt its way forward month by month,
and there was no single occasion when I sat down and nutted out
exactly where I thought it should go next. For one thing, there
was too much else going on. Pete Atkin and I, still writing
songs, were beginning to entertain the idea that it might be
advantageous for him to make an album with a proper label so
that we could both become millionaires, but the plan rather
depended on a proper label having the same idea. Perhaps the
London Weekend song-show programmes would help with that.
But the two-man show with Russell Davies had to be done first,
and before I could start with my share of writing the pilot, I had
to clear my Grub Street deadlines. After an exhausting week of
work I had done so, but I was in no great shape when I shambled
into the London Weekend office to meet our executive producer,
David Reed. Russell Davies, who was leading the same kind of
life as I was but with possibly even less sense of ruthless efficiency,
looked as vague as I did. We were both late for the appointment
by several hours. David Reed, a small, dapper man who later
proved to have a kind nature, wasn't a bit kind that day, and I
can't blame him. In any branch of show business, there is nothing
quite so depressing as to be put in charge of young people intent
on blowing their opportunity. 'Don't,' he said quietly, 'waste my
time again.'

   From that moment I was careful not to miss an appointment
with anybody, and eventually timekeeping became a fetish.
Today, I would rather hire a helicopter than be five minutes late
for a speaking engagement – an expensive obsession, when the
speaking engagement is in the local bookshop – but that's to leap
ahead. On the day in question, Davies and I, suitably abashed,
pooled our talents along with our hangovers to come up with a

title and a format. The title we thought fitting was *Think Twice*: because there were two of us, you see, and we would be doing quite a lot of thinking. (Years later, Joan Bakewell, possibly having forgotten that I was in the show, told me she thought it was the most irritating single television programme she had ever seen, and that her irritation had begun when she heard its name.) We sketched out possible items about our interests: jazz, movies, out-of-the-way literature. Today it would be called a standard postmodern emphasis but it was unusual for the time. David Reed picked out the subjects he thought might suit the pilot and we were given a desk at which to write the actual scripts. This proved to be a lot harder than sketching the outlines. Several times, as we sat and worked, Stella Richman went by, smiling nicely at her unconventional new talent. Eventually she and David Reed gave us our very own producer, a tall and improbably handsome young man called Paul Knight. Later on, for Goldcrest, Paul Knight produced the only solid television hit that ill-fated organization ever had, *Robin of Sherwood*. But at the beginning of his career he got us. He was very nice about it, but also very firm. He said that most of our subject matter was beyond him, but if we couldn't write it so that he could follow the argument, it would be beyond everybody. This was sound advice, embodying a principle I have tried to stick to ever since: the more abstruse the topic, the clearer you should be. (The converse holds: if you are reading deliberately abstruse prose, it has almost certainly been written about nothing.) Thus supervised, we wrote steadily until the day of the first pilot, which we taped nearby in a studio not much bigger than a bathroom.

I had ditched the beard by then, with some regret because it was the best of my beards to date, less like the old salt on the Player's Navy Cut cigarette packet and more like Dinwiddie, master swordsman of the Elizabethan age. The beard had been a sign of my unwillingness to compromise, and its disappearance was a sign of how my unwillingness could be overcome by the prospect of getting more of my face on screen. The space left by the beard's removal also left room for the knot of my tie to show: a relatively plain tie this time, although there was nothing plain about the shirt, which I remember as some sort of Liberty print on brushed nylon, fresh out of Carnaby Street after falling off a van from Yugoslavia. 'It's only a pilot,' muttered Paul Knight, but he and the studio director had bigger problems with me than that. Davies took easily to the teleprompter as he took easily to everything – he could play most musical instruments as soon as he picked them up and could probably have flown a plane after a few minutes to study the controls – but I had trouble grasping the simple principle that the teleprompter would scroll its message at the same speed as I spoke. I was under the impression that I had to speak as fast as the teleprompter was going. Since reading a text aloud at high speed had always been one of my party tricks, I read faster and faster, unable to believe that the teleprompter was following me, not I it. In those days the teleprompter, not yet called an autocue, stood separately to one side of the camera, so the effect I made on screen was of a man talking rapidly sideways to an invisible window cleaner. But Stella liked the pilot even though some of her fellow executives didn't (one of them threatened to resign) and she scheduled two days in studio to shoot a set of six.

The scheduled shooting days were only a few weeks ahead, so we had to write like a pair of convicts petitioning against an imminent death sentence. By night we wrote in pubs, in Wimpy bars, at the Angus Steak House. By day we were in our corner of the open-plan office, somehow finding room for our elbows among the coffee cups, sandwich crusts, and foully heaped ashtrays. Off to one side, behind a glass partition, sat Paul Knight, shaking his head over our scripts. Beautiful young secretaries queued up to take him coffee. None of them came near us: we had to make our own. I can still remember one of our script segments as being not half bad. It was about Michael Frayn, who had not yet begun his second career as a playwright. But as a columnist and novelist he was an inspiration to both of us.

Frayn's 'Miscellany' column in the *Guardian* had been one of
the things that made my life seem worth living even during my
first winter in England. The thought that I might never have to
be so poor and cold again no doubt gave my share of the script
wings. I wrote the exposition while Davies, armed with a copy
each of Frayn's paperback collections *The Day of the Dog, The
Book of Fub* and *At Bay in Gear Street,* worked on the voicing
of the extracts. His powers of mimicry were our best weapon,
and the whole office would stop when he tried the voices out.
My job was to provide the framework for his virtuosity.

Rehearsed in the studio, the result gave at least a hint of how
that kind of arts presentation could look and sound: rich in
content and unforced in vocal style, even if one of the voices,
mine, belonged to a Benzedrine addict being held at gunpoint.
The rehearsal came in useful for staving off at least one incipient
blunder on my part. Paul Knight emerged from the control
gallery to gently disabuse me of the idea that I should reinforce
my vocal points with physical gestures. I had made the classic
mistake of assuming that the illustrative use of the hands might
be useful on television merely because it was so useless on radio.
The assumption is natural but exactly wrong: rather than raise
the hands into shot, it is less distracting to sit on them. Rehearsals
were so prolonged that fatigue set in, which proved beneficial for
me, because I slowed down and even managed the occasional
pause in my tirade. A pause on radio sounds as if the world has
come to an end, but on television it looks like thought. I had
learned something. When we went for the tape I looked less like
a man about to be shot and more like a man who had been shot
already. You could call it relaxation, of a kind. Because the
programmes were wiped as soon as screened – it was still quite
rare to keep a tape after transmission – I can safely say they
weren't bad. They went to air in a graveyard slot where they were
immune from criticism, because nobody was watching except
Joan Bakewell.

The song show was to be called *The Party's Moving On.* Pete and Julie were already hard at work rehearsing for it. Though required to be in attendance to help supervise the format, I had much less scripting to do, which was lucky, because the *Observer* had sent me a book to review. In those days the *Observer* was the most important Sunday paper by a long mile. Edited as a family fiefdom by David Astor, it had arts pages that left those of any rival paper for dead. Not even the *Sunday Times* came close. The *Observer*'s arts editor was Terence Kilmartin. During the war, Kilmartin had saved Astor's life somewhere behind enemy lines. Doing a favour in return, Astor gave Kilmartin a free hand to run the arts pages as a kind of university campus. The roster of the faculty was dazzling. Although Kenneth Tynan was no longer reviewing regularly, he was still writing features. Penelope Gilliatt was the latest film critic in a line that went back to C. E. Lejeune. Katharine Whitehorn, author of *Cooking in a Bedsitter*, was a style-setter for woman journalists writing about all the practical matters of everyday life that had never previously got a mention. Edward Crankshaw, author of one of the best books about old Vienna, wrote on politics. John Weightman wrote so authoritatively about French literature that the French government gave him a decoration for his buttonhole. Even the man who wrote the round-up review of crime novels, John Coleman, was a recognized wit. John Silverlight, one of the section editors, was an outstanding example of a type now vanished: the expert on English usage who kept a strict eye on grammar and syntax throughout the paper. The whole thing was required reading every Sunday for the brightest million people in the country. For a Grub Street foot-slogger to get the nod from Kilmartin was like being commissioned in the field. Overawed at being asked, I over-wrote my first article to the point of sclerosis. Would-be epigrams met each other, fought and froze. Pointless erudition and strained jocularity formed a rigid amalgam. Correctly estimating that the result could have been written by no one else, I mailed it in. Fortunately Kilmartin was used to that reaction from new writers and instead of spiking the piece he called me down to the *Observer* office to discuss it. The office, in that era, was in the old *Times* building on Printing House Square, near the City end of Blackfriars Bridge, about a hundred yards south of the point where Ludgate Hill, plunging down from St Paul's, changed its name to Fleet Street. Let's say that name again. Fleet Street! I couldn't believe it. Nowadays, with the newspaper offices scattered all over London, the personnel who remember when they were still concentrated in and around Fleet Street are dying off like old soldiers. At the time when I made my way to the *Observer*'s door, however, such a diaspora was still inconceivable. Fleet Street was a boulevard of unbroken dreams and the *Observer* was the dream I held most dear. If Kilmartin turned me away, the Thames was conveniently nearby. I could just jump in.

He didn't turn me away, but he did scare me half to death. Not that there was anything terrifying about his manner: quite the reverse. Rising politely from his plain chair behind the book-piled desk in his book-lined office, he held out a dry firm hand that must have detected the residue of the sweat I had just wiped off against my trouser leg, but his face registered no disgust. It was too busy registering handsomeness. Kilmartin was as good looking as a man can be without ceasing to look intelligent as well. Of Irish origin, he was self-admittedly of the type that his countrymen call Desperate Chancer. There was a story that he once spent a night in jail in Paris after getting into a fight with the police. But none of that showed. He looked like the ideal English gentleman, in the exclusive sub-category of ideal English gentlemen who wield natural authority, speak perfect French, are charming to women and read ten books a week. It was a face to lead men into battle. There was only one item missing from the full kit of a commanding manner.

Scarcely a minute into our first conversation, I realized that he took a while to say things. Between any two words he said either 'um' or 'ah', except when either of these sounds occurred twice, in which case it would be separated by the other. The effect was to stop time. 'Your, um, piece, ah, needs, um ah um, some, um, attention.' By then we were sitting down, he had put on a pair of half-glasses, and he was pointing at my first paragraph with a blue pencil. 'Where, um, you, um, say, um ah um, this, ah, hugely, ah, impressive, um ah um, novel...' Then an extraordinary thing happened. Suddenly several words came out uninterrupted. 'I should have thought we didn't need the "hugely". I mean, if you call it "impressive" then you're already...' There was a pause, as if to recuperate. After a small eternity, normal service was resumed. 'Either, um, you're, ah, impressed, or, ah, you're, um ah um, not.' We were three lines into the piece with about ninety-seven lines to go. He was right, of course, and I quickly saw that my manuscript was going to end up a lot shorter. But it was equally clear that I was going to end up a lot older. I never doubted, however, that I was in good hands. Twenty minutes later, the fourth paragraph that had given me so much trouble to get right revealed why: it was all wrong. Trying to say too much at once, I had constructed a sentence out of clauses that should have been sentences in themselves. With apologetic regret, he prised them apart. Writing in my head, I supplied new beginnings for each. 'That, um, sounds, ah, much, um, more, um ah um, natural.' His secretary brought tea. At this rate she would have to bring us food and medical supplies.

But he was right every time. At the speed of a glacier, my overwrought piece was brought back in touch with living speech. It was my conversational tone, he told me, that he was after: there was no need to get up on stilts. It took him a long time to tell me, but that probably helped to drive the lesson home. 'We, um, can, ah, print, um, this, ah um ah, now.' It would have been an affectation to show my delight, because I had realized in the first few minutes that he wouldn't have been taking the trouble if he had thought the piece beyond salvation. But there was another wonder to come, and this time there was no holding back a laugh of disbelief. He showed me a row of upcoming books and asked me which one I would like to review next. No doubt it was the slush pile left over after the big stuff had been sent out to the name reviewers, but being granted access had to mean that I was in. Instantly I conceived a whole new ambition. Just as I aimed to write a piece for Miller that would make him smile, so I would aim to write a piece for Kilmartin that he would print without consuming more than an epoch to take me through the manuscript. Simultaneously exalted and exhausted, I limped along Fleet Street past the celebrated landmarks of my new trade. Outside El Vino's, the most famous of all the Fleet Street hostelries, a byline journalist whose face I recognized from photographs was standing on the edge of the gutter, gathering his concentration for the six-inch descent into the carriageway. He was so drunk that he swayed in the wind of a passing cab. A hundred yards further on, I looked back, and he was still in place. But not even he could depress me. He might be standing on the edge of doom, but I was walking on air.

5. NIGHT OF THE KILLER JOINT

But it was my effort in Grub Street that had led to my first toehold in Fleet Street, and, for a while yet, Grub Street would continue to be my main base. There could be no base more shaky: it was like Khe Sahn in there. You had to be on the alert twenty-four hours a day just to hold the perimeter, or you would wake up sharing your sleeping bag with several small men in conical hats. To keep up with the punishing requirement of putting an income together out of piecework, the temptation was to find a neutral style and just fill the various spaces as specified. But my instinct dictated otherwise. I tried to give each piece everything, composing it as if it were a poem, with every word considered before it was placed, as if I were a mad bricklayer building a garden wall out of precious stones. If I had known how to write with less effort I might have written more. Luckily the extra lolly from London Weekend took off some of the pressure, so that I never got to the point, quite common among veterans of the genre, where I was not only jobbing all over the place but doing each job with cheap materials, like a cowboy plumber. It thus became possible for me to overfulfil a specification: a possibility which, I later concluded – once again I didn't realize it at the time – is one of the keys to attaining a recognized competence in any field, and also of escaping from it when the moment comes.

If you just do the minimum you will get stuck. Give it the maximum and you will make your employer feel that you are doing him a favour, instead of he you. An example of this was when Ian Hamilton asked me to do a round-up review for the

TLS of Edmund Wilson's last few books. I thought Edmund Wilson was not just America's most comprehensive man of letters, but the greatest critic alive anywhere: and now he was on the point of death. Writing about him anonymously for Britain's most hallowed literary institution, the *TLS*, I would be giving him a send-off worthy of his stature. (One measure of the stature was that his English publisher had gone on bringing out his books right to the end, even though they went straight to the remainder shops: heavy evidence that commitment to quality can be a commercial disaster.) Anonymity would work for the venture instead of against it, because it would be the institution talking, and not just some Australian swagman humping his bluey through the early stages of the road to Hullaboola. Hamilton would have been content if I had wrapped the task up in two thousand words. I gave him eleven thousand, plus a suggested title, 'The Metropolitan Critic'. Hamilton cut it back to ten thousand, kept the title, and the piece ran, filling several pages of the paper. I'm not sure what the effect was on Wilson – I like to think it was not necessarily a bad sign that he died a few days after the tribute appeared – but it had a stirring effect on some other established writers, who might have quite liked the idea of one of their number being celebrated as a crucial figure in modern intellectual history. If him, why not them? No doubt inspired by motives rather more exalted than that, Graham Greene asked the *TLS* chief editor Arthur Crook who had written the Wilson piece. Crook having spilled the beans, I duly received a letter from Greene himself, telling me that he, too, held a high opinion of Wilson, but that he was very glad someone so young should have written the opinion down. Flatteringly avuncular, Greene suggested that I might consider the discursive critical essay as my destined field of operations. The piece wasn't as long as the letter I wrote in reply, which was probably the reason I never heard from him again. (I had not yet learned that any writer, even when much less prominent than Greene, is swamped with correspondence and should never be communicated with at any length greater than a single paragraph. A single sentence is plenty.) Still, I had that first letter from him, and there were many other letters from other people to back it up. I had done something right, and had done it, not with one eye on my ambitions, but by submitting myself to an obligation.

The lesson was not lost on me, although I was a long time figuring out the full range of implication. The range can be summed up thus: given the choice between personal opportunism and public duty, go with the duty. The rewards might not show up straight away, but they will outlast the quick returns for cynicism. Since rewards are still in mind, that interpretation might seem opportunistic in itself, but only because of a supervening paradox: virtue resides in the taming of a baser instinct, not in its elimination. Our baser instincts act in our interests, to get us fed, to make us loved, to keep our children safe. For all but the saints, neglect of one's own interests limits the power even to be altruistic. One gets more free time, but only to interfere. It must have been just about then, in her *Observer* column, that Katherine Whitehorn wrote, 'You can recognize the people who live for others by the haunted look on the faces of the others.' I didn't have to write it down: it went straight to memory, which may have displaced some of the words, but the balance of the sentence was unforgettable. With the best writers for the Sunday papers and literary magazines in those days, one of the pleasures was their confidence of aphorism – a confidence generated, as always, by the receptivity of the audience. The resonant sentence has been a basic form throughout the history of philosophy; a form in which all the best writers sound the same and time collapses into a permanent present. Consider one of my favourite moments from Seneca, his warning to the tyrant: you can kill as many enemies as you like, but your successor will be among those who survive. It's an insight anyone can have, but made penetrating by the compactness with which it is put.

I loved the idea of talking that way on the page. It had only dimly occurred to me that the same sort of thing might be possible on radio, and as yet I had no idea at all that it might be possible on television. (Not for me, at any rate: it was already the quality I admired most in veteran broadcasters like Rene Cutforth, Robert Kee, Charles Wheeler, Ludovic Kennedy and numerous others in those great days of the overqualified front man.) But the success of the piece on Wilson was the beginning of my confidence in a tactical approach to print journalism by which I might get away with combining the apparently antagonistic roles of wiseacre and smart alec. After all, if a reasonable proportion of the audience read such a long piece to the end, I must have got the tone right. Otherwise there would have been cancelled subscriptions en masse.

Thus glowing with self-esteem, I was better equipped to handle my status as gooseberry when Pete and Julie went to studio with *The Party's Moving On*. Though my name was on the roller somewhere as writer and script editor, the humbling truth was that my contribution had ceased to be useful after Pete had set my lyrics to music. Needing the full range of cameras and lights, the shows were taped at the old Rediffusion studios in Wembley, a district no lovelier then than it is now. All the tapes were wiped long ago, so once again it is safe to say that the results were good. They had enough impact at the time to help Pete get his first recording contract, with Philips: part of a tangled story that would have dominated my life in the first half of the 1970s if I had been doing nothing else, and came close to breaking my nerve even though I was. More of that later, because, for the moment, *The Party's Moving On* shows were sheer euphoria for the two of us who had written the songs, and I shouldn't let those real feelings of satisfaction be blunted by the unearned maturity of retrospect, which is always a false perspective if it invalidates past emotions. It's like belittling a lost love: you are calling yourself stupid for ever getting into it, when actually you were at your best, and you would not be wiser now if you had not been foolish then. When I watched Pete and Julie singing our songs, I was as proud as I have ever been in my life: I thought we were all on the road to immortality. The long truth was that we had no chance of general popularity as song writers, but in the short run it felt as if we had, because there was our stuff, right there on television. As Pete would be the first to admit, Julie was the radiant centre of the appeal. She looked and sounded like a blessing, and you would have sworn – you and almost any showbiz executive who saw and heard her in action – that she was headed for great things. Whether or not she would accept her destiny was up to her. If, in the course of time, she did not become one of the biggest stars in the world, it can only have been because she chose not to.

For those of us less gifted, the choice is not so open. We have to chase our luck or else run out of it. Making the dreary train journey to Wembley for what often seemed no good reason, I soon found that my opinion of myself as a spare wheel was not shared by Stella, who gave me all kinds of credit for the song shows, which she somehow decided I had been supervising by telepathy from my position in the canteen or, more often, the bar. Any impression of mental puissance might have been increased by the fact that I was usually to be seen working hard with notebook and biro, shaping up a new book review or a linking script for BBC radio's *Kaleidoscope*, on which I had graduated from occasional contributor to semi-regular front-man. In aid of these projects, books would be stacked up on the table at which I sat. For television executives, who are more likely to err through an excess of respect for the clerical life than through a deficiency, there could have been no more convincing evidence of cerebral fecundity. People must have tiptoed to Stella's office and told her that I was reading, writing, drinking and smoking simultaneously. Stella in her turn must have been further convinced that she was hatching a new Leonardo da Vinci. She informed Paul Knight that I was to be regarded as the key man, the potential presiding genius, for a new series of light-entertainment shows that would exploit the coruscating talents of all my young graduate colleagues. The conversations between Paul and Stella took place high up in LWT's office building near the studios. Had Paul but known it, this was the exact moment to strap on his parachute and step out of the window. Even if, the parachute given insufficient time to deploy, he had arrived in the car park at terminal velocity, the quick journey downward would have been less painful for him than what was to happen next. But he didn't know that yet. Later in his career, he would be better equipped to detect the shadow of an oncoming turkey. I can take some credit for sharpening that awareness.

Back in the Angus Steak House in Swiss Cottage, I got together with my troops. In a kind of Round Table conference with yet another notched tomato-half as a centre piece, we persuaded ourselves that a good title for the new spectacular would be *What Are You Doing After the Show?*. It is never a good idea for a title to ask a question, because in the event of mishap the question is an open invitation for sardonic onlookers to supply the answer. As time would prove, the answer to 'What are you doing after the show?' was 'I am going to crawl away behind a dung-heap and die in agony.' But we didn't know that then. Prescience came after the event, as it almost always does. Before the event, we were high on the possibilities of replacing the moribund traditions of television variety with the teeming, tumbling enthusiasm of our bright young selves. We were partly right about the moribund traditions – if *The Black and White Minstrel Show* wasn't still on the air, it hadn't been off the air long – but we were wholly wrong about having the wherewithal to replace them. My troops were clever and in some cases brilliant, but as far as material went, they had just about enough new ideas in stock to furnish a single show. It should have been evident to me that the series would run out of substance soon after it was launched. It would be a Chinese paper skyrocket. More accurately, consider-ing the size of its budget, it would be a huge new ship sliding backwards down the slipway and continuing its trajectory until it disappeared under the waters of the Clyde, leaving a lot of people with rattles in their hands silently examining a vast area of foam.

Perhaps this likelihood, not evident to me at the time, should have been evident to those who had hired me, but it would be unfair to blame them. After all, I had done my share of talking them into it, and nobody who has ever complained about his unique vision being stifled has a right to object when the supposedly repressive forces remove the pillow from his face and give him permission to rise up and strut his stuff. Later on I made a lot of bitter comments about how Stella and her executives had no real idea of what originality was. Stella, in particular, kept saying that she wanted 'something new, like the *Laugh-In*'. At the time, *Rowan and Martin's Laugh-In*, freshly syndicated from America, was making everything else on British television look horse-drawn. The show was fronted by the two men with their names in the title. Their names were practically all they had to contribute. A pair of cocktail-lounge hacks as far below Dean Martin and Jerry Lewis as you could get before arriving at Abbot and Costello, on screen they reprised their perennial on-stage relationship in short front-of-curtain numbers between sketches featuring the show's true talents, a bunch of young eccentrics ranging from Arte Johnson to Henry Gibson, by way of Lily Tomlin and Goldie Hawn. The ideal *Laugh-In* sketch was scarcely longer than its own punchline. I learned a lot from watching, but the part that I should have studied harder was the roller. The names of the writers went on for ever. In other words, the on-screen talents, almost without exception, were not writing their own stuff. So when our executives said they wanted 'something new, like the *Laugh-In*', there were actually asking for a large-scale operation without any logistical support.

But I could have pointed that out, had I been wiser. Paul Knight would have listened. A bit later on, as the disaster unfolded, he was the first to spot that we needed to recruit other writers pronto. Any writers: V. S. Naipaul if he was available.

Had I foreseen the necessity, I could have cast myself in the role of co-ordinator and catalyst. On the *Laugh-In*, that very role had been played by an Australian wanderer called Digby Wolfe, who remains, to this day, one of the unsung heroes of a TV revolution. (Another was Ernie Kovacs, whose fame as a performer eclipsed his influential originality as an ideas man.) In an earlier phase of American TV, programmes like *Your Show of Shows* had a table of writers so numerous that Mel Brooks, Woody Allen and Dick Cavett were lost among them. But the tumult could be kept under control by the central ego of the single star, such as Jackie Gleason or Sid Caesar. The *Laugh-In*, with a whole bunch of stars, needed someone to channel its writing staff. Digby Wolfe was the right man. From this distance, I no doubt tend to idealize him, but I should be quick to say that my estimation of his importance did not come from him. Indeed I never met him. He would have been hard to know anyway, as the buccaneering showbiz writers so often are. But I know them as a type, and have fondness for them. Buck Henry was one of them. Terry Southern was another. Southern was unclassifiable until he hit the big money in Hollywood. Not surprisingly, considering his personal habits, the big money hit him right back. By the time that there were no substances left to abuse, he had disappeared into an endless mess of aborted projects – first finished but useless, then unfinished, then half-finished, then unstarted. But the essence of the man was never on the screen anyway: not even in *Easy Rider* or the best bits of *Doctor Strangelove*. The essence was in *Candy* and *The Magic Christian*, and in some of the factual stories in *Red Dirt Marijuana*. I never stole anything from him but I admired his colloquial tone. (Listen to Aunt Livia in *Candy* and ask yourself if Ring Lardner, J. D. Salinger or Philip Roth ever eavesdropped on everyday conversation with quite so acute an ear.) It was easy to guess that Southern's judgement of pitch had a lot to do with his itinerant life. He was a pirate. Fancying that I, too, sailed under a black flag, I forgave him too readily for his compulsive urge to screw up almost every task he took on.

I should have realized that he had not forgiven himself: hence the capacity for self-destruction. Though a direct product of his fecklessness, his appetite for mind-altering drugs was a proclivity I was less inclined to be understanding about, and had no urge at all to emulate.

The evidence of what drink could do to me was by that time impressing even me, and there was obviously something wrong with the logic of replacing alcohol with dope. The counter-culture's growing population of drug experts were vocally certain that marijuana provided a more benevolent high than alcohol. There may have been something to that argument, since even today I know people from that time whose long-term relationship with the weed has lent them a lasting mellowness, in sharp contrast to the many drunks I have known who crashed early, and – the worst aspect – took innocent civilians with them. I may go into this subject further at the appropriate moment. For now, enough to say that the notion of hash as a substitute for alcohol, whether the proposal is valid or not, must surely be dependent on the premise that the intake of sweet smoke should be moderate.

Unfortunately I found that my intake of funny cigarettes was no easier to control than my intake of ordinary ones. I never exactly lit one joint off another, but there was only a short pause for contemplation, right up until the point when a state of suspended animation left me deprived of power to reach for a cigarette paper, lay down a line of tobacco, and sprinkle it with expensive crumbs. At somewhere about this time, our colony shifted from Swiss Cottage to Gibson Square, a rundown but finely proportioned Georgian feature of the not-yet-fashionable Islington. I can't remember a single detail of how we made the move, and you can guess the reason. I'm fairly sure that I had to be carried. At Wembley I was never high in the daytime. Circumstances there were so desperate that I would probably have sobered up within seconds even if I had arrived stoned. At the rate it was going, *What Are You Doing After the Show?* would run out of material entirely somewhere in the middle of the third instalment. The performers were too busy rehearsing to come up with new sketches even had they been inspired to. Since I was not on screen myself, in theory I had plenty of time to write material, but somehow, even under the gun, I found it hard to write lines for anyone except myself. Thus I became a large part of the problem. I thought I knew the answer: persuade any Footlights writers, present or past, to rally to the flag. Paul gave me carte blanche, and a budget, to do the persuading. The prospect of getting paid lured some of them to attend meetings at Wembley. But I had forgotten that most of the Footlights writers I had known in recent years had never produced more than three sketches a year for term-time smoking concerts, and, of those three sketches, only one would make it into the May Week revue, where it was usually performed by the writer himself, and not always to a storm of applause. Now engaged in the early stages of a career in the responsible professions, but still hankering for a time when they had trailed small clouds of thespian glory, these wistful luminaries seemed keen enough for the task. But when they went away to write something for us, they usually came back with something suitable only for themselves. Often they did not come back at all, which left me making explanations about their mercurial individuality.

Even more humiliating, I arranged a meeting with my fellow ex-President of Footlights Graeme Garden at the Salisbury pub in St Martin's Lane, where I did an upright version of going on my hands and knees. The vertical grovel tended towards the horizontal as I finally grasped that he had no reason to take the bait. He, Bill Oddie and Tim Brooke-Taylor had something else in mind. They had already slogged for several years each in sketch shows and were cooking up a format that would sustain itself without the exhausting search for a punchline. Eventually *The Goodies* would out-rate even *Monty Python*. The standard gag about *The Goodies* was that half the ratings consisted of Orson Welles, who for some reason found the three bumbling chums exquisitely amusing. But the standard gag was simply envy talking. Liberating its three stars from the deadly treadmill of sketch humour, *The Goodies* was a solid hit. It was still just an idea at the time when I was begging for my life from Garden, but it was a real idea, and he had needed only to hear my sales pitch to realize that our idea wasn't. Paul Knight, with typical realism, analysed my dilemma on the basis of results. Leafing through the pitifully small heap of our scripts, he told me the truth. 'We are in deep shtuck.' I had seen the word printed, but had never heard it said, so I hadn't known that it was pronounced to rhyme with 'book'. Perhaps provoked by the way I seemed to relish what he was saying rather than being disturbed by it, he went on to explain how most of my admittedly gifted colleagues invented material only when the mood took them, and that what we now needed were professionals, who would turn the stuff out against the clock. He then amplified on his preliminary remark. 'We are in deep, deep shtuck.' I savoured the expression even as it plunged me into gloom. I liked his style. For some reason he also liked mine, even though I had helped get him into the profound ordure that would close over our heads if something drastic were not done soon.

Having determined the true nature of the emergency, Paul whistled in the first two of what would eventually be half a dozen writers previously unknown to us even by name, but who had solid track records as suppliers of material to the sort of variety shows we theoretically despised. The first two were called Mike and Dave. They were very young. Their attire seemed designed to demonstrate that the 1970s would be an era unprecedented for its ill-judged extravagance of men's clothes. I won't go into details about the synthetic materials and the clash of colours. Enough to say that when Mike and Dave stood close together they created static. If you scanned them from their platform boots upwards, your capacity for response was already sapped before you arrived at the part where their faces should have been separately visible. Standing up, they were already hanging loose. Sitting down, they were a shambles. A luxuriance of hair, sideboards and moustache, punctuated by two pairs of rimless dark glasses, made it hard to tell if they were awake or even alive. They spoke in a relaxed, combined mumble that transmitted little beyond an abstract amiability, but they proved commendably flexible in adapting their writing style to ours. Indeed they did so with daunting ease. The same proved true with most of the other writers who were brought in to join them. After our first studio date yielded a show that made it clear we were already running out of our own stuff, reinforcements arrived by taxi. Without exception they were object lessons in professionalism.

Long before I grew older and wiser, I could already see that these peripatetic writers were the essential logistic element of British comedy, as crucial to a long campaign as the PLUTO pipeline was to the Allied invasion of Europe. Today, if you want to get the history of what happened in British light entertainment from music hall and ENSA onwards through radio and into television, you would be wasting your time asking even the best qualified academic. The people to ask are jobbing script doctors like Barry Cryer. In the course of about a hundred years Cryer has written for almost every comedian and tells a better story than all of them. But he has always been too canny to squander his personal stories on the air. Instead, apart from a little touring stage show that fits into a suitcase, he largely confines himself to after-dinner speaking, by which he makes unimaginable amounts of money. Laconically recounted, his anecdotes stem from hands-on experience of every showbiz era since Ralph Roister-Doister devised the first greased-pig-and-flaming-fart act at the court of Edward II. In our era, Cryer was working on every show in the building except ours. We couldn't afford him. Sometimes on the elevated railway platform at Wembley I would meet him. He was comfortably insulated by a fleece-lined car-coat against the wind. Even at that slightly earlier stage of his long career he could have been travelling in the back of a Rolls had he wished: but like most of the more prudent people in show business he believed in keeping the costs down. As we gazed out over square miles of urban blight that the Luftwaffe had never summoned the energy to bomb, he kindly predicted that the biggest thing I would have going for me in my career was that I performed my own stuff, so I would never be able to fire my writer, even if I felt like it.

Though he phrased this as amiable banter, actually he was touching on a theme crucial to the whole field of comedy in whatever medium. But the theme is rarely mentioned, because the cult of celebrity gets in the way. It is really quite useless to talk about the career of Tony Hancock, for example, without taking notice of the fact that he did not write his own stuff. His talent was solely for delivery. Fatally for him, he grew much too fond of being called a genius, and much too reluctant to admit that a proper script was essential. Ego duly eroded judgement, and he got rid of his best writers, Galton and Simpson, hoping to prove thereby that he had never needed them. His subsequent decline proved that the need had been desperate. Morecambe and Wise, on the other hand, were always smart enough to admit that they relied on the writing of Eddie Braben. Trace back the tradition of television comedy and you arrive at the radio studios where a hidden elite of writers served nearly all the famous names. Within the business, the writers were famous names themselves. A comparable figure to Cryer was Barry Took, who had always done valuable work as a radio writer behind the scenes. But the moment came when he was offered executive power in television, and he saw the virtues of taking a rest from the hard graft of personally turning out the funny stuff. Instead, he would supervise other people while they did it. Unfortunately for me, this was the moment. Rupert Murdoch was on the point of taking over at LWT. Stella Richman was feeling the cold. *What Are You Doing After the Show?* was less than a triumph – the few people watching it were still waiting to find out what it was about – and Barry Took discovered, no doubt to his alarm, that one of his new executive duties was to make our bright idea look worth its budget.

He was in a difficult position, but it's a rule of the game that if the man in charge of you is in a difficult position, it will never feel quite as difficult as yours. Barry Took had a lot of experience in script construction and unlike many weathered veterans he was not jealous of his turf. Later on, as a light-entertainment executive at the BBC, he helped the *Monty Python* crew when he could easily have hindered them. Showbiz journalists, who are always looking for an angle, often identify Took as the secret genius behind *Monty Python*: an opinion which, when it began to circulate, he was understandably slow to contradict. In cold fact, and in a far more complicated story than any journalist had the patience to unscramble, the Pythons, one and all, had climbed bloodily through a string of less original shows and had learned to look after themselves individually long before. But when they finally got together, undoubtedly it was Took who made sure that the door was held open while they trooped through it. He thus had some right to have his name embroidered on the nappy of their brainchild. He would probably have done the same for us if our brainchild was still in the womb. But it was already in the world, and it was ill. Took, therefore, was not just in the position of marshalling talent. He had to supply some talent of his own. Talent he unquestionably had, but he lacked the further talent of being tactful about it. He knew better than us. He might have been right about that, but by sending our stuff back for review after Paul Knight had already approved it he inevitably trod crushingly on our immediate mentor's well-shod toes. The suave Paul was a hard man to ruffle, but when he emerged from his first one-on-one meeting with Took he had a disturbing new variation on his standard theme of despair. 'We,' he said thoughtfully, 'are in deep Took.'

At one point Paul confided to me that any potential faith he might have had in his new commander evaporated when he ran into him in a lift. 'He started imitating Skippy the Kangaroo.' No doubt Took, for whom the aforesaid Skippy was an important item on his curriculum vitae, had merely been trying to establish an atmosphere of ebullience, but Paul wasn't the ebullient type. Everyone who prattles would like to drawl, and Paul was a drawler. As a consequence he gave Took the jumps. With our two big wheels turning out of synch, the whole engine shook itself to bits. After a particularly disastrous script meeting at which Took informed me and the assembled company that our latest batch of scripts needed the kind of excellent jokes once so prevalent on *Round the Horne* – he recited several of these from memory – I told Paul that I saw no point in staying. Paul let me go with depressing ease. He was well aware that I had played a large part in creating the problem that Took was failing to solve. Deprived of my help, the show looked no worse than before. Though there were plays by Ibsen that were funnier, and several Noh dramas with more pace, very few of the people who continued to tune in actually sued for damages, and apparently a financial problem accounted for the family that committed suicide. But it was a mercy when the show was taken off in mid-series. When the Murdoch buy-in was a done deal, one of the first things he did was to pull the plugs on *What Are You Doing After the Show?*. It seems that his own answer to its interrogative title had been: 'Not wasting my money.' There is never any argument with that, and any young writer who thinks there is had better stick to poetry. I always have, by the way. Especially in bad times, it can help to be alone with the pen and paper, working on a self-contained creation that the money men can't stop. But it might also be something that they will not publish. Best to have something in the bank, then, before you start feeling brave.

Unjustified self-righteousness helped to ease my retreat. I did some of my usual talking to the troops about how 'the system' had conspired to frustrate us. But experience was already playing its valuable role of chastening delusion, and this time I spoke less fluently. It might even have been that I spoke less. A help towards taciturnity, and perhaps towards heart's ease, was the dreaded weed. Mike and Dave resembled the Fabulous Furry

Freak Brothers not only in their appearance but in their unlimited supply of high-octane dope. Either in Swiss Cottage or in Gibson Square – I forget which, and given the circumstances I would have forgotten the location even had it been Easter Island – they showed up one evening with what they called a baggy. The baggy turned out to be a sack of hash so thick and rich that you could have bitten into it like a bar of chocolate. Today a stash that size would get you executed in Singapore, and in Thailand they would want to execute your relatives as well. From then on, I and selected members of my squad got used to lighting up with Mike and Dave. I should hasten to say that Pete never touched the stuff, perhaps because he had noticed how it robbed me of my judgement. The lyrics I composed under its influence were the nearest I ever got to writing perfect nonsense, and after trying out a few chords he would wait for the sober version. Nevertheless he was tolerant, which he had to be, because the sweet smoke was everywhere, turning the house into one big tunnel for the Marrakesh Express. We would never have got away with it at the Wembley offices, which were open plan, but at home the very air was heavy with the perfume of burning angel's wings. On the day I resigned from the show, Mike and Dave promised me a present for that evening. When they arrived at Gibson Square, they had the present in a flute case. Reverently they opened the lid. Inside, lying in a trough of worn blue velvet, was what they told me was the World's Biggest Joint. The flute case could have been a suitcase and the super-joint would still have been prominent. In the context of its modest container, it looked majestic, like a zeppelin. Mike and Dave, guiding their creation out of its hangar, assured us that the calculations for building it had been precise: this was as long and fat as a joint could be without collapsing under its own weight. Much of the weight, it was explained, consisted of the active ingredient, sprinkled on the loose tobacco to a density never previously achieved by man. 'You have to imagine,' murmured Dave, 'a car-park full of tumbleweed, and then there's this rain of shit.' They bent close over their masterpiece. Mike's voice came, as always, from a distance. 'We make these all the time,' he mumbled. 'But this is the biggest.' Dave lit a match.

If this book were pure fiction, I could say that my encounter with the super-joint marked the end of my period of Experimenting With Drugs. (Nobody ever explained how stoking yourself with proven narcotics could plausibly be called 'experimenting', or why the expression 'experimenting with alcohol' had never been heard even from the kind of drinker who wakes up in the police station after driving his car through a bus queue.) In truth, however, the facts are seldom so tidy. My terminal experience didn't take place until the next night. On the night of the super-joint, I deeply relished every drag. Hidden in the stereo system of the living room, Sandy Denny sang 'Who Knows Where the Time Goes?'. She could sing that again. Grouped around the dining table in the kitchen, we passed the super-joint around from hand to hand, or rather, in the early stages, from both hands to both hands. The quality was as outstanding as the quantity. After a few turns I was coining philosophical aphorisms, and after a few more turns I couldn't understand them either. One of the dangerously charming effects of pot is that it lends your most banal comments an alluring depth in your own ears, which is probably the main reason you make exactly the same comments again. Drunks can usually tell that they are being boring but they can't stop. Pot-heads really believe that they are Socrates or Dorothy Parker. At one point, offering unsolicited comments on Cocteau's experience with opium, I attempted to quote his aphorism about the only useful help you can give to an aspiring young artist: open the door and show him the tightrope. 'Open the door,' I said very slowly, 'and show him the tide.' I had run out of energy, but Dave nodded in agreement. 'That's good. Room full of ocean. Who was that again?' With a last burst of effort, I said the name again. 'Cock. Toe. Cocteau.' Mike said he had once worked with him at Thames Television.

Next morning I woke up in bed, but felt unusually hot. It was because I was still fully dressed, including shoes. My head felt clear, however: much more so than it would have done had I been drinking. After a hard day at the typewriter, carving into the first of the half dozen deadlines I needed to catch up on, I began to fancy that I had life well worked out. If I could just wean myself away from the sauce to the grass, I would have a dependable release from the anguish of writing that would not interfere with the brain that produced the words. Look at the piece I was writing now, for example: how vibrant in argument, how bold in its use of metaphor! I was alone with my inspiration. The boys were all off in Wembley for the studio day of the final show, and would not be back until late at night, after the inevitable wake. Tough on them. After dining on fish and chips – the fish identical in texture to the chips – I knocked out the final paragraph of the day. It seemed to me that Swift had seldom been so pungently clear, Burke so meticulous in his control of rhythm, Hazlitt so universal in his understanding. Then I settled down in front of the television with my notebook and the makings of a small joint. Compared with the super-joint, of course, all joints were small, but this one really was quite modest: no bigger than a gorilla's little finger. In consideration of its diffident proportions, however, it seemed permissible, nay mandatory, to be generous with the magic sprinkle. I crop-dusted the tobacco with the prodigality of an American child decorating a scoop of ice-cream with uninhibited use of the toppings supplied. If these metaphors are mixed, they are no more so than the ones I had been concocting during the day, in the flow of a creative confidence I had thought uncommonly lucid. As you will have already guessed, I was still high from the previous night. But I had no means of knowing that, because even my movements in rolling this shyly harmless new spliff were of uncanny precision. The finished product was as tight and neat as a fresh tampon. Almost a pity, really, to set it on fire. At the time there was a catchy Californian expression: 'Don't Bogart that joint.' I not only Bogarted that joint, I Lee Marvined it. In about ten minutes it was gone, and in about twelve minutes so was I.

As I recall, there was not even a brief period of tranquillity before the unpleasantness began. The wave of nausea came straight up the beach, flooded the highway, knocked down the motel, and washed me upside down into the trees. Ever since childhood, the moment I knew I was about to vomit had been a blessed relief from the agonizing hope that it wouldn't happen. This time the moment of certainty never came. I just felt that the fish and chips were stuck between floors. Meanwhile I myself was steadily ascending, yet for some reason the ceiling got no closer. I was falling upwards, yet not moving. Once again, it would have been a relief if I had. I could nestle against that plaster rosette up there and wait until my stomach made up its mind. But I was pinned to the couch. After about the time it took to build the Sydney Harbour Bridge, I managed to manoeuvre through ninety degrees, hoping to feel better if I lay down.

I felt almost incomparably worse. It was like being taken out to sea by a rip tide. Theoretically you should go with the rip until it brings you back in further along the coast, but there are sharks out there, so you try to swim against it. You get very tired: too tired to lift an arm so that the lifesaver can see you. Lounging superbly in his elevated chair, the lifesaver is checking out the apricot bottoms of the bikini girls on the beach, choosing the one that he will peel and slowly suck the juice out of back in his room while the Great White is biting you in half. The thought that you will soon die is overwhelming. I was having exactly that thought on a ratty mock-leather couch in Islington. I was sweating peanut oil yet my hands were dry: how could that be? My sinuses were full of molten lead. Somehow I knew, without being able to reach down and verify the fact, that my genital area was being redeveloped as a shopping mall. The project would take years to complete, but I didn't have that long. My life would end in another five minutes. And then another five. All right, another ten. The television screen said goodnight and shrank to a fizzing white dot, the universe ending with a small bang and a long whimper. Time must have a stop. But it doesn't. We do.

I do. What a way to spend eternity, with a growing but forever unconsummated belief that you are about to dump your guts. When the boys finally came rollicking home and asked me what was wrong, I had to answer them with the shortest words I could think of, the words widely spaced by long clenchings of the teeth, as though I were posing for a very old camera with a long exposure time. The clenched teeth held back a blob of ecto-plasm the size of a water bed that I could feel occupying every cubic centimetre of my alimentary tract. 'Joint,' I said. 'Too,' I added. 'Much.' From far away there came a voice. 'Christ, it's an overdose.' Then another voice. 'Never. You can't O.D. on pot.' The first voice again: 'He can.'

The first voice was right. People who say they have an addictive personality are usually just transferring the blame for their deficiency of resolve, but if there really is such a thing as an addictive personality, then I have one. The night of the killer joint was just further proof of a propensity that had been manifest since childhood. Partly as a result of my marijuana experiments, I was able to avoid the harder drugs that were soon to become fashionable. The mere thought of heroin made me remember what had happened to Frank Sinatra in *The Man With The Golden Arm* when I first saw the film at Ramsgate Odeon in the early 1950s. Actually I had quite liked the thought of being soothed against the luscious bosom of Kim Novak. Sexual experi-ence looked like a good thing to have, even at the cost of sticking a needle in your arm. But the drastic result of the needle being withdrawn looked all too convincing, and from that time forward the cold-turkey episodes of my life – cutting out my daily packet of Jaffas, for example – had been accompanied in my mind by a Saul Bass title sequence and the music of Henry Mancini. As to cocaine, I could never see the point, because the people I knew who were burying their heads in heaps of white dynamite seemed to attain no higher state of mental alertness than the one that I was doomed to live in all the time. At one point a medical friend, kindly acting as an unpaid consultant in a period when I was actively shopping for some means of relief from my perennial melancholy, assured me that although it was unlikely that I was naturally secreting $C_{17}H_{21}NO_4$, there is indeed such a thing as a constitutionally determined hyperaesthetic state. The idea checks out with my introspection, to the extent that I have time for it.

To put it in non-technical language, I have a metabolism like Colombia. Unfortunately it is no better governed, and will immediately demand industrial amounts of anything it likes the taste of. In the first volume of this memoir I recorded how I had been the only infant in my district to overdose on marshmallows. In my early teens, down at the local shopping centre, I bought my mother a box of Winning Post chocolates for her birthday – if I have told you this before, it is because the shame has never left me – and ate nearly all of them before I got home. (Presenting her with the almost empty box, I said that there had been an accident. Her reception of the story armed me for life against any reliance on the classic excuse about the dog that ate my home-work.) In late adolescence and early maturity, I quickly out-stripped my contemporaries as a smoker, and would have done so as a drinker had I possessed a hollow leg to match my thirst. Even today, I can't buy a roll of Extra Strong peppermints – indispensable equipment for the secret nicotine addict – without swallowing them all one after the other after chewing each no more than twice. Don't Bogart those sweets? What else are they for? No use asking me to be moderate. Just steer me towards something safe that I can overdo. After a whole roll of instantly inhaled Extra Strong peppermints, for instance, the lips develop a chlorinated tingle, as if after drinking from a swimming pool. Nor does high expense temper the intake. A pot of caviar, no matter how big, rings empty in a few minutes, even though, absorbed at that rate, the soft black buckshot converts the interior of the mouth into a whaling station. Cursed with this tropism, I have never found anything strange about the more decadent Roman emperors and their raging quest for satiety. On the contrary, I marvel at Nero's restraint.

6. WAKING UP ABSURD

But the night of the killer joint spelled the end of the affair between me and marijuana, and, by extension (I hope it will bear being said again), of any possible flirtation with the more serious drugs that were already creeping into the scene. At the time, the pot-head lobby was still peddling the message that their beloved weed was the gentle alternative to booze. Even today, I know adepts from the period who have built their recreational lives around hash while sidelining the bottle, undoubtedly to the benefit of their personalities. One of them, among our most prominent novelists, is the nicest man I know. He would probably still have been sweet-natured even without his rare knack for growing an infinitely renewable crop of vintage hemp in the window boxes of his apartment, but the stuff certainly didn't hurt. The second message of the pot brigade, however, sounded dubious even then. Moderate indulgence in the gentle habit, it was alleged, would stave off any urge to get involved with smack. Implicit in this argument was the notion that getting high would somehow increase one's sense of consequence instead of diminishing it. The time soon came when needle-freaks could be heard announcing that their consumption of brown sugar was well under control. They were seldom in a position to announce this very loudly. Quite often they were in the sitting position, drowsily engaged in the search for a vein, and often enough they were in the supine position, persuasively impersonating a dead Christ by Cranach.

Wishful thinking and drugs are variations on the same theme, so it was no surprise that nothing on the subject sounded true except when said by someone who had been all the way to the limit and somehow contrived to return. Decades before, in the truly alternative society of jazz, Charlie Parker, in one of the rare moments when he was not strung out like a line of washing, had insisted that anyone who thought he could play better when he was high was dreaming. Keith Richards is unlikely to agree with that: after all, he still plays his instrument better than almost anyone else. He could also say that the needle has given him a range of extreme insight that lends depth to his playing, although it is hard to see how music can transmit the experience of flying to get your hair cut in Switzerland and waking up in Tokyo. But no reliable account will ever come from paid-up citizens of the artificial paradise. There is a certain glamour, however, to the way they fantasize: a glamour, and even an authority. Vice always finds it easy to make virtue look naive. Yet it is noteworthy that the knowing voices of the stoned can say so little in rebuttal when a veteran adept tries to point out that the drug thing was always a mistake even though Nancy Reagan said the same. John Phillips of the Mamas and the Papas, during a reprieve from the effects of combining all the habits it was possible to have, said that his long personal disaster began with the delectable fumes of marijuana, because they helped to normalize the expectation of getting high. All over the world, old-time hippies who were still dreaming about California greeted Phillips's admonitions with an orchestrated silence. They just breathed in and waited for what he said to go away.

The same could be said about Carrie Fisher's excellent debut novel *Postcards From the Edge*, which remains one of the most fearlessly penetrating memoirs about what cocaine can do to an original intelligence. It doesn't make the intelligence less intelligent. But it does make the intelligence less able to apply itself: a high price to pay for the bruised charms of an outlaw vocabulary. The remorse that saturates the book's enchantingly colloquial prose is concentrated in a single moment of the movie version, when Gene Hackman, playing the film director, calls the newly sober actress played by Meryl Streep into the looping studio to show her the scene she thought she had done so well, and she realizes that she made a mess of it. For any kind of artist, that's the worst feeling there is, and drugs are more likely to ensure you will feel it than to stave it off. There might be such a thing as a self-controlled user who can still create – it was Keith Richards who could play a duet with Chuck Berry, not me – but for those of us who can use up a lifetime's supply of anything in a fortnight, drugs are out of the question. That was the conclusion I reached when I woke up at about five o'clock in the evening on the day after the night I have described. I went down to the King's Head and sat alone while I made my resolution. A half pint of lager in one hand and a cigarette in the other, I vowed to stick to the devils I knew. In Cambridge, when the baby arrived, I saw myself as a model of probity, cherishing in my mind a silent pledge: though I might breathe beer on you and blow smoke in your face, I probably won't drop you out of a window or leave you forgotten in the back of a car. Not that we had a car. Come to think of it, if I didn't double my output of journalism we wouldn't even have a roof. Time, as we say in Australia, to take a good pull on myself.

A family would need a house, or at least a bigger flat. The wherewithal was thin on the ground. Sometimes I still dream of it: a sparse blizzard of little cheques. In reality, the cheques were bigger than snowflakes, but in my nightmares they are as tiny as the amounts of money written on them. The cheques for the monthly *Listener* TV column were the nearest to being a predictable event, like a female sparrow's period. There were other cheques from the different newspapers and magazines. There were the occasional cheques for appearing on BBC radio panels, the more occasional cheques for chairing the panel, and the very occasional cheques for contributing material for a radio series like *I'm Sorry, I'll Read That Again*, with which I had a loose connection but no regular contract. The songs would of course make millions one day but so far, with Pete's first album still

waiting for release, they had earned only the standard payments
for being played on the radio: payments that were collected by
the Performing Rights Society and extremely occasionally transformed into the smallest cheques of the lot. (Sometimes they
were for less than a pound.) Nowhere among these drifts of
unimpressive bits of paper was there any mention of a pension
or insurance. If I got sick for a week, our whole financial system
shrank to fit my wife's not very startling salary as a junior
academic. I had long been accustomed to more than my fair
share of that, but always on the understanding that my creative
efforts would eventually generate the cash to pay her back and to
pay my way, with something left over so that the family might
flourish.

That result was still in prospect, but it was all very chancy.
So far the baby didn't do much except eat, but it wasn't hard to
imagine her wanting other things: clothes, a bicycle, ballet lessons. From that viewpoint, I couldn't afford to have flu or even
a bad cold. I avoided snifflers in trains. Anxiety had barely taken
hold, however, before an invitation came from Granada Television. In those days, most of the best programmes on British
commercial television were produced by Granada. *All Our
Yesterdays*, *What the Papers Say* and *Cinema* were all Granada
programmes. For a long time I had been under the impression
that Granada Television was broadcast from Spain: an offshore
enterprise like pirate radio. Actually Granada was a company
based in Manchester, where it was presided over by Lord Bernstein, one of the great generation of Jewish grandees who
enriched Britain's post-war drive to educational justice with their
combination of money-making efficiency and an unquenchable
philanthropic urge. Possessed of cultural taste and the financial
wherewithal to spread its benefits, they played a crucial part in
extending cosmopolitan enlightenment to ordinary people. They
had seen civilization brought to the brink of ruin and they
wanted to bring it back. Bernstein was the pick of the bunch.

His flagpole programmes did what the BBC was meant to do but all too often didn't.

Among those programmes, *Cinema* had the biggest audience. Michael Parkinson, otherwise the best-known sports journalist in the Midlands, had made his television name as the presenter of *Cinema*. Now he had decided to move south and to move on. Granada was auditioning for a replacement. The producer of the show, Arthur Taylor, was a young man of rare qualities. He had not risen to his position from the usual Oxbridge background. He had got there by natural initiative. One of the marks of his originality was that he had actually seen a few episodes of *Think Twice*, a feat of selective attention comparable to having noted down the number plate of the Loch Ness monster. More stunning still, he had picked me as a possible substitute for the suave, neatly dressed and very personable Parkinson. Then as later, the mark of Parkinson's style on screen was to look as if he was hardly trying. Later on, as a critic, I was to make the mistake of echoing this common opinion in print. The fact, of course, was that he knew exactly what he was doing. But even then, when I didn't know how he did it, I doubted I could have the same effect of taking it easy on the air. On radio I had managed to slow myself down a bit by that stage, but I still got jumpy enough to swallow the front of every sentence. Couldn't stop doing it. Kind of verbal impressionism. In a rare fit of honesty, I conveyed some of these doubts to Arthur Taylor by telephone: briefly, because I was worried about the cost of the call. I told him that, too, and he said that a train ticket would be waiting for me at King's Cross.

The ticket was a first-class return. Today you could fly to Budapest for the cost of a first-class return to Manchester, but the ticket represented a considerable sum of money even then. A quick mental calculation told me that if I was that much ahead I might as well drink the difference. The first-class steward, who had once worked on the *Queen Mary* and looked distinguished enough to have been her lover, brought supplies of excellent beer to my seat. Luckily, nerves offset some of the effects, so that when I arrived in Manchester I was able to complete the journey to the Granada studio on foot instead of in an ambulance. Nevertheless, Arthur Taylor must have wondered what he had let himself in for. I had another beard going, even more nautical than the last, plus an abundance of hair swerving down the back of my neck and sticking out at the sides, thus to offset, in my view, the bald patch that was conspicuously surfacing on top of my head like an albino volcanic island. The slurred voice emerging from these cranial enhancements might as well have been singing 'What shall we do with the drunken sailor?' When I told him there was nothing wrong that a hair of the dog wouldn't fix, he told me the truth: Granada was a dry house, but there was plenty of coffee. While supplying me with a gallon of that, he mercifully neglected to say that the hair of the dog was already around my chin. He himself was clean shaven and immaculately clad in a well-cut leather sports coat, plain shirt with plain tie, and dark trousers with a knife-edge crease. My own shirt was the usual misjudged polyester paisley extravaganza, topped off with a new semi-suede belted jacket that was already showing signs of having been worn too close to a vat spitting hot oil. At no time did Arthur object to any of these features. Instead he gave me a brief outline of what would be required and led me into the biggest TV studio I had ever seen. There was almost nothing in there except a backdrop, a stool, a camera, a monitor, and a teleprompter. This was the entire kit with which Parkinson had made himself famous. If I got the audition right, it could be my turn.

This chapter would be more fun if I could say that I got it wrong. But my guardian angel descended, radiating benevolence. Later on I was told that the guardian angel was wearing the face of Lord Bernstein, who was watching on closed circuit in his office. By rights he should have taken one look and had me thrown me out of the building, with Arthur landing on top of me. But he decided to listen while I did the stuff that saved me.

The script on the teleprompter was to be recorded paragraph by paragraph between a string of film clips that would be played in on the monitor. The girl on the teleprompter control desk was of heartbreaking beauty and magnificence of bosom, so even when dazed I marshalled the energy to show off to her. I had learned a few things when doing *Think Twice*, and I ripped through the script without a fluff. My tiny, deep-set eyes turned out to be a plus. If I held my head straight, it was hard to tell from the screen that I was glancing sideways. This remained true even after the lighting gaffer tried to give me some eyes by setting a 10K lamp (it was called a 'brute') on the floor in front of me, pointing upwards. It lit up my cheekbones like Bela Lugosi thirsty for blood but there was still no telling which way I was looking as I prattled on. The film clips had to be rewound in real time, so there was a pause before the next run-through. During the pause, I did something that would have been really smart if my brain had been involved. Powered by the urge to close the physical distance between me and the pretty girl, I leaned over her angora-clad shoulder and told her how every piece of link material should be rewritten. From that angle, her breasts looked like a couple of nuclear submarines nosing out of harbour, but I managed to concentrate.

Writing in my head, I slipped in a back reference to some detail in each of the clips I had just seen, plus a forward reference to some detail in the next one. I can remember how I got in a pretty good crack about Jack Palance: something about how his first meal had been the midwife's fingers. Little did I know, as I inhaled the fragrance of the young lady's hair and she inhaled the fragrance of my breath, that I was in the process of nailing down a job. When we did another run and I made the cameraman laugh with the re-vamped script, I still didn't know. Later on I learned that Bernstein, from his office, had telephoned Arthur in the control room to ask if anything could possibly be done about my hair. Arthur correctly deduced that this meant Bernstein thought I should be taken on: he wouldn't be asking for modifications to the appearance of someone he was about to reject. Arthur replied that my beard was probably non-negotiable, being, as it was, a symbol of my refusal to compromise with bourgeois values. (Actually if he had asked me about that, he might have found out that my rebellious stance was flexible when faced with the prospect of losing out on a regular income.) Arthur agreed with Bernstein, however, that the wings of lengthy back-hair that stuck out at the sides, giving the effect of two squirrels hiding nose to nose behind my head, would have to go. When Arthur raised the question tentatively with me, I was too dumb to realize that I was being offered the job. I thought we were discussing a change of costume preparatory to another rehearsal.

But over drinks in the late afternoon, the sweet facts sank in. We took the drinks at a mid-town private club called the Grapes. Arthur explained to me that Granada was dry at Lord Bernstein's insistence. He had some old-fashioned idea that people worked harder if they weren't pissed. Granada personnel who wanted a beer during the day had to get it at the nearest pub, and not to be observed when going there. Apparently there was a cir-cuitous route that could not be seen either from the executive floor or from the front desk in the lobby. Threading down fire escapes and along behind annexes, this route was known as the Ho Chi Minh trail. One of the trail's branches led to the Grapes, where alcoholic drinks were served even outside pub hours. The Manchester United star footballer George Best, then in the last phase of his career but more famous than ever, was often there, attending to his business affairs. 'Attending to my business affairs' was a phrase he often used when answering questions from the tabloid reporters who were seldom far away, although mercifully they could gain no access to a private club. At the time, Best owned a Manchester boutique which was inexorably going broke while he sat in the Grapes pulling birds. He was present while Arthur and I had our discussion. Sitting only a few tables away, Best was communicating by telepathy with two attendant blondes while he threw beer coasters in the air and caught them without looking. Arthur assured me that this process was known as a Business Discussion. Our own business discussion seemed equally fantastic to me. I was being offered a contract that would bind me to recording two half-hour shows every second Wednesday for £60 a week each, plus first-class travel each way on the Midland Pullman and a night in the Midland Hotel after the day of recording. There would also be a full day's work per week in London at the Granada annexe in Golden Square, Soho, where the film clips for the shows would be marked up and the skeleton script worked out, mainly by me. It sounded like a lot of work but in those days £60 a show was big money for a beginner. A guaranteed first series of thirteen shows would produce something like a regular income even if they dropped my option afterwards.

Suddenly I was a breadwinner. As far as I can examine my own motives from this distance, the income was the main consideration, although I suppose the prospect of sudden fame was not without its attractions. The show had made Parkinson well known enough to earn the envy of his fellow journalists – the envy being expressed in the form of vituperation, as usual – and there was also the spectacle, edifyingly close to hand, of George Best and his supporting courtesans. They were looking at him as if he could work miracles. Since the only miracle he was currently working was to toss a beer coaster in the air and catch it without looking, this should have been evidence of their stupidity. But they didn't look stupid. They looked like the kind of Scandinavian air hostess who could speak four languages and fly the plane if the pilot died of food poisoning. So it should have been clear to them that their hero, when away from the football pitch, had little to offer except a snarl of lechery. But it didn't work that way. Fame was a universal solvent. Up went the beer coaster, and their eyes flashed as he caught it. You could tell that their underwear, if separated from their bodies, would just hang in the air, like a cloud. I said yes, and somehow made it to the Midland Hotel before I collapsed. I woke up again in time to catch a meal in the dining room before it shut down for the night. I can remember sitting there alone, trying to find my key so that I could prove to the waiter that I was allowed to sign the bill. The key, of course, was in my room, on the bedside table where I had left it after stripping my pockets. It was all very confusing. Something had gone right.

Something else went right not long later. Within a few weeks after taking over the show from Parkinson, I established a working rhythm for the first time in my professional life. Actually it was the first time that I thought of myself as someone who might have a professional life. Until then, everything had been an extension of my student days, minus the academic requirements and plus a sporadic financial reward. Student journalism in Cambridge had been a transition. Hand-to-mouth freelance journalism in London had been a further transition. This was the thing that the transitions were a transition to. This was actually it. I kept all my deadlines going and wrote more poems and songs than ever, but I also had a set task from week to week. Every Thursday I would be in Golden Square, viewing film clips all day and sketching out a commentary. Films that I hadn't actually seen could be viewed at other times: that didn't count as work. But choosing the clips was quite demanding if it were to be done well, and I wanted to write something more engaging than factual filler. Luckily, for a new movie the clips were already specified by the film companies, so there were no agonies of selection. There were sometimes agonies about what the film companies had been foolish enough to release, but there was no way out of that.

The day's work was sealed by a few beers with Arthur at Soho's most notorious drinking club, the Colony Room. Nothing about the Colony Room was more notorious than its proprietress, the notorious Muriel Belcher. She had a lot of notorious clients, most notoriously the painter Francis Bacon, but they were all outdone for notoriety by Muriel's face, which was a study in unrelenting hatred. I somehow got the idea that she hated me in particular. Perhaps she remembered me for the day in the early sixties when I had been in there in the role of gooseberry at a meeting between Robert Hughes and Colin MacInnes. I had distinguished myself on that occasion by my unfortunate trick of increasing the volume of my voice as it lost coherence. But she had seen plenty of drunks who did the same thing. No, this, surely, was a whole new loathing. I was probably putting too specific a value on her general manner. I thought she had a way, when I was ordering my round, of looking at me as if I were the suppurating corpse of a crushed toad. But she would have done the same for anybody. She looked that way even at Francis Bacon himself, who was often to be seen hulking notoriously beside the bar. He looked like what he was, a mad painter, and Muriel looked as if he had painted her. It was a frightening symbiosis, but it made me feel part of the action.

There was more action later, when Arthur left to catch his train back north and I headed off unsteadily to the Pillars of Hercules. At the Pillars, Ian Hamilton held his usual position at the bar, all set to receive incoming manuscripts and shred them in the presence of their perpetrators. Often I had a manuscript ready to receive this treatment, but now I had more confidence than usual, because I was at the end of a day's work that was, incontrovertibly, work. If I had done the work reasonably well, I was all set for the trip to Manchester every second Wednesday morning on the Midland Pullman. From the culinary angle, the Midland Pullman was the most luxurious thing that had yet happened to me in my life, with the possible exception of a few nights out with my future wife and her friends in a little restaurant near Santa Croce in Florence, in the days when I was too green to know that the pimps and hookers who infested the place were eating like royalty, and that those tiny slices of beef were as good and real as meat can get. Even today I am not much of a one for caring about food, as long as it isn't trying to kill me. Sequestered in my apartment while working on a book or a long essay, I am not quite the kind of slob I might have been if

I didn't care at all what I ate. I take pride in my timing. When heating the contents of a can of stewed steak, I keep a watchful eye on the saucepan to make sure I stir the stew at the exact moment when the first bubbles appear. Sometimes I wander off, start fiddling with a sentence, and notice only from the thick smoke and the smell of a crashed oil truck that something has gone awry. But usually I remember to stay near the hob. I try to keep an aesthetic measure to my simple needs. When cutting the corner of the plastic bag of the boil-in-the-bag piece of cod in white sauce, I try to cut it in a clean straight line so that no sauce gets on the scissors. The women at home don't let me eat cod – something about the world's stock being dangerously depleted, apparently by me personally – so when I eat cod in my apartment it tastes like a stolen truffle. But I couldn't care less about presentation. The stew goes into a bowl and the cod goes onto a plate, often with some green stuff added – spinach, beans, broccoli or those sweet little peas from a can – so as to stave off scurvy. The resulting visual arrangement is a legitimate cause for pride, in my view, but I don't call it presentation. On the rare occasions when, usually for business reasons, I am trapped in an up-market restaurant, I have been known to gaze at the exqui- sitely arranged main course – usually a small edifice of sprigs, shavings and sprouts in the middle of the plate – and wonder aloud when the food is coming. I have never been back to any restaurant where three waiters lift the silver dish covers simul- taneously at a murmured signal. They look like a brass band and you'll be eating their sheet music.

Later on, as we move further into a context of financial adequacy, I might return to this theme, but suffice it for now to say that breakfast on the Midland Pullman was a nice change from the Angus Steak House, even though the same notched tomatoes were a feature. In those days it was still true that the secret of eating well in Britain was to have breakfast three times a day. The Midland Pullman breakfast was what the British Indians of today have learned to call an English. Nothing that could make you fat was left out. Even the bread was fried. The black pudding was an ice-hockey puck soaked in the same fat that had drowned the bacon. The sausage, when cut, bled a thick, rich crude oil. The fried eggs were scorched brown around the edges like flying saucers after a battle in space. It was all brought to your table by waiters who expected to live and die in the service of British Rail. Later on I was to see the same dedication in the Qantas stewards of the airline's glory days: swervingly tactile Judy Garland fans who brought a deep love of choreography to the task of treading on the passenger's feet, they would present the next bottle of chardonnay as if it were a newborn baby to which they themselves had given birth. If a Midland Pullman waiter was troubled by the spectre of lingering class divisions, he didn't show it. You were called 'Sir' when asked if the massed calories already supplied were sufficient to fuel your next heart attack, or would you like an additional plate of fried bread?

Having washed it all down with a couple of beers, I would arrive in Manchester several pounds heavier than when I left London. Under my beard, my first double chin was arriving with the same inevitability as my temples were retreating, but I was still young and dumb enough to feel fighting fit. I had my script ready and I was ready to deliver it. I had kept the rule of having two beers only. They would wear off by the time we went for the tape. I hadn't forgotten the consequences of going on stage drunk at Hampstead – I still haven't forgotten – and I can truthfully say that I was always careful, even in my most dissipated years, never again to get tight before the show. The thought that what I did after the show might be damaging me anyway, with a steadily more devastating effect, had not yet occurred to me – partly because, no doubt, of the thoughtlessness induced by the steady massacre of the brain cells. But there were enough brain cells left over at that stage for their owner to figure out that a certain precision of delivery might be a useful characteristic to cultivate, with benefit for the reputation. And indeed I soon became pretty good at hitting the words in a visual ten-second countdown from the floor manager, and at reciting the long paragraphs without a stumble. In the dressing room before rehearsal, I went through my tongue-twister drills. 'Unique New York,' I intoned. 'Red leather, yellow leather.' There was a useful couplet from Edith Sitwell. 'Pot and pan and copper kettle/ Put upon their proper mettle.' If my tongue felt thick I cooled my head in cold water.

In the studio I could go for hours without a fluff. This ability was doubly important because in a clip show like *Cinema* a fluff could have large consequences. The clips were arranged sequentially on a single roll and were played in on time no matter what, because there were no editing facilities to clear out dead air. If a fluff screwed the cue, the clip roll had to be rewound to the start in real time. A presenter who mangled his words could be there for days on end. Hitting all the marks, I got a reputation as the One-Take Kid. Actually, in the long term, this was a dangerous reputation to have, because, after instant-start tape machines and electronic editing came in, a presenter who never wasted any time was simply setting himself up for putting too much work into the day. But at that time it was not only good manners to get it right first crack, it was a requirement. As I told Arthur over drinks in the Grapes afterwards, I was quite proud of meeting the demands. He smiled tolerantly, which was very nice of him. So I told him again. At dinner, I told the beautiful teleprompter girl the same thing. Under her angora twinset, her magnificent breasts stirred with emotion as she leaned forward and murmured something that was to live long in my memory. 'I don't think I've ever gone off anyone so fast.' But if I had trouble accepting the fact that I was a married man with a family – a thousand years later I am still struggling with the concept – there was at least a glimmer of awareness that my working life was acquiring a sense of order.

7. SQUARE-EYED IN DARKNESS

The opportunity of restoring it to chaos soon arose. At the *Observer*, Terry Kilmartin was printing my book reviews with sufficient frequency to attract the attention of the editor, David Astor, whose position at the paper was made no less influential by the fact that his family owned it. The paper was looking for a critic who could give the TV column the same sort of currency as the film column. When Penelope Gilliatt wrote the film column, people read it even if they never went to the cinema. The *Observer* bigwigs naturally assumed that the paper's intelligent, upper-crust readership couldn't possibly be watching television regularly. How, then, to make the TV column into a talking point like the film column? They decided that they were looking for a TV critic with a similarly identifiable prose style. Actually they already had a stylist on the job, Maurice Richardson. But Richardson was getting to the end of his career. Early on he had been a substantial name, author of a little classic of humour, *The Exploits of Engelbrecht*. Richardson was never as prolific as Paul Jennings, but he was in the same camp as a colloquial fantasist, and at his best he was of the same rank. Unfortunately he had developed idleness into an art form. He had got to the stage where making a minimum effort shows up in one's prose as a repetitive bag of tricks. He took on a book review mainly with an eye to selling the book afterwards, and had grown so dependent on the book-reviewer's classic perk that he would raid Terry's office at lunchtime for books he could sell even when he wasn't going to review them. His long voyage was ending in a slow shipwreck. I had already seen a few similar cases around Fleet Street and was starting to wonder how I could avoid the same fate for myself. The recurring picture of decrepitude seemed always to be connected with alcohol. There was a conclusion to be drawn from that, but the prospect of drawing it was so depressing that it drove me to the pub, where Terry would assure me that it was a bit early to start worrying about the end of my career. Terry, who found the English social consciousness tedious, enjoyed the company of off-trail vagabonds. By the way he laughed in disbelief, I could tell that he found my naked ambition refreshing, especially because I seemed less ambitious for anything in particular than for everything at once. As for me, I had found yet another father figure.

But this father figure gave me no clue that the job of TV critic was about to fall vacant, and that I might be up for it. Instead, I was invited to lunch by two of the paper's senior staff, Richard Findlater and Helen Dawson. The lunch took place at Bianchi's, the most written-up media restaurant of the period. The word 'media' might not yet have arrived in the language as a singular noun, but the actual thing, regarded as a collectivity, most definitely had arrived in the social fabric, although its personnel had not yet taken to writing mainly about each other. If you ate in Bianchi's you were part of the new communications meritocracy. Until recently I had been part of the communications underclass which ate at Jimmy the Greek's. Still haunted by the identical cockroaches that had blocked the way to the toilet during my first year in London, Jimmy's was on the same block in Soho as Bianchi's. In fact its distance from Bianchi's could be measured only vertically, because Jimmy's was in the basement and Bianchi's was on the first floor, practically in a straight line upwards. The distance was about fifteen feet but it could seem like fifteen miles to a young man with aspirations. People could lose their hair and gain an extra stomach as they made the climb. (Only Melvyn Bragg ever arrived at the top looking the same as when he left the bottom. In fact he looked younger. Eventually he arrived in the House of Lords looking as if he had just finished a game of conkers. Nobody has ever been able to figure out how he does this.) Breathless from the climb, I was pointed to the table by the front window where Findlater and Dawson were sitting. On the way I stopped to satisfy the curiosity of Nick Tomalin, who was holding court at a table of his *Sunday Times* cronies. Ever the investigative journalist, he asked me how I had got in. I told him that I had no idea. His tilted glance sparkled with suspicion through his thick glasses as I moved on. It was my first experience of table-hopping, a practice that I later came to disapprove of. But apart from murder, bank robbery and rape there has never been much I disapproved of that I didn't try out first, and I was aglow with that wanted feeling as I joined my hosts. The *padrona*, known only but universally as Elena, had just brought them a carafe of wine. Included in the round of introductions, she told me that she never missed an episode of *Cinema*, collected my book reviews in a special folder, and had not realized that my body, now visible at full length without the restrictions imposed by the small screen, would have such an athletic appearance, although she should have guessed it from the strength of my features, so unusually definite for one of such sensitivity. It was easy to see why she was the designated den mother of a thousand male misfits all thirsty for flattery. Her face glowed with maternal concern. I thought I detected the same fond look in the eyes of Helen Dawson, but for some reason her smile had developed a curl of the top lip. Findlater stared into the far distance, perhaps remembering what it had been like to be young, clueless, and still thrilled to have set foot on the road ahead. He was all too aware that the road ahead led around the block and, unless you were lucky, back down to Jimmy's.

Sharp cop, vague cop. It took me a while to figure out what these two were after. Unnervingly familiar with my monthly *Listener* TV pieces, they asked me why I treated the mass-entertainment programmes at the same length as the important stuff. I told them what I thought: that the mass entertainment was even more important, because a popular programme actually embodied social values, whereas prestige programmes merely examined them. By then this was a theme that I had worked out in detail, and I spared my hosts none of the nuances as the wine started to do its work. As I banged on, Findlater's eyes glazed over like the devilled kidneys he and I both chose for a main course. Later on I was to realize that his eyes were usually that way: I had merely failed to notice. There had been a time when Findlater, as a theatre critic, was level-pegging with Kenneth Tynan, but an era had passed, and now Findlater was one of those figures who haunted the corridors as they worked out their time. His very availability for this mission to size me up was in itself a bad sign, because Helen Dawson, lunching off a leaf of lettuce, was clearly the brains of the outfit. Her tongue was keen to match. Even when she approved of what I said, she spoke as if I were trying to sell her a used car, and she met any loose opinion with plain scorn. Her level of aggression was rare for a woman in an English context, and would have been rare for a leopard in an African context.

Not long later, that must have been one of the qualities that made her appealing to John Osborne, who was unusual among playwrights in his propensity for staging a scene in real life. Indeed he got to the point where he would rather do it there than in the theatre. After he married Helen Dawson, their conversations must have been like the plays he might have written instead. They lived in a large country house, which no doubt gave Osborne plenty of extra rooms in which to conceal himself. In Bianchi's I was at the future Mrs Osborne's mercy. Feeling as if I were somewhere in the middle of Act Two of *Look Back in Anger*, I nevertheless pressed on, as if stimulated by her sour interjections. The penny dropped when she asked me if I thought I could keep up a weekly schedule. Writing once a month in the *Listener*, she informed me, I might be able to scrape a thousand words together from intermittent viewing, but writing once a week would be a full-time job. At last it occurred to me that a full-time job was on offer. Suddenly I became taciturn. It was because I was stunned and frightened, but it must have looked as if I was indifferent. Not for the last time in my life, it didn't hurt to let the bait drift by instead of lunging at it. Findlater came momentarily into focus. 'What can we do to persuade you to come to us?' Mentally I replied that a large salary would help. Then I heard myself saying it. 'A large salary would help.'

Helen Dawson liked that. It was her kind of talk. 'How about an ordinary salary?' At least that's how I remember what she said. She might have said, 'Don't be a prick.' Whatever she said, I felt emboldened to explain that my stint on *Cinema* would not be something I would willingly give up if Granada renewed my contract after the first series, so I would be letting myself in for working night and day. It was clever of me not to say that I was already working night and day. In fact it was more than clever: it was an outright suppression of the truth. More accurately, it was a lie. But with my remaining powers of reason, I thought it might be better to secure the offer first and then figure out what to do next, rather than pointing out the impossibilities in advance. The sharp cop must have known that she was being hustled, but perhaps she was pleased to meet a whippersnapper who was ready for anything. Findlater, who had snapped his last whip long ago, was calling for the bill. The effect of waving to the waitress took all the energy he had left. His companion's parting shot was something about how refreshing it was to meet an Aussie so patently on the make. She even pronounced 'Aussie' correctly, which was an unusual skill among English journalists in those days. But her sardonic bent carried the virtue of honesty. The job, she said, was mine for the taking. Suddenly I was looking at the furniture of Bianchi's as if I had become part of it. In the distance, the suspicion framed by Nick Tomalin's horn-rims had become a certainty. He was smiling at an angle.

I can remember the restaurant, but I can't remember how I left it. Whether horizontal or vertical, I should have been feeling ten feet tall. A more reasonable estimate, however, would be ten millimetres, because even in a state of euphoria I could see a problem looming that would tax my reserves of moral courage a long way beyond the limit. Karl Miller would have to be told, and told before rumours of this offer reached him. Since Fleet Street ran on rumours the way that a sperm whale ran on krill, I had about a day to get to him before I found him sitting there with a cocked shillelagh on his desk. Asking myself to do this was like asking myself to get to a dentist just because a tooth was hurting, or to open a brown envelope just because it was marked FINAL NOTICE in red. But a dimly flickering sense of rectitude told me that for once I had better shape up to a potentially unpleasant confrontation. Next day, after only a few tours of the block and an unprecedented visit to St Whatname's in order to study its entablature, I entered Karl's office to face a character analysis that began with flagellation and went downhill from there. On a technical level he was so brilliant that he must have had his stuff ready. Perhaps he had figured out that if I was turning up before my next piece was due I could only be there to tell him that I wouldn't be writing it. More likely, he had already heard the news overnight. The *Observer*'s internal security was not great, and he had close friends in the building. Either way, he was well prepared with invective. There was none of the standard headmaster stuff about letting myself down along with the school. Instead there was quite a lot about treachery, duplicity and the spiteful biting of the hand that fed. The same man I had seen sitting behind his desk with an open umbrella above his head to ward off his troubles showed no humorous self-deprecation today. The deprecation was all for me. Falsely assuring me that he lacked the words to express his contempt, he invoked historical parallels with Culloden, Vichy France, the suppression of the 1956 Hungarian uprising, and other episodes in which devious opportunism had played a role. The historical overview expanded to embrace the cosmic: Satan himself had probably been an Australian. In his peroration, he expressed his relief that at least he would never have to clap eyes on me again. But just before I left, he wanted me to know that I shouldn't feel too certain that my readiness to serve the enemy would ensure a glittering future: Vidkun Quisling had once felt the same about his prospects in Norway. Awaiting the disloyal, he reminded me, there was a circle of Dante's Inferno which punished them with each other's company in perpetuity, so deeply shut off from the civilized world that nobody virtuous had ever heard their screams. Never, he whispered hoarsely, never did any of them return to the sweet light of day. Finally it was all over and I was removed from his office in sections.

Later on, when I recounted the episode to fellow writers of more experience, I was told I had got off lightly. By Karl's standards, it had been a caress, and indeed he was speaking to me again after less than a quarter of a century, telling me fondly that he had always found my sensitivity and diffidence quite touching. At the time, I was poleaxed. A reluctance to tell people what they don't want to hear has always been among my worst weaknesses of character. It still gets me into trouble today, but early on it led me into a kind of paralysis, and would have earned me a crippling reputation for deviousness if I had been less lucky. This confrontation with Karl was proof that the reluctance had a deep purpose, because to overcome it might hurt, and I was ill-equipped to take the hit. Above all, I hated making an enemy. Ian Hamilton, reigning supreme at the Pillars of Hercules like John Calvin in Geneva, once told me that he counted it a bad week if he didn't make a new enemy. I told him that it was one of those things I couldn't understand about him. I told him that I brought suffering upon myself and others by a psychotic inability to say what was on my mind. Sipping a Scotch through his fixed sneer, he said, 'You're a very complex character.' Instantly I realized that he wouldn't mind making an enemy out of me either, if it came to the point. Cravenly I vowed to myself that it would never come to that. But it had come to that with Karl. Remembering his anger, I lost sleep. But I was going to be losing plenty of that anyway. When I told Arthur Taylor that

I planned to take on the *Observer* TV column, in addition to *Cinema*, he said, 'You're going to do *that*?' as if I had outlined a plan for splitting myself in half so as to be in two places at once. In attempted mitigation, I explained, with some element of truth, that with a steady commitment in a Sunday paper I could cut back on some of the casual journalism that had been filling my spare time, and thus lead a more efficient working life.

He swallowed it because he had to. My Granada contract specified exclusivity only for television. There was nothing to stop me taking on a full-time job in any other field: nothing except sanity, which was clearly not among my attributes. As for the *Observer*, they could not restrict my outside activities either, as long as I did not write about television for any other weekly newspaper. They could have controlled more of my time if they had taken me on staff, but David Astor, after one look at my beard, nylon corduroys and brown reinforced wool tie with electric-blue shirt, had instructed his accounts department to offer me only a freelance contract. Himself a picture of the gentlemanly Establishment – even his underwear must have been tailored in Savile Row – he probably thought that anyone who turned himself out like me could not live long. Eventually I heard that it had been Terry who persuaded Astor to offer me any kind of extended deal at all. Astor had a solid track record of hiring refugees from Europe, but they were in flight from persecution. I was an Australian in flight from nothing except ordinary standards of personal appearance. In fairness, however, it should be said that Astor was a genuine connoisseur of writing. I would like to think that my writing, even though still in a raw state, had something that would have led him to set aside his fastidious objections even if his most trusted troops had not told him that he should. But perhaps this is wishful thinking. A freelance contract, after all, was close to being an invitation to drop dead as soon as possible. No staff privileges, no pension, no nothing except a fixed fee each for forty-eight pieces in the year ahead, the deal terminable at any time with only three months' worth of fees as a pay-off. If I had had an agent, she would have told me to get a lawyer. If they had ever fired me, I would have been on the scrap heap, because it would have been plain for all to see that I had tried and failed. But I didn't plan to get fired. In the same way, my hero Evel Knievel, when he took off from the ramp on his motorcycle to leap high in diamanté-studded white-leather outline against the dazzling nightscape of Las Vegas, didn't plan to end up in hospital with his bones being joined back together by metal pins.

Although careful, for once, to play myself in slowly, I got lucky with the *Observer* TV column from the start. By 1972 the sports commentators were operating in full force and the screen teemed with real-life characters richer than anything in the soap operas or the police series. A fashion parade of sheepskin-lined car-coats and sporting hats, David Coleman, Ron Pickering, David Vine and Alan Weeks continued to be reliable sources of unintentional innuendo. ('And once again Tompkins pulls out the big one!') Heart-rending in their unguarded patriotism, they provided one quotable double entendre after another as they praised British contestants not for how well they played the game, but for having taken part. ('And he is inside Podborski! He is inside Podborski by a long way!') I won't indulge here in too much quotation from myself. What I wrote in those years is available in my 1991 collection *On Television*, or would be available if the book were available. It is out of print now, but there are still some young would-be writers who are kind enough to look for it second-hand. When they find it, they are bound to conclude that many of the contemporary references have gone out of date. But history consists entirely of contemporary references that have gone out of date, and what I was writing was a kind of social history, as it was transmitted through the voices, clothes, hairstyles and mannerisms of the people on screen: not the actors in the dramas, but the permanent staff who were bringing us their interpretation of reality, and creating a whole new alternative reality by doing so. If my approach clicked, it was because the audience already thought the same, but had not previously written it down.

The key element of the column's gratifying impact was that its readers were already talking that way at home. They had not only been watching much more television than the *Observer* bigwigs suspected, they had incorporated television's repertory cast of presenters and pundits into their folklore and frame of reference. They made cruel jokes about Fanny Craddock. The thinly rewarded jingoism of the sports commentators ('And Wilkins quite content with his fifth place. He can build on that') was as hilarious to them as it was to me. Thus one of the best things about Britain – the readiness of its educated class to see the funny side of a fading dream – worked in my favour. I covered the serious programmes too, and indeed, right from the start, I spent more time praising than blaming. The praise drew a bigger response when it was unexpected. I thought, and said, that the unknown women who had written, produced, and directed a series like *The Girls of Slender Means* were worth all the famous males in the West End. When I praised many of the popular programmes as if they were more serious than the solemn ones, it was meant as the endorsement of a value, not as the mocking of it. Good comedy, I argued, was better than bad drama because good comedy was more dramatic, and almost always better written. Sometimes I spelled such principles out in what was meant to be an aphorism, but gradually I learned to illustrate them by implication.

There could be no doubt, however, that outright denigration was the most fun to read, and easiest to remember. If I am remembered as an attacking critic, that was the reason. It was never really true, but there is no point complaining now, and I had no call to complain then. Letters flooded in. Journalists commonly call any number of letters greater than two a flood, but this really was a lot of mail. It was waiting for me on my desk every Friday morning when I came in to type up the column. Until I was instructed by the management to answer every letter,

I dealt with the correspondence by putting it in the bin after having read it. Since most of it was literate and thoughtful, and some of it was signed with names I would later have recognized, to dump it was unwise as well as intolerably rude, but I have always had the twin bad habits of treating praise as my due, and the acknowledgement of it as a depletion of precious energy. Nowadays, I try to be more grateful, but a considerate personal letter is still likely to go into my Must Answer By Hand file, where its paper will dry and its ink fade as the years elapse. In the early seventies I just automatically ditched everything, using youth as an excuse. In the early seventies I was already in my early thirties, so the excuse was getting rusty. But I had trouble grasping that all this attention was quite real. (Being unable to accept praise gracefully is quite compatible with needing a lot of it: in fact the second failing is often a direct product of the first.) I felt the same way about life itself: if I stopped running even for a moment, there would be nothing to hold on to. The speed was keeping me upright. Compulsively productive, I couldn't even get drunk without working on my next piece of writing somewhere in the back of my addled brain.

With time off for my *Cinema* obligations, and for all the literary journalism assignments that I had promised to cut back on but in fact allowed to increase, I was writing the TV column in my head all week, even as I made written notes in my workbook while actually watching the little screen. Much of the viewing I could do at home in Cambridge. This would have made me popular if it weren't that a man watching television all the time was effectively as absent as an astronaut orbiting the Earth. On the Thursday night I was in London, going through my notes and deciding on the running order – the right term, because my column was essentially a one-man Footlights smoking concert in miniature form. It needed an opening number, a monologue, a love song, a knockabout sketch, a closing number, and a spontaneous encore. And they all had to happen in a thousand words. That took thought, which I recorded as a skeletal frame, listing and shuffling the desirable events, outlining the themes, joining them up with arrows. Next morning, I was in the open-plan office at my assigned desk, which during the week had been used by other people doing other things. Nothing in, or on, the desk, was my property, not even the typewriter, into which I fiddled my first sheet of self-carbonating paper at about ten a.m., with the deadline set at noon. Double spaced, a thousand words filled three and a bit sheets of foolscap. I filled them as if they had offended me through their ever having been empty. For two hours my hands were a blur, reappearing in focus only when I ejected a full sheet of paper and reached for the next.

I was soon told that I was an infuriating spectacle while doing this. Manning desks all around me and far into the distance, there were a lot of full-time journalists slogging dutifully at their mandatory tasks, and for them it was no pleasure to see a part-time carpet-bagger earning the full whack in two hours, hammering away as if being fed his whole piece by dictation through an electrode implanted in his skull. Apparently the least prepossessing element was my tendency to rock with silent laughter at my own jokes. There was a reason for that. The jokes were the last aspect to form on the page. I had the line of argument already worked out, but when a tricky thought suddenly condensed into a gag I was surprised every time. When the piece was done, I took it to Findlater for editing. Out in the middle of a nominally open-plan office with acres of people all subject to one another's scrutiny, he had managed to build himself a cubicle out of filing cabinets and bookshelves. Inside this cubicle he might or might not be hiding. Invisible even when he was there, for much of the time he was absent, slowly stalking the corridors, where he would meet other, similarly venerable corridor-stalkers who were taking leave from self-constructed cubicles of their own. But he was usually in residence at the appointed time to receive my copy, on which he would make a few marks with an antique fountain pen – almost certainly a school prize – that looked as if it weighed a ton. It moved as if inhabiting the gravity field of Jupiter. The marks it made were usually helpful but he had a bad tendency to put a comma in at random near the middle of a sentence if he thought it had been going on too long. Because I had already devoted several years to developing a style that would crack along instead of hanging about, extra commas affected me like mosquitoes that had got in under the net on a hot night. Ready to fight for once, I would demand that the commas be taken out again. The demand no doubt sounded more like a tearful plea, but Findlater found it easier to comply than to resist. Lying back in his chintz easy chair – how had he got it into the building? – he looked up at me as if wondering at his own part in creating a monster. But he took out the commas. Later on, after Findlater had finally faded away altogether and his cubicle had been dismantled, Terry Kilmartin personally took over the task of editing my copy. Though untroubled by my calculated dearth of commas, he proved a much harder nut to crack if he thought that some extravagance I had committed needed to be taken out. Much of my lexical intemperance had already been torched out of me by Karl's acetylene scrutiny, but there was plenty left for Terry to purse his lips at. He stared at me over the top rim of his half glasses as his blue pencil softly struck. Findlater rarely questioned an excess, perhaps aware that anything stupid would be picked up later, at proof stage, when Terry would see the piece anyway. Findlater wanted a quiet life. The trouble he had gone to in order to secure it was impressive even to a tyro. He had everything in that nest of his except a hip bath. Burrowing my way out, I would go to lunch.

Lunch, at first, I usually took at the Black Friars pub, an *Observer* haunt only a few steps away. John Silverlight used the place to run an informal seminar on English grammar for all who cared to listen. Many did, in those blessed days when the precision of the language, in the city where it first flowered, was still thought essential to its beauty. Terry was often there and we would eke out the beer with a few sausages. After a couple of months we took to lunching à deux at Mother Bunch's, another

Observer filling station, where you could order an actual plate of something, instead of eating it with your fingers. Later still, the occasion acquired extra personnel, as I shall relate, but in my first days as a working visitor to the paper I was regarded, and regarded myself, as a strange bird strictly passing through. This worked my way, because I was allowed to break rules. It was correctly supposed that I didn't know what the rules were. After lunch I went back to read my proofs. Sometimes there had been drastic subtractions because the legal department, which had been separately reading my carbon copies (they were called 'the blacks'), had objections on grounds of libel. Some of these objections struck me as foolish. In a paragraph about the burgeoning human traffic on the peak of Everest I had written: 'Régine has plans to open a restaurant up there.' The lawyers pointed out that unless she really did have such plans, she could sue. I thought she would be more likely to send us a case of champagne, but I had no choice in the matter.

Quite often the lawyers were right, and saved my skin. Other subtractions were done by Terry. In most cases he was right too. I would put in a plea for a cherished phrase and sometimes save its life by allowing a slight modification. None of this was regarded as troublemaking. It might even have registered as an uncommon care for detail. The trouble started with what I did next. It was an unwritten rule that no journalist could enter the downstairs composing room where his prose, after being set up in type, was laid out on the flat table called 'the stone'. Unaware of the rule, I would turn up at the stone to see what they were doing with my stuff. In the days of hot metal it was a compositor's skill to read the blocks of type back to front, like Leonardo's mirror writing. I had the same skill from my stint at the *Sydney Morning Herald* in the year after I left university and before I sailed for England. Charged with putting the leader page to bed every Friday night, I had learned quite a lot of the technicalities. The *Observer* compositors, every one of them a member of the only union that could hold Fleet Street to ransom, found themselves being instructed to make adjustments. If I found a line turnover was interfering with the balance of a sentence, I would ask for an extra word to be set up and inserted, or another word to be removed. When a new midshipman turns up on the gundeck to suggest a better way of loading the cannon, the gunners have only two courses of action: either to pitch the little bastard over the side, or else to adopt him as a mascot. Unbeknownst to me, the compositors had a quick chapel meeting and decided on the second course. I got adopted, and for as long as hot metal lasted I was allowed to turn up and help sling the lead that was turning my voice into print. Unaware that it was a privilege, I took it as a mutual recognition of the fact that the piece wasn't finished until the presses rolled. When they rolled, they shook the building. I had already left, but I knew exactly what I would see under my name on Sunday morning.

8. STAR ENCOUNTERS OF THE FIRST KIND

That a million other people would see it too was a datum whose full impact was slow to sink in. After all, the paper was full of good writers. But I had the best subject. When Edward Crankshaw reviewed a book about Stalin, he had to spend the opening paragraph giving the readers a potted history of the Soviet Union. My readers already knew what I was talking about. By that stage, television was a household experience, the first frame of reference in everybody's mind. So I could spend my whole time being as allusive as I liked. In the long term, this privilege was to make all the difference. Because TV took in everything, I could take in everything too. It was the ideal set-up for a cracker-barrel philosopher. The possibilities, however, were slow to dawn, and for the moment my *Observer* column felt like a holiday from *Cinema*, which was the job that counted. For one thing, the job was growing, like the spaceman's hand in *The Quatermass Experiment*. I was still recording the two shows back to back in Manchester every second Wednesday, and preparing for them in London every week, but there was a new policy to supplement the regular shows with irregular specials, which would add up to a series all on their own: a string (not yet called 'a strand') of interviews with the movie stars. Some of the movie stars were quite big, but even the small ones were hard to lure up to Manchester. The first star was very small indeed, although in my own eyes he loomed larger than Betelgeuse. He was the veteran lyricist Johnny Mercer, the very man who wrote 'The Summer Wind' and 'One For My Baby', which today still sets my standards for the way a colloquial phrase can be multiplied in its energy by

how it sits on a row of musical notes. But to *Cinema*'s audience
he was known only, if at all, as the author of 'Moon River', which
everyone knew from the charming way Audrey Hepburn almost
managed to sing it in *Breakfast at Tiffany's*. Mercer had prominence, but scarcely stardom.

Mercer's relative obscurity was a lucky break for me, because
there were few repercussions after I stuffed up the interview so
badly that it couldn't be transmitted. Knowing a lot about him,
I spent far too much time proving to him that I knew it. An
interviewer should certainly be well prepared, but only so that
the answers won't catch him flat-footed. I made the beginner's
classic mistake of including the answer in the question. This left
my puzzled guest with little to say beyond 'yes' and 'no'. The
interview was done on film in a specially rented room of the
London hotel where Mercer was staying. When Mercer had gone
back to his own room, no doubt wondering why he had bothered,
Arthur sat down in the guest's vacated chair and read me the
news. 'We can't use this.' I sat there on the verge of tears while
he gave me a quiet but unforgettable lesson in the necessity of
asking a plain question so as to make the guest look like the
interesting one, and not the host.

Well aware that I had made an expensive mess of things, I
took the news in, and it formed the basis of my modus operandi
from then on. Though I have always choked on such standard
questions as 'How did you feel when . . . ?' and 'What was it like
to work with . . . ?', it is better to ask them, or something like
them, than to load a question with the very information that it is
designed to elicit. I tried to overcome my squeamishness about
appearing ignorant to the instructed viewer. The instructed
viewer is rarely watching. It's the uninstructed viewer that you're
after. Another basic interviewing skill was even more elementary
but harder to master: listening to the answer. If you ask someone
'What did you do when you left school?' and he answers 'I
murdered my mother and buried her under the patio,' the next
thing you say should not be 'And then I suppose you went to

university?' Eventually I got better at that one, but luckily I got better straight away at not upstaging the client. The Mercer debacle, plus the subsequent tongue-lashing from my producer, threw a real scare into me. It seemed logical to conclude that I should try to learn from the humiliation. Much, much later, I learned to count this ability to recover from catastrophe as one of my most useful qualities. I could put it down to sensitivity, but it is more likely to depend on the opposite. I have seen some highly talented people put out of action by a failure. They take it for a just estimation of their abilities. I never questioned that I had a right to be there, even when the people who thought I hadn't might seem to have a good case, handed to them by me. No matter what disasters had driven me out of it, I always returned to the centre of attention. The spotlight healed my wounds. I had a thin skin, but a brass neck.

An interview with Richard Burton went better: well enough, in fact, to reach the screen. Burton had a stiff movie to push and was therefore available. Even in those days, you could get the stellar names only when they were flogging a dog. Burton's movie, called *Hammersmith is Out*, barked and chewed bones. I don't think even he ever sat through it. I did, as part of my preparation. Something had gone wrong with every part of the movie. The action never started. On the other hand, it never ended. As a token that the plot was going nowhere, Burton spent the whole movie standing around. When he walked, it was so that he could stand around somewhere else. Nobody would give a toss. But he was still a star. When Granada proposed to Burton's people that he should be interviewed in Manchester, they proposed Monte Carlo. London was the compromise, but at least we were in a studio. I can't remember which one it was – they all look the same from inside – but I can remember exactly my first impression of Burton. In the press profiles he had always been called stocky, and as his career declined, the journalists took to calling him short. Later on I realized that journalistic estimates of physical stature are always relative to perceived status, but I was still at the stage of believing what I read, so it was a shock to find that Burton was quite tall. What made him look less so, especially on screen, was the size of his head. It was as big as a tea chest. You had to lean sideways to look past him. On the front of that vast expanse of cranium, the features were arranged like a caricature of Richard Burton. I was still getting used to the fact that the stars look so like themselves: it is the first, and sometimes the only, characteristic they have. Burton seemed quite tolerant of my beard. He would probably have been tolerant if I had been dressed as a Maori chieftain. Though upright, with his bulky shoulders squared, he was barely awake. He was sober that afternoon, but the previous day had taken its toll, along with the previous half century.

Fortune decreed, however, that he had his answers ready, whatever the question. I courted disaster only once, when I hesitated to join in with his estimation of Joseph Losey as some kind of genius. If Burton had been in, say, *The Servant*, this might have been a proposition that he could plausibly illustrate, but the Losey film he had been in was *Boom*, which I had once watched go by on the big screen like a stricken luxury liner limping home to port after its passengers all died in a mass outbreak of boredom. As a blacklisted Hollywood director who had gone into exile in Europe and made a string of literate films in conditions of great difficulty, Losey was much revered among British film people: to admire him was a mark of seriousness. But he was short of humour, as his occasional attempt at comedy proved, and his concomitant solemnity – general recognition of which would eventually deprive his back catalogue of its prestige – was perfectly apparent even at the time to anyone not blinded by his legend. My guardian angel stopped me from saying so, and Burton was free to burble on with detailed reminiscences about Losey which were all taken out in the editing, on the correct assumption that the audience wouldn't have known what he was talking about. But I made sure that I dug out of him all the best stories about his more popular movies. Some of them, after all, were pretty good, especially *The Spy Who Came In From the Cold*, which I thought masterly. He was pleased to hear that, although he would have been less pleased to hear that I thought Oskar Werner attained a naturalness on screen which Burton had never dreamed of. Happily I didn't say that either. Most of the opinions came from the client: a desirable imbalance, because the viewers, on the basis of their own experience, can decide for themselves whether the interviewee is talking nonsense or not, and even if they decide he is, they still find him a lot more interesting than the interviewer. I even managed to look excited when discussing *Hammersmith is Out*, which is more than I can say for Burton. But although never more than half awake, he was also never less than intelligent and civilized. Discounting the occasional flash of his undying belief that his alliance with Elizabeth Taylor had raised him to new artistic heights unknown to the Stratford Memorial Playhouse or the Old Vic, Burton handled his end of the business pretty well, and I was almost as impressed by him as I was by his one-man entourage, a black heavyweight who drove the car and arranged the details. After the heavyweight loaded Burton into the back of the limousine so that he could finish waking up, I was glad to find that I had my producer's favour. 'We can use that.'

When I saw the trimmed version on screen, I could see that it was no triumph for either party. But it wasn't bad. An interview with Robert Mitchum went better still, mainly because Mitchum was more interesting all round. Burton, to prove himself alert to the English language, had to quote Shakespeare or Dylan Thomas. Mitchum could quote himself. There are people you can't take your ears off when they talk, even when they mumble. Mitchum was one of them. His mumble, however, was formidable. Operating through a spokesman in his retinue, he demanded to audition us over lunch at the Dorchester. Arthur and I were there early, and well dug in. Mitchum turned up on time to the minute but we couldn't understand what he was saying. 'I seem fine squaws rive earl.' A trained simultaneous translator from Geneva would have told us that he had said, 'I see my firing squad has arrived early.'

Theoretically Mitchum was on the wagon at the time, but he must have taken one look at my beard and changed his mind, because when the waiter asked him if he would like something to drink he made the waiter bend down and spent a long time whispering in his ear. The whispering was accompanied by illustrative movements of his hands, as if he were passing on arcane secrets in the art of flower arrangement. When the drink arrived it was about two feet tall, changed colour on the way up, and had foliage sprouting from the top, like a core sample from an Amazonian swamp. All it needed was a toucan perched on a branch. There was always the chance that this concoction had no alcohol in it, but it certainly had some kind of active ingredient, because after he had inhaled about half of it, Mitchum's voice suddenly came into focus. It was still, however, pitched very low. It has always been a practice of the big male movie stars to pitch the voice low when off screen, so as to make the interlocutor lean forward. The angle of inclination is an index of prestige. For a movie star, being interviewed on television counts as being off screen, so the volume is duly screwed down, which duly increases the amplitude of the timbre. This can give a TV sound engineer unmanageable problems. I had seen an interview with Lee Marvin during which I had to lean my head against the TV set, which shook to the reverberation. Here was Mitchum doing the same thing in a restaurant. If he did the same thing in the studio, we were dead. Inspired by fear, I decided to play it deaf. Nowadays it would be no trick, but then I had to fake it. Mitchum took pity on a fellow actor and raised his volume into the range of the audible. Greatly daring, I offered not to ask him about his early stardom in the first-ever celebrity marijuana bust. 'Go ahead.' This answer cleared the air nicely, and the following conversation flowed without a hitch, except for his reluctance to expand on an anecdote after giving us its bare bones. Afterwards, Arthur told me this was a good sign: the client was saving his best stuff for the air.

He did, too. In studio he was tremendous. He liked it that I knew about the off-trail movies as well as the mainstream ones. *Build My Gallows High* was a favourite film noir of mine and I could have proved it by reciting the dialogue from memory, but I had learned my lesson and let him recite it instead. I was a big fan of *Thunder Road*, the low-budget thriller about the best moonshine-liquor driver in the mountains. ('He sets a pace that only a madman can match.') So was Mitchum: the project had been his idea, and he was instantly off and running about the difficulties of getting a pet idea financed and filmed within the prevailing system. His rare intelligence was in every sentence he spoke, and for a wonder he spoke every sentence clearly, although he was still no louder than a mole in hiding. But compared to Lee Marvin, Mitchum was Cicero. It went so well that we asked him if we could keep rolling long enough to turn the footage into two programmes instead of one. He agreed on the spot. It was as if he didn't want to go home. I didn't either. Finally the electricians pulled the plugs, Mitchum wandered off into the gathering dusk, and I waited with some confidence for Arthur's accolade. 'We can certainly use that.' Arthur went off to catch the train to Manchester, where he would have three whole weeks to edit the first of the two programmes.

Early the next day he was on the phone to Cambridge to break the bad news. Mitchum's people had double-crossed us and made their star available for the *Parkinson* programme two weeks from now. Parkinson's BBC talk show was still building up at that stage but it was already the thing for a visiting star to do, and the studios were already working on the principle that to turn down the exposure just because of a previous promise would be a quixotic price to pay for a little thing like integrity. It was no use complaining to Mitchum himself, who probably had no idea of what was going on. The only answer was to edit the first of our programmes immediately and get it on the air before *Parkinson*. A ticket awaited me at Euston. I was direly enjoined not to have too big a breakfast on the Pullman and to be sure to write my introduction on the way, because we would have to tape it as soon as I got there.

Drinking nothing but orange juice and water, I wrote the script on the train, taped it successfully when I arrived, and sat in on quite a lot of the editing, which was a revelation. We were cutting film, not splicing tape, so it took two moviolas and a pot of glue to accomplish in an hour what an Avid machine would later do in five minutes. The revelation lay in what you could cut out and still keep the sense. Next morning I left them to it and went back to London on the early train to write my TV column, feeling like a fighter-bomber pilot flying multiple missions to the Falaise Gap in 1944. This was the life.

Or to put it another way, this was madness. Military analogies are always the tip-off that a writer is dramatizing himself, but there could be no doubt that I was outrunning my supply lines even as I stormed forward. An example of what madness looked like was provided by Burt Lancaster, who suddenly became available after our first Mitchum programme was successfully screened. We managed to get it on the air a few days before the *Parkinson* interview, which duly undercut the impact of our second programme that followed later. But on any objective assessment I could say truly that Mitchum did better with us than with Parkinson. Like all people with a feel for language, Mitchum was reluctant to say the same thing again in the same words, so he gave Parkinson a more circumlocutory set of responses. It wasn't Parkinson's fault. But I had a subjective assessment going along with the objective one, and I preferred to think that it *was* his fault. I was a bit chippy about Parky's having jumped our claim. Nevertheless, we had got our first programme into the leading spot, and Lancaster's people were sufficiently impressed with what they saw to think that we might do the same for their man. For them, it would be good advance publicity for a Michael

Winner movie called *Scorpio*, then in the last stages of filming at
Shepperton. The deal was that I would interview Lancaster at an
exterior location, somewhere not far from the studio but far
enough to ensure that it would be difficult to control the sound.
Open-air interviews are hard for just that reason. Unless you are
using two cameras at once, noise in the background makes the
footage hard to edit, so that you are always going for another
take on an interchange that might not have gone very well
already, but will be certain to go worse when you shoot it again.
Arthur told me it would be good practice, and anyway, this was
our only chance to get Lancaster, even though his career was in
the doldrums by then. After personally revolutionizing the Hollywood production system so that actors acquired real creative
power for the first time, he had clung on too long to his status as
the magnetic leading man. (Later on, when he allowed himself
to be cast as the old timer, his career entered a second phase of
glory, with movies like *Local Hero* and *Atlantic City* being built
around his hulking but always gracefully moving presence, whose
boundless vitality had at last mellowed towards the bearable:
he became less of a ham as he lost vigour.) But if, at that stage,
he was no longer what he was, he was still a huge name. We
would have said yes if he had been in jail.

So down we went to the location, in an open field where there
were tents for dressing rooms, tents for offices, and tents for two
different grades of dining hall, one for the dogsbodies, and the
other, a hundred yards further away, for the director and the star.
One glance at the film's prospectus told me that it was a tired old
spy drama that would be released only into oblivion, like a blob
of spit aimed at a hot stove. But I had no reason to despise
Michael Winner and indeed I still don't today. *Death Wish* might
be a favourite movie among gun nuts but it is not without a
measure of narrative drive, and at least Winner got his movies
made, when so many other British directors were sitting around
moaning about their wounded artistic purity, which they didn't
mind compromising by making commercials anonymously.

Recently I read Winner's autobiography and it wasn't half bad. It was three-quarters bad, but only because of its many thousands of superfluous exclamation marks. Clear those out into a skip and the book would be a fascinating, if much shorter, story of diligence rewarded, told in a prose admirably forthcoming if not always edifying. One of the sub-stories in the book concerns Winner's love–hate relationship with Burt Lancaster. You might wonder why it wasn't hate–hate. Once, on location in Mexico, Lancaster had grasped Winner by the throat and hung him out over a high cliff. It's either kind or craven for Winner to remember this behaviour as somehow an indication of Lancaster's lovable volatility, because it sounds exactly like homicidal mania.

On location near Shepperton, things were more restrained, but still very weird. The unit was between set-ups when we arrived. Sitting intensely in a canvas-backed folding chair marked BURT LANCASTER, the star stuck a cigarette in his mouth and waited. He had to wait only a few seconds before Winner shouted, 'A light for Mr Lancaster!' A factotum bounded forward with a cigarette lighter already spouting flame. After the next shot, lunch was called. The smaller mess tent for the star and the director was in plain sight, about two hundred yards away. Lancaster stood up from his chair, but that was as far as he went by himself. He stared at Winner with a weary impatience. Winner took the cue and shouted, 'A car for Mr Lancaster!' A black Mercedes 600 longer than a school bus loomed across the grass and stopped precisely so that the action hero could step directly into it after the back door had been opened by the assistant director, the PR attaché, and other members of the door-opening party that I could not identify. The Mercedes set off on its epic journey across two hundred yards of grass, arriving at the sacred tent only a short time before the rest of us arrived on foot. Lancaster's door remained firmly closed until it was opened by the chauffeur, the assistant director, the PR attaché, the other members of the door-opening party, and Winner himself. Winner congratulated Lancaster on his successful voyage in terms which would have embarrassed

Lindbergh after his arrival in Paris. It was a graphic demonstration
of the perennial need for the institution of monarchy: because
there is a total, ineradicable potential for subservient ceremonial
bullshit in the universe and it all has to go somewhere.

I would have been open-mouthed if Arthur had not conveyed
to me in a whisper the vital necessity of keeping my trap shut. I
already knew that Lancaster had not attained his position as one
of Hollywood's most powerfully creative figures by self-denial
and humility. His company Hecht, Hill and Lancaster had
changed the industry, making it possible, for the first time, for
a star to be in full charge of his career. Lancaster had not only
starred in more than his share of important movies, he had
produced them, and often developed them from the initial idea.
To do all that, he had to get some respect, and had frequently
got it by imposing his personality with the full force of his
improbably gleaming teeth, sometimes implanting them in the
outstretched neck of a courtier he found insufficiently supplica-
tory. But this stuff on the *Scorpio* location went beyond self-
assertion. This was megalomania. Lancaster wasn't precisely
carried into the tent, but its flaps were held aside by two men
who had clearly learned their flap-holding skills at the court of
Hailie Selassie, and the business of making sure that Mr Lancaster
sat down safely would have been familiar to Louis XIV. As
Lancaster, once a champion acrobat and still in superb physical
shape, lowered himself from the standing to the sitting position,
Winner, from the other side of the table, flung out one hand in a
gesture of caution, as if the star might be putting his life in peril
from the speed of transition and change of altitude. You could
see the instruction hovering on the director's lips: 'A parachute
for Mr Lancaster!' From our position in one corner of the tent, I
watched Mr Lancaster eat. Chesterton once said, on the subject
of innate human dignity, that it all depended on the presence of
the holy spirit, and that it was otherwise hard to take the human
body seriously, belonging as it did to a creature that nourished
itself by pushing food into a hole at the bottom of its face. But

everybody at Lancaster's table watched him eat as if their fate depended on the proper functioning of his digestive system. I was disappointed that there was nobody to taste his food first, in case of poison, but would not have been astounded to learn that his excrement was weighed afterwards, in the same way that the output of the Chinese emperors was examined for portents.

After lunch, the interview took place in another tent at the edge of the compound. Once again, Lancaster was transported by limousine. But in our preliminary conversation he seemed to like my references to his early career as a gymnast. Flying on the high bar, Lancaster had forged in a touring circus the magnificent athleticism that made him, on screen, so beautifully poised even when he was standing still. It is always a plus, when warming up a difficult subject, to get him or her talking about their formative skills. This gives them a chance to instruct you. I hadn't yet formulated this as a principle: I had got it right merely by luck. It was flattery, of course, a version of 'A light for Mr Lancaster!' But it worked. He scaled down the hauteur considerably. Instead of being Louis XIV, suddenly he was merely Napoleon Bonaparte. By the time our cameras rolled he was practically mortal. From *The Crimson Pirate* onwards, I got a good story out of him about every movie that counted, and from each story he emerged as a model of reason, taste, and judgement. There was only one moment when he seemed insane. When I made the mistake of praising Alexander Mackendrick, director of *The Sweet Smell of Success* – by common consent the greatest film that Lancaster was ever in – the star said that Mackendrick had been so slow with the set-ups 'we almost fired him'. By 'we', of course, he meant 'I', and my jaw, against strict instructions, dropped. But my moment of revulsion could be cut out of the finished interview, and forty years later, from a detailed biography of Lancaster, I found out that he had been telling the truth. Mackendrick's slow shooting threatened to put the masterpiece a mile over its budget, thus threatening Lancaster's finances. His film company was the biggest of the independents, but it was still betting the farm on every project. He really was a brave, intelligent, and original man, although I always thought him a ham actor until time forced him to commit less energy. But I left that unmentioned, and at the end of the interview he indicated his satisfaction in a way that had been lighting up the screen for decades. His teeth looked like tombstones anyway, and when he bared them in a smile it looked like a carnival in a graveyard. Film stardom has more to do with presence than with acting, and Lancaster had always had so much presence that everyone else felt absent. He still had it. Getting away from him as far as possible seemed the only thing to do. As Lancaster, once again surrounded by his entourage, prepared to enter the limo for the awe-inspiring journey to the tent next door, and I followed our crew towards our humble van, Arthur muttered, 'Don't say anything. He might be listening.'

The Lancaster interview looked good on screen, but it made me wonder if I was really cut out for soothing the frailties of these fabled beasts. The mild-looking ones could be as dangerous as the known killers. Riding a tiger was one thing, but stroking an antelope could cost you your eyesight if the creature rounded on you and stuck out its tongue. Already I was wondering if I wanted to go on much further with *Cinema*. Pete was about to go into studio with the first album of our songs, the *Review* and the *TLS* were hungry for copy, the *Observer* TV column was nominally a full-time job anyway, and there was always Louis MacNeice showing up in my troubled dreams like Banquo's ghost. Did I really need the anxiety of talking to madhouse people with household names? The question was settled by my next big *Cinema* special, an interview with Peter Sellers.

Universally acclaimed as a comic genius, Sellers, after *Dr. Strangelove* and *A Shot in the Dark*, was still on a high plinth, but the cracks were starting to show. There were stories that he was driven by his own version of Tony Hancock's fatal reluctance to admit that a comic star might be to a certain extent dependent on those who supplied the words he said. As I mentioned earlier, but always feel bound to mention again, when Hancock heard too often that the scripts provided for him by Galton and Simpson were essential to his screen persona, he met the threat by firing them. His final destruction duly followed. Sellers wasn't as stupid as that, but he had already reached the dangerous state, for a comedian, of wanting to be cast as a romantic lead, as if he had more than comedy to offer. Successful comedy is already 'more than' almost anything else, but there will always be comedians who regard their reputation for getting laughs as a cruel diminishment of their real qualities. It had become known that Sellers was one of these. It had also been attested that his famous range of mimicry included no character that could reliably be identified as Peter Sellers himself. He bought a new car every week, changed women every few months – usually after giving a press conference to declare that the latest tie was eternal – and generally showed all the signs of someone short of an identity trying to supply it with a sufficiency of fancy toys, ranging from the latest automatic camera to Princess Margaret. All of these things I had read about but most of them I had discounted, on the assumption that he had attracted journalistic envy.

There could be no safer assumption than that, but within minutes of meeting him I realized that the press had been giving him an easy run. The encounter took place at some swish restaurant whose name I have repressed: it might have been Odin's. Sellers and his latest agent were in position at the table before Arthur and I arrived. While Sellers was regaling Arthur with a superb imitation of John Gielgud, the agent leaned in my direction and said, 'He's a vegetarian this week.' The implication was that the star didn't want even to smell meat, so Arthur and I ended up eating a small pile of vegetables each while Sellers became Laurence Olivier, Ralph Richardson, Richard Burton, and Alec Guinness. In broad daylight, it was a jamboree of spectres. When a student, I had loved his Alec Guinness routine in 'The Bridge on the River Wye' sketch, and here it was again, the replica of a replica. He went on to become Field Marshal Montgomery, President Nixon, Bing Crosby, Winston Churchill,

Adolf Hitler, and Marlene Dietrich. The only dud in the range was when he was pretending to be himself. His beautifully produced standard BBC English had the unmistakable gleam of a freshly forged banknote. But it was what he was actually saying, in this voice purportedly his own, that rang the alarm bells. He launched into an account of how Blake Edwards, the director of *A Shot in the Dark*, had screwed up the billiard-room scene. As his agent studied the ceiling while looking down at his plate – the trick needs a practised pair of eyeballs – Sellers moved pieces of cutlery about to demonstrate that whereas on screen the sequence had gone like that, it should have gone like this. Edwards, apparently, had deviously seemed to agree with Sellers' suggestions on the sound stage, but had double-crossed him in the cutting room. As the well-modulated tirade went on, Arthur and I exchanged the glance shared by two coal-miners when they hear water coming down the tunnel. Arthur told me later that this was the moment when he started thinking about the relative ease of dealing with Burt Lancaster. I was thinking of *A Shot in the Dark*. Sellers had come up with the perfect face, voice, and set of movements for Inspector Clouseau, but he was everywhere abetted by well-planned scenes that could only have been the work of the director, because they were the product of concentration, and Sellers was clearly incapable of concentrating on anything for five minutes, except, probably, on Sophia Loren in the passenger seat of his new Ferrari.

According to him, however, the movie was all his. Transparently untrue, this contention was a sign that he was already far gone in the fatal delusion that the people who helped him to succeed were conspiring to his downfall. The sure sign of a weak man who ascends to glory is that he can't tolerate having strong men around him. But it would be a long time before I figured that out as a general principle. At that moment, I was too busy remembering the scene in which Clouseau hurls himself at the door of the upstairs concert room in the castle, hurtles across the room in long shot, and is then seen, in the exterior shot, bursting through the window and falling, still running, into the moat below. Out of those three shots, his stunt double could have done the second and almost certainly did the third. In *The Pink Panther*, also directed by Edwards, Clouseau, preparing for a rare night of passion with his wife, heads into the bathroom while holding a bottle of pills. Of course, being Clouseau, he will spill them. But when he does, we don't even see him. We just hear the pills hit the tiled floor. The camera is looking at Capucine, who doubles the laugh by putting her hand over her eyes in resignation. Clouseau is present only as an idea. The joke emerges from the character, who has been created not just by the actor but by the writers and the director. How could Sellers be so ungenerous as not to concede that? He could even have been proud of it, because without his talent at the centre, none of all these other talents would ever have formed around him. The answer was not long in coming. He was ungenerous because he was unrealistic. When Charles Chaplin thought he could do everything, he could provide the evidence to back up the claim, although the evidence ran thinner when sound came in and it turned out that his touch with a story did not extend to its dialogue. But Sellers had always needed other people. The need, however, conflicted with his nature, which was that of a solipsist. To be a solipsist is to be deluded about the world, which would not be worth living in if it did not exist independently from the self.

I was wrong, however, to suppose that Sellers thought the world revolved around him. He thought the cosmos did too, and history, and the fates. After the endless lunch had ground to its conclusion, we headed off around the corner to the hotel in which our crew had taken over a room to rig the cameras and lights. The moment that Sellers saw which hotel it was, the really weird stuff started. He had drunk nothing during lunch except some special water that had to be brought in by courier from high in the Himalayas, where it had been strained through the loincloth of a swami. So he couldn't have been drunk. But

suddenly he was staggered. 'Oh no,' he said, in a version of the
Sellers voice that sounded like his cockney accent in *The Wrong
Arm of the Law*. I suspected that these might be his true tones,
to the extent that they could be resurrected. Resurrected was
the right word, because he looked like living death. 'Oh no. No.
Can't go in there.' While he stood staring paralysed at the hotel's
front door, his agent whispered to us fiercely: 'Jesus, what made
you pick this place? He can't go through the door.' It turned out
that we had chanced on the very hotel where Sellers had begun
his liaison with Britt Ekland. Their eternal alliance having ended
with the usual bitter abruptness, bad karma had gathered around
the doorway of the place where the universal catastrophe had
begun under the guise of bliss. Evil spirits walked and groaned.
Voodoo tom-toms, inaudible to us, pulsed. Negative feng shui
enveloped the building. All of it, apparently, except the roof.
When Arthur explained that there was no time left to hire another
venue and reposition the camera, agent asked client if there was
any way of getting into the building that would not offend its
incorporeal guardians. Blinking as if called upon to assent to the
sacrifice of his immortal soul, Sellers whispered that an indirect
approach might be all right. 'We could go in over the roof.' It
took ten minutes to navigate upwards through the building next
door, Sellers giving autographs all the way, with the terrible smile
of the condemned. You could imagine Christ ascending Golgotha,
asking the autograph hounds to hold their books still so that he
could sign one-handed while dragging the cross. The transition
over the rooftop would have been quicker if Sellers had not been
bailed up by a particularly hostile spiritual presence speaking
Swedish. Sellers spent several minutes negotiating with thin air.
Inside the hotel, certain corridors had to be avoided. Our small
party was exhausted when it finally attained the room full of
lights, cameras, and technicians.

The interview itself could have been worse. Sellers decided
to impersonate a normal, even reasonable, human being. In a

position, by now, to realize that this was the most remarkable acting feat of his life, I managed, while the magazines were being changed, to keep him occupied by proving myself familiar with the details of his more off-trail achievements, the ones we weren't talking about on camera. I was further struck, however, by the way he was not in the least surprised to encounter someone in possession of all this knowledge. He thought everyone knew it. Like every egomaniac, he behaved as if everybody else spent their day being as interested in him as he was. Even at the time, I had enough sense to mark this down as a lesson for life. Self-regard would get out of hand, if it were given the power, so watch for the symptoms. Sanity would be hard to get back if it were ever let go of. At the end of his career, Sellers would show signs of wanting to get it back. After a long and progressively disastrous series of scripts chosen on the grounds that they presented him as an irresistible sexual object, he elected to star in *Being There*, a movie about a man minus a personality who rises to prominence because people can read their dreams into him. Perfect for the part, he was able to go out on a high note. His whole career might have been like that if he had always been so judicious. But it would have been a lot to ask. He had a conspicuous individual talent, but it was interpretive, not directly creative. He could never have emulated Chaplin, Keaton, or Jacques Tati and set up a whole project by himself, controlling its every detail even if the task took years. But there is no point carping. He had such a protean capacity that it would have been a miracle if he had been in full command of it. Those of us with less to offer earn no points for ordering our lives better. Wagner couldn't compose unless he was living in Byzantine luxury, worshipped as a living god. You and I aren't quite that nuts, but we didn't write the Magic Fire music in the last pages of *Die Walküre*, either. When Sellers was far gone on the road to self-destruction, I tried to remember him as Dr Strangelove, strangling himself with one black-gloved hand. It was all too symbolic. But it was also his idea, a moment of brilliant improvisation. He just thought of something perfectly expressive on the spot, and hardly anybody can do that.

When the Sellers interview went to air it looked a lot more interesting than an exercise in hagiography. There was information and the occasional cause for amusement. And Sellers was undoubtedly a vivid illustration of the truth that the new, classless arts-media elite left the old social Establishment looking as tedious as a pair of green wellingtons caked with mud. An interview with the Governor of the Bank of England would probably have had less brio, unless he could do card tricks. But I was already making up my mind that my time on *Cinema* had run its course. After three series of thirteen regular weekly programmes, I had learned all I could about writing a clip show. When the time came for the tapes to be wiped – as, in those days, nearly all tapes were – one of them was preserved and given to the National Film Theatre, for the collection that was later to form the core of the Museum of the Moving Image. I chose the representative show myself: it was on the subject of the Hollywood Heavies, and I was quite proud of the bit about Lee Marvin. But anyone who saw it today would soon spot that I had a formula worked out. The prize for finding a formula is that you can pack more in. The penalty is that you will quickly exhaust the possibilities. The troubled but inexhaustibly inventive Kenny Everett, who really was a genius in a way that Peter Sellers was only talked about as being, was currently in the hilarious process of developing a television formula that could be elaborated for ever. Indeed other people are still elaborating it today. But for mere mortals, a television formula soon becomes a cocoon. (The great thing about a pre-industrial art form like poetry is that there is no formula to find: it's a new start every time. Not even Dante exhausted the possibilities of the terza rima, and Shakespeare, had he wished to, could have gone on writing sonnets for ever.) The specials, had I gone on with them, might have led to a more expansive layout than the simple interview with written top and tail, but there was an inhibiting factor, looming already even in those early days of rule by PR: the studios, in control of access, also limited the tone. No new movie could be dismissed as worthless. Everything the star had done was important and nothing was a waste of time. These precepts might have been a guarantee of decent deference – which on the whole I really felt, because I respected public opinion too much to believe that anyone ever got famous for nothing – but they were undoubtedly restrictions on expression. In the TV column I was much more free to let rip.

9. A LUNCH IS BORN

This last point was part of the message I had been receiving from the *Observer*. The paper's numerous corridor-stalkers were of the opinion (they spent a lot of time being 'of the opinion') that my exalted freedom as a critic could only be compromised by the lowly pressures of television. Exerting subtle but relentless pressure of their own, they sent the opinion down the descending layers of corridors until it reached me. Terry was disposed to ignore it. He gave me the courage of his convictions as well as my own. He had no respect for the corridor-stalkers. They reminded him (he didn't tell me this, but I worked it out from secondary sources) of the same distinguished boneheads who had chosen to call him a troublemaker when he pointed out that the persistent absence of the preliminary safety-code group on the messages from Holland was a clear indication that the safety-code group had in fact performed its function. The people sending the messages were not our agents. They were Germans. The corridor-stalkers, persisting in their belief that no circumstance so inconvenient to themselves could possibly be true, went on sending in more agents, who ended up in Buchenwald if they were not tortured and shot on the spot. Corridor-stalkers are placemen, more concerned with protecting their position than exercising judgement. At the *Observer* their position was ideal: worshipping, as well they might, the publication from which they still drew a salary even though they no longer actually wrote anything, they had a free hand to cherish 'the spirit of the *Observer*'. There was something to it. The *Observer* was still a great newspaper, and perhaps I was being cavalier in making my column look like a casual concern, instead of my main effort. Without doubt there was an anomaly when I sat at Richard Burton's feet on *Cinema* and then, in the same week, talked in my TV column about his gala television appearance with Bob Hope as resembling two drunks trapped in a revolving door. If it didn't actually feel like a conflict of interest – a conflict of interest rarely does – the point still niggled.

Add all these considerations together and they amounted to a reason to call it a day. But perhaps I was just restless. By other journalists I was already being called ('dubbed' as they would have put it) the *Cinema* man. If I wanted to escape an imposed identity, the time to make the break was sooner, rather than later. It could also have been that I was sick of the Midland Pullman. No doubt I had been remiss in not more assiduously exploring the marvels of Manchester, but apart from a few pre-Raphaelite paintings they seemed to consist mainly of George Best pulling birds in the Grapes. I hated the pre-Raphaelites and had seen enough of Best tossing beer coasters. Arthur took the news depressingly well. Never in favour of my holding on to the *Observer* job, he had probably concluded that my divided loyalties were bound to wear me down in the end. He made a civilized offer to try talking the Granada bean-counters into raising the stipend, but we both knew that the offer was just routine. Ego demanded that he fall to the floor, hold on to my ankles, and beg; but he had an ego of his own. So at the Midland Hotel we had one of those last suppers where you say far too much but forget it in the morning. When the morning came, the Pullman took me to London. In the future I would return to Manchester many times, mainly to present *What the Papers Say*, but I had renounced my chance to be a cherished adopted son of the great house. There could have been a psychological component in that refusal, because in the future I was to do it several times again, with other institutions equally venerable. They threatened to put a crimp in my lust for unbelonging. I don't exactly like being alone, but I prefer to be seen that way. There is something about a mentoring arm around my shoulder that makes me want to cut and run. Too well groomed, that comforting presence. I can smell the grave in the aftershave.

With *Cinema* out of the way, there should have been time for other things. As always, the spare time filled up overnight. The success of my *TLS* piece on Edmund Wilson gave me a Quixotic taste for writing articles longer than requested for pay that did not commensurately increase: a whole new way of doing more for less. Spotting this, Ian Hamilton gave me a chance to write a long piece for the *Review* for no pay at all. Though it meant that I would be conspiring to starve my own children, I found myself accepting the assignment. How Hamilton inspired this suicidal commitment from his writers remains a matter of debate. Some talk of hypnotism, others of a kamikaze commander's knack for instilling a sense of shame in any of his flyers who acquired the urge to come back alive. The second explanation was closer to the mark in this case. The subject was *The Savage God*, a new book by the redoubtable A. Alvarez. It was a treatise on how the purportedly unique pressures of being an artist in the twentieth century had led a disproportionate number of the greatest practitioners to untimely death, all too often self-inflicted. Ian asked me whether I could find time in my demanding show-business schedule to treat this undoubtedly serious book at some length. From subtle signs, I got the sense that if I turned the job down I would be confirming his estimation that the bright lights were eroding my sense of purpose. 'Or are you too busy being sucked off by starlets?'

For length, my resulting review of Alvarez's book left even the Wilson piece behind. I had a lot to say, and possibly too much of it consisted of cultural references brought to the siege in order to hammer at a wall already crumbling. Alvarez had a point about the number of modern suicides. But there was a corollary that he left unexamined, as if it would carry itself by default. He gave the idea that a suicidal commitment was necessary for quality. Since Philip Larkin, for example, had shown no signs of wanting to kill

himself or of favouring the same course in anybody else, he was
ranked automatically below Sylvia Plath. This idea seemed false
to me, but not patently so: it needed rebuttal, and I piled on the
historical examples in the attempt to match the easy flow of
Alvarez's prose. He had always written and spoken with the
natural authority of a man at ease with the big subjects. As Philip
French had once famously said, the best way for a newcomer
to survive on the BBC 'Critics' programme was to say, at any
awkward moment, 'I agree with Alvarez.' I was disagreeing with
Alvarez and I wanted to look as if I had the qualifications to take
him on. There is a possibility that my attempts to evoke the full
range of cultural history since ancient Athens had an element of
showing off, but a more likely motivation was nervousness.
Though not very big in physical dimensions, Alvarez was a giant.
This was my first giant-killing mission since I had taken on
George Steiner when I was an undergraduate. I had spoiled that
effort by taking far too much delight in cutting him up. He took
umbrage, and in short order I saw that he had been right. (He
forgave me later on, although he had no need to: the best kind of
forgiveness, when you think about it.) With that in mind, I took
care, in the Alvarez piece, to give the devil his due. I can safely
recommend this practice to any young critic preparing to make
his way forward over the corpses of sacred cows. As long as it is
in defence of a value, there is nothing wrong with writing an
attack: any critic would be too bland who never did. But even
if responsible for some obvious pile of steaming ordure like
The Da Vinci Code, most of the authors who achieve a regular
following do so because of some quality. It might not be an
especially admirable quality – it might just be the elementary
ability to narrate some dumb story so that you can't help vaguely
wondering if the stolen virus will destroy civilization – but by
saying he hasn't got it you automatically denigrate all those who
think he has, while laying yourself open to accusations of envy.
Those accusations will quite often be right. After Tynan attacked
Noel Coward in print, he was impressed when, after meeting

Coward by chance in a hotel dining room in Switzerland, he was
asked by Coward to sit down. Actually he said: 'Tynan, you're a
frightful shit. Sit down.' The true wording makes Coward's
magnanimity even more striking. In recording this, Tynan might
have added a further truth. Though Tynan seriously thought that
the politically committed theatre after Brecht had put paid to
the old West End world of Binkie Beaumont (upstage French
windows, 'Anyone for tennis?' etc.), Tynan, at a deeper level,
knew that his own achievement in criticism was outweighed for
permanence, and even for entertainment, by the least line in
Private Lives. In other words, he was envious of Coward's place
in the theatre.

I was envious of Alvarez's renown as a literary critic and
would have quite liked some of it for myself, but I can honestly
say that I had a better reason for going after him. I thought he
was wrong, and wrong on an important theme: one on which
the young ought not to be misled. From that viewpoint, I can
regard my capacity for going overboard as a virtue. Almost
always I have written from a true impulse, even when it is
counterproductive. Dismantling somebody's arguments can be
counterproductive indeed – he might reassemble his strength
and go for you – but you are more likely to get away with it if
you remember that your chosen enemy is a human being. This
is not just good tactics, it is civilized behaviour, which you
yourself are trying to embody anyway, or you shouldn't be
writing. As you can tell from my tone, I could give a course of
lectures on this one subject. It is because I have a lot of guilt
churning. Critics who actually enjoy causing pain have an easier
time, but there is a name for the uniform they should be wearing, and invariably they are soon forgotten, because memorable
prose simply refuses to be written below a certain level of human
decency. It should always be kept in mind that the notion of a
critical 'attack' is strictly a metaphor. A Rottweiler attacks a
human being. A critic judges what a human being does. I could
go on, but it would be better to do so later, because at the time

we are talking about I was still a long way from working most of this stuff out in detail.

Alvarez, when he saw an advance copy of the issue in which my piece was front-paged, thought that I had got him wrong but asked me to dinner anyway. Comfortably installed at Bianchi's, he proved delightful company. For the young literatus on his way up the greased ramp, nothing quite beats hearing the veterans growling away about what they once said to T. S. Eliot while William Empson was pissing in the pot plant. And here I was, getting in amongst it. When the magazine officially came out, my Alvarez piece, called 'Big Medicine', caused a gratifying stir in the literary world. It should be remembered that the literary world was still a very tiny part of the galaxy, in those days before the Booker Prize and a dozen cultural supplements created the conditions by which its population could be multiplied by thousands of people with no literary gift whatsoever, except for publicity. When the literary world was still small, there was an automatic mitigating circumstance for the naked urge to get in amongst it. We're talking about only a few hundred people. But they were among the brightest people in the country, and there was nothing slavish about wanting to earn their regard. While an undergraduate, I already knew enough about how the British cultural establishment worked to find F. R. Leavis absurd when he attributed a herd instinct to its literary component. The reverse was clearly the case. Cliques had often formed; there would always be a mafia of the talented; but an all-embracing orthodoxy there had never been, and couldn't be. Nothing like the *gauchiste* dogma that engulfed the post-war French intelligentsia had happened to its British equivalent. The English were just too eccentric. For one thing, there were too many Scots among them. There was not much chance of a herd instinct forming when someone like Karl Miller could still hold a blue pencil. Karl had been a student of Leavis, but remembered his own roots too well to put lasting faith in clerical rule – which, of course, Leavis was trying to impose. Leavis was John Calvin in another cloak. The spectacle of a collegiate martinet accusing the metropolitan culturati of orthodoxy should have been too funny for words. Unfortunately, it was. People choked on the subject. Though patently more batty by the day, the good doctor was still draped in an awe-inspiring prestige. Bewailing this anomaly one Friday while at lunch with Terry at Mother Bunch's, I hit on the idea of making Leavis's mad fantasies of a London conspiracy come true by actually starting one up. Couldn't we whistle in a few recruits and make the Friday lunch look like a plot to control the collective mind of the capital? Terry, no doubt recalling the long-lost days of the SOE, thought the idea silly enough to work. But true inspiration hit me when I thought of giving the proposed cabal a title drawn from the paranoid fantasies of Leavis himself: the Modish London Literary World.

So that's how it started. In the long run I am fated to be written out of the history of the Modish London Literary World, because so many more illustrious people joined it: Martin Amis, Julian Barnes, Ian McEwan, Mark Boxer, James Fenton, Craig Raine, Christopher Hitchens, Russell Davies, Piers Paul Read, to name only the junior regulars. Kingsley Amis and Robert Conquest counted as senior regulars, with Peter Porter somewhere in between. Among the irregulars there were several women in the early days, but the lunch quickly settled – ossified, if you like – into the sort of all-male scene that would be frowned upon today. Perhaps I am lucky that I no longer feature in folklore as its instigator. But as I sink towards obscurity I grow less inclined to have my few original moves forgotten, and the Modish London Literary World was one of them. In the course of time its name contracted to the Literary World, and finally to the Friday lunch. The location changed, as with a floating crap-game. In the course of more time still, the frequency changed too, as people became less available, the senior participants because they were getting older, the junior because they were getting busier, almost everyone because they were either getting married and starting a family, or else (even more time-consuming) getting divorced, married again, and starting a second family while working a double shift to meet the payments on the first. But for years the thing went on, achieving endurance because it fulfilled the simple need for what the Spanish call a *tertulia*. It was a talking shop where you could actually talk shop, while pursuing any other topic that emerged. Quite often that meant scandal, which in that era could still be enjoyed aloud. After the gossip requirements of the expanding number of upmarket media outlets filled even the literary world with snoops, spies, and delators, you had to assume that the enemy was always listening.

Apart from Terry and myself, who recruited each other, one of the first recruits was Russell Davies, already embarked on the same sort of chaotically multiple career as my own, although possessed of many more talents to help drive him to distraction. A musician and an actor as well as a caricaturist and a writer, he had the mimetic gift that often goes with a musical ear, and the actor's skills to project it, although he rarely raised his voice. People would come just to hear him speak in tongues. If the subject was Robert Lowell, for example, Davies would become Robert Lowell. Since the impersonation gained wit from jokes thrown in, it was better than having the actual Lowell present. (A lot better, as I was to find out.) Another founder member was the freshman novelist Martin Amis. You will notice how I avoid the air of portent. ('Compactly stylish in appearance, already surrounded by a small cloud of glory from the succès d'estime of his first, trend-setting novel, this shy but somehow dauntingly self-assured young man was called Martin . . . Martin Anscombe.') Actually a note of portent would be appropriate, because he was clearly destined for great things. You could tell from his conversation, which was not just wise in judgement – precocity can sometimes deliver that, although not often – but wonderfully funny. Clearly, if he could get that kind of talk on paper, he would have no trouble emerging from the shadow cast by his father's fame. For all those of us who could recite passages of *Lucky Jim* by heart, Kingsley Amis was a big star, but the young Martin generated his own light: he wasn't just a planet. The effect of his conversation was multiplied by the fact that he rarely smiled to signal the arrival of a joke. There was a reason for that, beyond the requirements of elementary tact. The victim of an orthodontic condition that would eventually threaten his general health, he preferred to keep his teeth in the background. He had already developed the tic of raising his hand to his mouth when he laughed. We called it a victory if we could make him laugh before he could get his hand into position. Actually the dentition thus revealed looked perfectly ordinary, but it didn't feel that way to him. He was carrying a permanent headache in his mouth. As his early novels were to suggest, he had nightmares of spitting his teeth out a few at a time, as if after a fist-fight. The point is worth noting for the sake of justice, because much later on, in the years of his worldwide fame, the swarming parasites of the British cultural press were to turn on him for the supposed excess of his having had cosmetic dentistry. They might as well have attacked him for having had a failed gall-bladder removed. But early on he was still living with his condition. It formed part of a general self-consciousness about his physical appearance: a self-consciousness which, when expressed in his early novels, enslaved a generation growing up in the media culture that rated sex appeal as a virtue rather than a characteristic. The paradox, in his case, was that beautiful women were drawn to him like pigeons on their way home. He only had to stand there and he was in like Flynn. He would have liked to have been a few inches taller, but the same went for Alexander the Great and Josef Stalin, and neither of them ever made a table rock with laughter. When Martin was on song, men who fancied themselves as wits laughed helplessly, glad to concede that there were in the presence of a superior practitioner. Those not so glad felt guilty at their own churlishness.

But the full flush of the Modish London Literary World lay somewhere in the future, like any semblance of equilibrium for the self-generated dogfight that I did not yet dare to call my career. Having consistently lost money with the *Review*, which came out only occasionally, Ian Hamilton thought of a way to lose a lot more money by launching the *New Review*, a quarto-format glossy that would come out every month. Swept up in this project, I initially committed myself to writing long articles. Tactically, if I had been capable of thinking tactically, this would have been a useful way of proving publicly (the *TLS* was still anonymous) that my name was good for something more substantial than the fizz and crackle of the TV column. Though I had foreseen that the TV column might prove more accommodating to reasoned argument than it first appeared, it did not offer the opportunity to write seriously at length, and be known to be doing so. The facts say, however, that I wrote my *New Review* pieces because Ian told me to, with the usual baleful implication that to turn him down would be tantamount to a betrayal of him, myself, and Western civilization. But it was my own idea to write even more stuff for the *New Review* under the name of Rudolph Regulus, thus to help fill the magazine's demand for copy, which proved insatiable from the jump. Most of this pseudonymous material was meant to be funny, and I hope some of it was, but there was nothing amusing about the way I had searched out yet another opportunity to overwork. When I turned up in Cambridge, I was a second baby to look after, with the difference that I could sit up in a proper chair and smoke. I smoked so much that I needed the hubcap of a Bedford van as an ashtray. I had found the hubcap lying in the gutter in Trumpington Street, and thought: 'That will make an ideal ashtray.' A man who thinks like that has to be a real smoker. From then on, with the help of the hubcap, I proved I was. At the end of the day – a phrase I usually like to avoid, unless I am actually talking, as here, about the end of the day – the hubcap would be full of cigarette butts. There was another baby on the way by then, which would make three. Playing the good provider, I had some excuse to be a burden, but it occasionally occurred to me that I must have been no source of joy. When it occurred to me, I worked harder, vaguely formulating plans for making a big enough score to hire a nanny. Still enjoying the blissful dawn of the two-career-family concept, like most toiling husbands I cherished the illusion that a toiling wife could be taken off the hook by a nanny, instead of saddled with the extra obligation to look after the nanny as well. Taken off the hook? Saddled? The mixed metaphor illustrates the mental confusion.

Pete went into studio with our first album at about that time and I would follow him in, so that I could sit around watching. I was convinced that the music business would provide the really big score that would set us all free of the alarm clock forever. In the popular-music business there were only two kinds of money you could make: not enough to keep a flea alive, and more than you could imagine. At the risk of sabotaging the narrative tension I feel bound to say now that we only ever made the first kind, but in the early days I would sit in the production booth of the recording studio and nurse the expectation that the sounds being mixed on the desk would not only satisfy the demands of uncompromising artistic integrity but also generate cash flow, as if a successful oil well could be sunk in the vegetable garden of a monastery. Yet there seemed some warrant for the expectation. Our music publisher, David Platz at Essex Music, had told us outright that if we couldn't get a hit single then our plan to make highbrow LPs would result in a long agony. Kenny Everett, however, thought we had written a hit already. At the height of his radio glory, before he rose to an apotheosis as the most original mind on television, Everett was still running a BBC show that all the bright young people listened to. If he spun your record, it could get you an audience. He took to one of the songs on Pete's first LP for Philips, *Beware of the Beautiful Stranger*. The song that Everett liked was called 'The Master of the Revels'. Perhaps seeing himself in the title role, Everett spun the disc on every show he did for weeks on end. He raved about it. Just as we were poised to take off, he got fired for making a libellous joke which allowed the interpretation that the Minister of Transport's wife might have had an easy time passing her driving test.

We found it hard to believe our bad luck, because the one thing we knew about getting a hit was that airplay was everything. Hence the life-or-death importance of the BBC playlist. If your record was on the playlist, it wouldn't necessarily get a bullet beside it, but if it was banned from the playlist you would get a bullet through the head. We had high hopes for a song called 'Have You Got a Biro I Can Borrow?'. The BBC said that 'Biro' was still a registered brand name in Hungary and that they therefore couldn't broadcast the word, because that would breach their house rules about advertising. Otherwise they would be glad to put the track on the playlist. Could I change the word? How about 'Have You Got a Ball-point I Can Borrow?' I had an attack of artistic integrity and said, 'Over my dead body.' Well, the BBC could arrange that. As far as that song was concerned, my body was duly dead. Unfortunately Pete's was too. What I should have done, of course, was cave in immediately. Even the Rolling Stones would change a word to get on the air. But I still had a bad tendency to look down on the fundamentals before I had submitted to them. It made me outspoken at the wrong times. The plain speaking that I directed pointlessly at the featureless face of the BBC monolith I should have employed in the recording studio for Pete's album, where I thought that a mistake was being made in mixing the vocal so far forward, so that the words reached the listener before the music did. Not out of modesty (definitely not), but out of a real conviction that a song should hit you in the knees first and climb to the brain later, I wanted the words to filter through, not leap out. I should have said so. It might have helped. But everybody else present, with Pete himself to the fore, was either a musician or a sound technician. I respected their expertise at the exact moment when an ordinary punter's view, the only thing I was good for, might have altered the balance. Still, it was undeniably an ego boost to hear my lyrics coming out of the loudspeakers, and there were people saner than Everett who seemed to admire some of the results.

Nick Tomalin was prominent among them. I inflicted the discs on him and he found time to listen. (In retrospect I wonder how that last part happened: at this end of my career, young people flatteringly weigh me down with more of their first records, novels, and books of poetry than I could possibly listen to even if I did nothing else.) Nick, whose opinions I respected about the fertile ground between popular and serious culture – respected them, I suppose, because they coincided with my wishes – would recite one of my own lyrics back to me and say that he thought there would be a market for our kind of stuff if we could only get it on the air. The lyric he quoted was called 'Carnations on the Roof'. It was the story of a dead metal worker whose hands, when he is cremated, burst into coloured flames because of the grains of metal embedded in the skin. It was my version of the Dyer's Hand. Nick liked the idea that I had once worked in a factory and had actually seen a man like that. It satisfied Nick's idea of journalistic authenticity, which, he believed, could only arise from the weighing and judging of observed reality. This was a pretty deep idea to follow on from hearing a pop lyric, and I thought that to arouse such a response would be a worthwhile reason to pursue our course to the limit, win or lose. The day was there to be seized. The most telling phrase that Horace attached to *carpe diem* was *spem non pone secutas*. Put no faith in the future. That idea came into sharp focus when Nick got killed.

He went to cover the Yom Kippur War. Somewhere on the Golan heights, he got out of the jeep and was no doubt glancing obliquely at an expanse of hot geography when the rocket-propelled grenade arrived. I must have been in the middle of typing up my latest TV column when the thing happened, because just as I was making my last corrections I looked up and saw Terry's assistant literary editor, Miriam Gross, standing up and holding the telephone as if it had just stung her. Still, today, one of the most beautiful women in London, Miriam in those days was the object of all male eyes and it was not unusual to look at her on any excuse at all. But this was different. In my childhood I got early practice at watching a woman receiving the news of death, so I guessed immediately what was up, although I would never have guessed who was involved until she said his name. She said his whole name. 'Nick Tomalin's been killed.' Silence raced through the open-plan office, and then the whole building, as the shock wave spread.

Scratch one more father figure. As usual I got the mental barriers up immediately. But there was no shutting out the sense of squandered promise. Later on it happened again when the gifted poet and political writer Francis Hope was lost on the DC-10 that went down outside Paris after some poor dunce at Charles de Gaulle airport jammed a cargo door shut instead of locking it properly. A ten-dollar RPG round, a door that should have been designed to open in instead of out: the discrepancy between cause and effect is part of the pattern, and a chilling reminder, for those who need it, that chance has no respect for what has been achieved. But Nick had already proved himself. What could I be said to have achieved if I were taken now? Time to look after one's health. Time for a long, life-enhancing drag on a cigarette. But above all, time to get serious.

10. PASTING IT TOGETHER

One way to get serious would have been to do something about Louis MacNeice. Alas, my few pages of notes reminded me all too vividly of my PhD thesis about Shelley, an opus that had never advanced far beyond an outline. A good general tip for would-be writers in any field is to beware of outlines. If you keep going back to elaborate the outline, instead of getting to work on the first of its listed topics, then the outline has become a substitute for the project, which will never get done. It works like a cargo cult: the natives lay out bits and pieces of junk in the rough shape of an aircraft, and wait for it to fly. They start fighting over who gets the window seat. But the thing never stirs, and eventually the jungle closes over its forlorn outline. Even on that level, my MacNeice outline looked skimpy. Lacking the nerve to tell Charles Monteith that I had got nowhere, I told Ian Hamilton instead. As he did so often, the world's least practical man came through with the right practical advice. He could do that for everyone except himself. On this occasion, while we both stood in the Pillars drinking beer for starters and Scotch for chasers, he cut my tale of woe short with his trademark amused sneer and said the thing that had never occurred to me. 'Give them another book.' This, he said, would help cure my chief problem. I had a blurred image. I was arousing resentment on all sides by playing with every toy in the kindergarten. The literati, in particular, were pissed off because I was writing articles out of what seemed no particular qualification except an urge to take their space. 'Everybody knows who you are, but nobody knows what you do.' I can remember these sentences of his because they stung. His advice was that I should collect all my literary pieces into a book, give it a title that made it sound as if it meant business, and thus promote the impression that my whole miscellaneous activity was part of a plan. 'Everything changes when you get a book out,' he snarled. 'Suddenly you're an author.' The Edmund Wilson piece, he suggested, would be a good lead-off for the book. Here, I made my own contribution to the scheme. 'I could call the book *The Metropolitan Critic*.' He nodded. 'Perfect. Sounds confident. Sounds arrogant as hell, in fact. Let the bastards argue with that.'

For the first time in my life, I sat down with a large pair of scissors to cut out my recent articles from their respective magazines and newspapers. There were quite a few that didn't make the cut, as it were. Already forming the resolution not to write anything that I couldn't at least consider for future publication in book form, I consigned them to the scrap heap. Those which I thought passed muster I further cut into column-width strips and pasted them onto sheets of foolscap. Haunted by distant memories of unsuccessful school projects, I nervously contemplated the crinkled and blotched strip running down the middle of each page, leaving room on each side for corrections, for rewriting, and for toning down. Plenty of that last thing proved necessary. Phrases which had only last year struck me as beaten gold now looked gimcrack. Actually too many of them stayed in, but I failed to spot them for the same reason that I had written them: lack of tone control. On a charitable view, faults of tone are the inevitable consequence of early exuberance: only a dullard is infallibly decorous from his first day. On a less charitable view, faults of tone are the deadly product of a tin ear working in combination with a loose mouth. But as I cut, pasted, and cursed far into the night, I could congratulate myself that a further stage was being reached. Somewhere inside the bumpy pages that piled up like popadoms, a picture was forming. This was the literary commentary of someone who had no academic job, no prospect of official preferment, and indeed no obvious credentials except as a common reader. Clumsy or not, it was all done for love. The finished manuscript just fitted into a box-file that bulged when I buttoned it shut. I tried to suppress the sceptical inner voice that said the box-file would become an actual book only if Faber agreed. Otherwise, like so many other unpublished authors, I would be merely toting a manuscript, like that mad don I used to see around Cambridge, endlessly carrying his stack of old newspapers on their random journey to nowhere. And my manuscript didn't even look like a manuscript. When I unbuttoned the box, the top pages came burgeoning upwards as if the paste were yeast. The Andromeda Strain! It's growing!

But Faber went for it. Charles Monteith, who must have guessed long before that the MacNeice project had the same chance of becoming operational as Blue Steel or Skybolt, even looked pleasantly surprised to be getting something out of nothing. He muttered dark obscurities about the difficulties of transferring the contract, but I was able to mutter back that my agent would be taking care of that. Yes, I had finally acquired an agent, or rather an agent had acquired me. Young, pretty, and still assembling her first roster of likely prospects, Christine Pevitt of Farquhar's had been following my work and roped me in at just the right moment. I often get asked by young writers about how one goes about getting an agent, and the answer is that I have no idea. Look busy enough and an agent will get you. She herself will probably be only at the start of her career, and on the lookout for clients. Later on, her client list will be full. Never mind: when you, the hungry young writer, succeed in getting a few big pieces published in magazines, or in placing a manuscript of any kind with a publisher, some hungry young agent will probably turn up. But agents themselves don't place manuscripts with publishers, or at least they didn't in those days. Publishers didn't take recommendations from agents, from other writers, or from anybody. Publishers were in the business of looking for publishable manuscripts, and they had paid readers of their own to aid them in the search. Similarly, the editors of magazines and newspapers commissioned articles directly from the writers of their choice. The agent's job was to look after the contracts, from whatever source, making sure that writer's take was negotiated upwards to the limit of what the market would bear, and that the resulting cash was collected in due time, instead of being conveniently left in the publisher's bank to earn interest for him instead of the writer. All this was quite a big enough job without the agent becoming a star too. Nowadays some of the agents are stars, occasionally rather bigger ones than most of their clients, and we are told that they handle a lot more than these mundane details, even to the extent of creating new talents out of nowhere. It seems more likely that they poach from each other names already established, and that all those routine requirements I just mentioned still apply. But the work is so painstaking that you can't blame the occasional agent for welcoming an attribution of glamour, which the culture-page journalists are increasingly eager to grant, even when the agent is not, as so often, a personable woman. In fact the unpersonable men have become the biggest charisma-merchants of the lot, sometimes even carrying code names, like terrorist masterminds in the kind of movie that Bruce Willis turns down so they get Jean-Claude Van Damme instead. (Imagine some dweeb adjusting his tie while he looks into the mirror and mutters, 'They call me the Vulture.') Though some of today's big-name writers have undoubtedly benefited from the kind of agent who is shown to the best table while demanding top dollar, whether the agent's job has really changed all that much is a matter for doubt. But in those days there was no doubt: the job was quite big enough, and no agent, however cunning, could turn a duffer into a desirable publishing proposition, just as no makeover, even if it includes plastic surgery, can turn an ordinary but glamour-struck young woman into Natalie Portman. This is only a brief disquisition about an extensive subject, but I put it in writing here because so many new writers, when they encounter their first disappointments, are driven to conclude that the reaction of the publishing world to their sincere and self-sacrificing efforts must be some kind of conspiracy, which could be circumvented if they had the right representation. There is no such conspiracy. There is only a market, which you can get into only by having something to sell – and something to sell means something that people want to buy.

That last bit is the poser. Quite apart from the obvious nutters, many a good soul has come to grief through failing to accept that nobody very much wants what they have to give. Since the necessary determination to press on in spite of failure – a determination that any artist must have – is indistinguishable from the futile determination to persist in a hopeless cause, the possibilities for self-delusion are almost infinite. You can even take universal rejection as a sign of your essential seriousness. You will take it to the grave, but there are worse ways to waste your life. With any luck, however, the penny drops, and the aspirant redirects his courage into one of the support branches of the art form in which he longed to shine. It is a desirable outcome. If all the accomplished but not especially interesting would-be writers became schoolteachers and taught grammar, the country would be on the road to recovery. The sky has more stars than it knows what to do with, but it can't do without gravity. I can give myself credit for realizing this quite early on, although for a long while I was too arrogant to give credit where credit was due. But I did manage to notice that almost every-one who gave service in the cultural world was an unpublished novelist, and that most of the published novelists had been forced, over time, to accept the fact that they might as well have stayed unpublished. After they accepted it, they turned, reinforced by self-knowledge, to other and more beneficial things. They had made something useful out of rejection, which is a far harder test of character than to make something useful out of acceptance.

For the moment, I had been accepted. *The Metropolitan Critic* was on its way to being a book. Somewhere in a back room at

Faber in Russell Square, the popadoms were out of the box. Christine was in no position to renegotiate the MacNeice contract's tiny advance, but she did somehow manage to rewrite the small print so that I was neither prosecuted for non-compliance nor deprived of the fee for delivery. As I remember, the total amount of money involved was about a hundred pounds – worth ten times as much in those days, but still not a lot. The author, however, felt as if he was rolling in it. Part of this euphoria was relief. I had been sprung free from a haunting bind, in relation to which everything else had been a displacement activity. Now I could concentrate on the displacement activities as if they added up to the main event. In practical terms they got in each other's way, but at least I wasn't pursuing them all as a means of dodging a promise. In Cambridge my elder daughter was up to about the fifth rung of the climbing frame. She won't thank me for saying that to me she looked more heroic than Sir Edmund Hillary at the peak of Everest. To mention her pixie hat will cost me a drubbing, but I can't leave out how, from my invigilating position on the park bench, I gazed upwards – well, if not precisely upwards, still a bit better than straight and level – with a mixture of pride and alarm. By the nature of my work and the nature of my nature, I was an absentee father who might as well have been serving in a nuclear submarine. If my wife was not to be crushed flat by the combined burdens of scrupulously fulfilling her duties as a don while simultaneously bringing up not just one of these things in pixie hats, but two of them, then I still had to make a big score. The book, when published, would, of course, make me millions. The music business would make me zillions. But not, in either case, yet.

＊

Meanwhile there was enough to pay the nanny: my one unarguably valuable connection. Myself useful only for lifting heavy objects, I tried to do my share of the cooking. I mastered the art of divvying up a batch of mincemeat into small dollops and

frying sixteen mini-burgers at once. Nobody except me wanted
to eat them and they went straight to my waistline. My shoulders
were still the widest part of me, but the body of the Australian
surfing hero was no longer what it was. I got some useful weight
training when I helped shift our stuff out of the flat at New Hall
to a small house in St John's Road, near Jesus Green. Staggering
along with one of about fifty tea chests full of books, I could
fancy that I was doing my bit. But being the helpmeet ate into
my time for being the good provider, which seemed the more
useful role, considering the fact that I couldn't even unpack the
books without sitting down to read one of them, and then
putting even that aside while I worked on a poem. Even a student
of Dante, who was famed for his ability to concentrate on his
poetry when swarms of Florentine factional street-brawlers were
stabbing each other all around him, is likely to grow impatient
if her nominal soulmate sits fiddling with a rhyme when he is
meant to be carrying a refrigerator. As he offered to do, by the
way. That's the worst of living with artists: they volunteer to do
things, and then they glaze over when the rapture hits them, and
they're gone, even when they're still there.

So I was in no fit state to turn down a windfall. After the first
year the *Observer* had offered me the same freelance contract
again, with a gratifying but not very startling increase. It might
have been more startling if I had not negotiated the contract
myself, without benefit of an agent, but my first contact with a
newspaper editor was always personal; and even after I was fully
armed with representation I was to go on, until recent years, with
keeping my newspaper deals to myself. I had noticed that a
newspaper will up the stakes just to cut down on the paperwork.
They might be screwing you, but in such intimate circumstances
you stand a good chance of screwing them right back. Both of
you are screwing the agent, who needs to be tolerant about being
cut out of the loop, but since the marketability of her asset is
likely to increase, all three parties gain. At that first try, however, I had not gained all that much. Staff members might have

thought otherwise. Sitting chained to their desks as I came and went, they tended to forget that they were also sitting on their pension. I never forgot it. Never much good at being properly fearful for my own future, I knew no inhibitions about being fearful for the future of my family. I had heard too many stories about the loved ones of some famous freelance being reduced to beggary. Tiny upturned faces in pixie hats! With the column steaming along from week to week, there might have been enough money going into the bank, but only just enough, because it was coming out again just as fast. How to get ahead of the curve?

The nagging question was made more so by the sudden prosperity of a friend, Bruce Beresford. In previous volumes I called him Dave Dalziel, for the usual reason: I was attributing to him inappropriate behaviour. But by then his youthful indiscretions were behind him. He was now a respectable, moderate man, instead of what he once had been, the one figure among his young Australian expatriate mates who could actually fulfil his priapic dreams, partly because he was so funny and good-looking, but also because – his secret weapon – he always earned some sort of salary and wore clean clothes. This sound practical initiative was a reflection of his realism, which, among the dreaming young, is forever in short supply. Realism had driven him to accept that if he wanted to make a feature film, the best place to finance it would be in Australia. The success of the 'Barry McKenzie' strip in *Private Eye* had opened a window. Barry Humphries, creator of the Bazza character and author of the words, had realized that if Nicholas Garland's pictures added so much, then moving pictures could add more. He and Bruce cooked up a script together, and Bruce flew home to raise the scratch. The Australian film industry being non-existent at the time, this was no easy matter, but Bruce, with typical persistence, had got it done. Philip Adams, later a huge name in Australia as an expert on everything, was a big help as producer, but he wouldn't deny that Bruce and Barry were the magic combination, perhaps partly because their combined first names sounded as if they had been inscribed on the scroll at the bottom of modern Australia's coat of arms. Together they had the right idea for the actor to play Bazza: a singer called (wait for it) Barry Crocker. Tall, gangly, and lantern-jawed, Crocker even looked like Bazza. It was like finding, to play Superman, an actor who could fly. The film was to be made in London and Bruce had a role for me. (I'm flashing back a bit here, as Bazza might have said: this first Barry McKenzie film was made in 1972, in the first year of my TV column.) I was disappointed to find what the role was. I would be playing someone who had passed out at a party. Bazza would step over my inert form. But at least I would be on the screen, even if appearing only one step above the carpet. And the pay was good: for a couple of days' work, ridiculously good. Extras who lay down got paid more than extras who stood up, because lying down counted as a stunt.

Having found that out, I was able to watch Bruce in action as he marshalled the teeming forces of a full-scale feature movie. In cruel fact, all directors look impressive when a film is being made, even if the results look nothing of the kind. The generalship involved is automatically awe-inspiring. I was stunned by how a contemporary I thought I already knew could be so in control of events. It made me wonder if I would ever achieve the same focus. Responding to the challenge, I put a lot into preparation for my role, practising endlessly to lie down at the right angle. When Bazza stepped over me, he was stepping over an actor who was not just pretending to be unconscious, but inhabiting unconsciousness. I had submitted myself to immobility by finding the essence of that motionless state within my soul. When the movie came out, I wasn't mentioned in the reviews. In the relevant sequence, indeed, I thought that the camera unnecessarily favoured Crocker even in the long shot, and in the close-up the audience had to imagine, from the expression on the star's face, that he was stepping over an unusually convincing unconscious person. But the movie, called simply *The Adventures of Barry McKenzie*, was a success, especially in Australia. The Australian film industry as we know it today was launched, and I felt that I had played my part. When Bruce hinted that there might be a sequel, in which my part would grow even bigger (talking like Bazza is almost impossible to stop once you start), my nostrils flared.

During my agonized wait for film stardom in the sequel, there were other things to do. Some of them helped with the mortgage, but as usual I felt especially drawn towards the ones that didn't. Lest I give the impression that I was always looking for a financial angle, I should record here that, in matters of a central stipend, my best reason for following the money was self-knowledge: given the chance, I had a dangerous propensity for lavishing prodigies of concentration on activities that not only failed to pay, but that I had to pay in order to pursue. Foremost among these activities was poetry. Mentally I was still living from one poem to the next, as I had before and still do today. But in the long list of editors unaccountably dedicated never to caring for what I wrote in verse form, Ian Hamilton was included, and that was a blow. Though he would print as much of my prose as he could extort, he inspected my proffered poems as if they were not even counterfeit money, but tiny banknotes hand-drawn in coloured pencil by a child. 'I don't,' he muttered, 'like this kind of poetry.' As his own poems proved, he favoured personal feeling, in the range between depression and desperation. Playfulness was the enemy. The typical poem that he thought legitimate, whether written by himself or by the handful of other poets for whom he felt respect (often, in the Pillars of Hercules, there was a quorum of them, looking like a morticians' convention), was no more playful than running blindfold across a busy highway.

He particularly loathed my poems when they tried to be funny and serious at the same time. He himself could be a ferociously funny parodist, but he kept his parodies in a separate category, and published them under a separate name. The name was Edward Pygge. Established poets lay awake in fear at the thought of being parodied by Pygge. Generously, Ian offered me the use of Pygge's name if I wanted to try the same trick. Immediately I saw the possibilities, and in the course of a month turned out Pygge versions of several different poets whom I thought were being denied the denigration due to them. When I showed Ian the manuscripts his reaction was gratifying. At the supposedly personal lyric poems written under my own name, he had sneered. At my Pygge poems he sneered again, but with the occasional baring of the teeth, a revelation which I had learned to recognize as a sign of uncontrollable mirth. Sparsely scattered in the jaws of a heavy drinker and smoker with an aversion to dental appointments, Ian's teeth were at odds with his otherwise darkly handsome face. They were dark enough, but they didn't fit the picture, so he usually kept them under wraps. If they were on show, he was either going to bite somebody or else he was amused. In this context, it had to be the latter.

Suddenly we were getting on at a new level. We had always got on, but often against the odds. In personality he was naturally dominant and I was naturally submissive. But I didn't like myself for being submissive, and I would like still less whoever made me feel so; and I would always eventually rebel, usually choosing the most unsuitable moment to declare independence. These quirks from both of us had led to several clashes already, with bad blood slow to drain away on either side; and the clash arising from our respective views of poetry was worse than all the others put together, because it never subsided below the level of threatening to break out all over again. As so often happens with boon companions, we were very unlikely friends. When two male friends both write poetry, the sensitivities go even deeper than sexual rivalry.

In that department, rivalry with Ian was pointless anyway. Other men, when running after women, found that they had to run faster because the women were running towards him. Though a star footballer in his daydreams, in his personal appearance he was one of those rare poets who actually look the part. He looked doomed. He didn't look unhealthy, which was unfair considering his habits of nourishment. These have been described by better hands than mine, and none of them needed to exaggerate. He really did order complete meals and do nothing with them except rearrange the food on his plate with a fork. He really did remove the lighted cigarette from his mouth only to replace it with the rim of a glass of Scotch, maintaining that steady rhythm throughout the day and far into the night. But he looked as fit as a welterweight contender, an impression added to by his broken nose. In the eyes of women, his nose was broken at exactly the right angle to indicate many a gallant fist-fight against their oppressors, and his thick black hair begged for their soothing fingers. His hair was a particular affront to those of us who were losing ours. Many years later, at a moment when his permanent financial crisis had reached the catastrophic point where he was being sued by the solicitor he had hired to help him out of it, his hair turned white and fell out in clumps; but typically, and unforgivably, it grew back again, and just as black. No, until the very end he never looked sick, or even frail. But he did look condemned. He had the knack of embodying self-destruction in an alluring form. He looked as if he needed to be saved, like Venice. Women keen to save him arrived from all over the place. They would give him their front-door keys, which he put on a key ring that shook the floor if he dropped it.

There can occasionally be some point in taking a moral stance about a man's sexual behaviour, especially if the man is oneself. But there is no point in taking a moral stance about a man's sexual attractiveness. If he's got it, he sure as hell didn't steal any of it from the rest of us. Ian lost several friends because women they desired fell for him instead, but those friends were foolish. It wasn't his fault: which, of course, made the fact more infuriating still. At the height of his pulling power, he never had to do anything to get a woman he wanted except fight off the ones he didn't, so as to give her a free run to the target. Her rate of acceleration could be disconcerting if you thought she was with you. I can honestly say, however, that if I bore any grudges against him in that area, they didn't go any deeper than general- ized envy. One got used to it. There was an occasion when we both did a reading in Oxford. I did my usual thing of entertaining the audience between poems. Ian just read his poems, saying nothing directly to the audience except, 'Can't you shut up in the back?' When it was over, a beautiful young blonde graduate student came up to us and hung gracefully on my every word about Auden and MacNeice while Ian sat impatiently glowering. I suggested to the poetry-mad young vision that she should drop into the Pillars of Hercules next time she was up in London. When she did, I lurched forward to greet her at the door. I was all set, in my role as guide to the lower depths, to answer any questions she might have. She had only one. 'Is he here?'

I wasn't even surprised. In the area of poetry, however, there was a gulf between us that could easily have remained unbridged. I only partly believed that what he was doing in poetry was as necessary as what he was doing in prose, and he didn't at all believe the same thing about me. If your friend takes your woman off you, he merely doesn't care about your feelings; but if he makes it clear that he thinks you are wasting your time with poetry, he doesn't care if you live or die. There had been a dozen occasions when our friendship might have been over, if we hadn't made each other laugh. It worked like a marriage, which can survive anything except lack of good will. But even the good will had been often under stress, and we would have called it quits sooner if the Edward Pygge connection had not intervened. As we stood there at the bar of the Pillars, we were joined by Pygge, the phantom impresario, in the spirit of a new enterprise. The scurrilous Pygge papers, an untidy array of typescript hedged about with pints of beer and glasses of Scotch, clearly had theatrical possibilities. We could do some of these voices our- selves. The rest could be done by Russell Davies, who could do anything. He could also write parodies to a high standard. Yet more Pygge products were in prospect! The very consonant 'p' became a provocation. At that moment, Davies himself walked in out of the gathering dusk, picked up my Pygge parody of the Welsh bard R. S. Thomas, and read it out with the appropriate accent. All within earshot fell about. The barman looked puzzled, but he probably wouldn't be coming to the show anyway. We already had a name for it: the *Edward Pygge Revue*.

I always loved that stage direction in one of Ring Lardner's little surrealist plays: 'The curtain comes down for seven days to denote the passing of a week.' To denote the several weeks it took to prepare the *Edward Pygge Revue* for its one-night run, let me make a slapdash collage of some of the other stuff I was busy with at the time. The more slap the dash, the greater the fidelity to a period of confusion. Looking back on it, I can see that this was a formative moment. In most of our formative moments, we do nothing much except lie around in a daydream, like a snake measuring itself for a change of suit, and we find our future purpose through discarding the false purposes of the past. But there are other formative moments when so much happens at once that there is no order to it, or even a chronology: opportunities arrive like a hail of bullets, and a circus performer who had previously to catch only one bullet at a time in his teeth finds himself snapping desperately at a fusillade. One of the bullets he swallows, and it turns out to have transforming properties, even though it tastes at first just like another mouthful of lead. Full of metaphors no less extravagant than that, my book *The Metropolitan Critic* finally came out. For stylistic brashness it invited the pillory, and its exterior appearance might have been designed as a provocation. Almost full size, my self-approving face, enriched with untrimmed sideburns, appeared on both front and back, as if appearing once were not more than enough. But some of the reviews were good, and one of them was better than good.

It was written by Philip Toynbee for the *Observer*. Before it was published, Miriam Gross kindly showed it to me in galley proof when I came into the office to write my TV column. Toynbee had praised me in sumptuous terms. His piece was the literary equivalent of 'Roll Over, Beethoven'. The new boy from the Australian bush, according to Toynbee, was a prodigious combination of style and exuberance: the ant's pants had met the bee's knees. George Orwell, look to your laurels. Dr Johnson, the jig is up. Montaigne, *rien à faire*. It went on like that. After memorizing the piece like a poem, I spent Friday night getting smashed in the Pillars, striving to share my secret with no more than one person at a time. As I explained to Ian that I was finding it a struggle to reconcile literary integrity with blazing success, was there an element of respect in his usual sneer? 'You're a very complicated character.' No, it was an element of contempt. But he would have to live with that. Lying on the floor of the last train to Cambridge, I rehearsed the speech that would prepare my wife for the life-changing impact of the *Observer* on Sunday.

11. WELCOME TO THE COLOSSEUM

The impact was all on me. As published, Toynbee's review of my book was only about half the length of the proof. Almost instantly I realized that Terry had been at it with his half-glasses, blue pencil, scissors, and axe. All superlatives had been excised. There was practically nothing left except a brief description of the book's size and weight. The previous day, the Saturday, in between my usual household tasks of lifting weights and searching for the goldfish behind the bookcase, I had toured Cambridge to tell our acquaintances that they might care to catch the *Observer* books pages tomorrow, after they had read my column. But now they would merely be puzzled. In London, there were dozens of my colleagues who would now, at this very moment, be rolling around with aching sides. My own sides ached for a different reason. I could hardly breathe for my sense of injustice. Screwed by my own editor! Kicked into the pit by my own Virgil! My wife, who had to live with injustice every day of the week (like any other female don, she was surrounded by suavely indolent male dons who sincerely thought they were doing her a favour by loading her with extra duties just because they knew she would carry them out), was faced once again with a husband's peculiar capacity to treat a setback as an international crisis, instead of as a petty local condition. In later years I tried to correct that discrepancy, but even today, when I have a cold, it is the worst cold in the history of the house. On that day, cruelly deprived of what I thought my due, I addressed long speeches of protest to the wall I was supposed to be painting white. I could see the words

flaming back at me, as if admonishing a DIY Nebuchadnezzar:
You have Been Weighed in the Balance and Found Ridiculous.
Early in the following week I found some moral courage for
once and called in on Terry to have the matter out, instead of
letting it simmer for a few years as I would normally have done.
I thought I had the moral high ground: Toynbee, after all, had
actually written such and such, and to cut out his true meaning
was an act of censorship. But Terry, staring at me over the top
rims of his half-glasses, soon reduced my high ground to a
molehill. Using far fewer ahs and ums than usual, he informed
me that a regular contributor to the *Observer* must not be seen
to be puffed by his own paper. That would, ah, do the paper no
good. The molehill became a foxhole when he added that it
would, um, do me no good either. He said I was no longer the
oldest living student, but well established as an indecently productive and successful young critic, and that I should avoid
being seen as seeking more of the validation that I had already
achieved: it was as counterproductive as to go on talking the girl
into bed when she was already, ah, lying in it. The trench I was
now standing in deepened, and my eyes were level with the
earth, when he added that Toynbee was an eternal enthusiast,
had once glorified Communism in the same terms, and that his
rapturous praise of a new saviour was a well-known equivalent
for the kiss of, um, death. The ground finished swallowing me
up when he said if he hadn't cut the piece he would have had
to kill it altogether. He was the literary editor, and ah, making
decisions like that was what the literary editor, um, did. From
my subterranean position, I tunnelled out under the foundations
of the building and headed for the Pillars of Hercules. Already
dead, I had no fear of being killed by Ian's laughter.

But he wasn't laughing, and he had a fate worse than death in
store for me. John Carey, an Oxford don already established as
the most deadly of the academic critics moonlighting in Grub
Street, had reviewed *The Metropolitan Critic* for the *New Review*.
Ian showed me Carey's typescript. With memories of my unfor-

tunate preview of Toynbee's *Observer* piece still fresh in my
lacerated mind, I would have been smart to leave Carey's manuscript unread. But the chance to do the stupid thing was irresistible as usual. Besides, Ian was insisting that I should know what
was in store for me, so as not to feel double-crossed when the
piece was published. I didn't quite see the logic of that. Does
someone who has mailed you a dead cat exonerate himself by
telling you that it's in the post? Not that Carey's piece was a dead
cat. It was a living cheetah. My opinions that I had thought so
bold were chased down, bitten through the back of the neck, and
dined off for their tender parts, with the bulk of the corpse
contemptuously left for the hyenas and the vultures. What made
this treatment worse, I reflected bitterly, was that Carey could
write. The bits of my prose that he quoted did indeed look
overwrought when put beside his. (As a general rule, a review
that doesn't quote you can never hurt you, and a dullard will
never quote you unless he is so stupid that he doesn't realize how
his own prose fails to shine.) As I read on in deepening despair,
Ian manfully forbore to smile, and even nodded in sympathy, but
there was a gleam in his hooded eyes that I had learned to
interpret. In the name of editorial integrity, he not only didn't
mind making enemies, he didn't mind hurting his friends either.
As I handed the typescript back – the hand failing to tremble
only because rigor mortis had already set in – he told me that I
could look forward to seeing the piece in the next issue. I nodded,
feebly voicing my observation that although it was not the done
thing for a newspaper to praise a regular contributor, it apparently was the done thing for a magazine to make a monkey of
him. 'Yeah. It's tough.' That evening I got an early train.

When in Cambridge, I still spent a lot of time in the Copper
Kettle, which had previously been my office when I was a skiving
graduate student. Directly opposite King's College, it was a good
place to go to ground. One of Carey's less devastating points was
that the virtues I claimed for the metropolitan critic as a recurring
type throughout modern literary history were rather undermined

in my case by my continued attendance at the university. It
would have been more devastating had it been fully true. But it
was only half true. I had no attachment to Cambridge University
beyond living in the middle of it. Even today, the family base is
still in the centre of the city. I suppose that by now we could
afford a bigger house out in the country, with a pond and a
couple of ducks. But I like the way the learned buildings wall me
in with their reassurance that there is really nothing wrong with
sitting down for half the day to read and write. At the time *The
Metropolitan Critic* was published, I did the reading and writing
in the Copper Kettle. When I lifted my eyes from the page, there
was none of the meretricious argument London always offers that
the sole real purpose in life is to hustle for a buck. Through the
window, I could see the crippled physicist from Caius who had
recently handed in his crutches for a motorized wheelchair. Now
he took less time to go past the window. There were rumours
that even his colleagues were puzzled by his explanation of the
universe. Later on he would lay out the explanation in a book
that puzzled people by the million, but even at that stage he was
clearly occupied with thought in its pure form. It was a useful
reminder that the mental life must be pursued for its own sake.
The reminder came in handy when *The Metropolitan Critic*, after
selling only a few hundred copies, turned over and sank.

But the heartening truth was that my very first book had
done me good. Apart from Carey's *stroncatura* – my wife, while
pressing cold towels to my forehead, had kindly supplied me
with the useful Italian word for the review that kicks the shit out
of you – the press had been tolerant at the very least. Some of
the critics had been kind enough to identify a new, peculiarly
Australian style that approached European culture the way Rod
Laver approached Wimbledon, as if what mattered wasn't the cut
of your shorts or the angle at which you bowed to the royal box,
but whether you could hit a cross-court running forehand. I liked
the sound of that emphasis. It had an echo of what Nick Tomalin
had once said about how the resident aesthete scores nothing for

cultivation, whereas the barbarian invader scores double. Really he was saying that it didn't matter if you talked with your mouth full as long as you were quoting Rilke in the original German. It was an insult to my country, but I took it as a compliment to me, and now I started to see the possibilities. Instead of narrowing my range of allusion to appease my critics, I would widen it to flatter my readers, who, I had guessed, quite liked the idea of someone treating the whole world of the arts as if it belonged not to any special caste or class, but to anyone with the interest and the energy, and who could possess the whole thing even though plainly having no background except the outback. (Actually, like the vast majority of Australians, I had been born and raised in a city, but in the British imagination at that time the whole of Australia was still the outback, which was somehow equipped with a beach. Later on, this outback beach acquired an Opera House and row of brick bungalows, one of them occupied by Kylie Minogue.) I resolved, however, to exploit the image only by countering its negative expectations, and never by reinforcing them. Suddenly the opportunities to take this course had increased. Now ranking as an author instead of a mere journalist – it was the journalists, not I, who thought in those terms – I had a whole new swathe of prominent outlets available to me.

Some of them were the wrong ones. I should never have tried to write for *Punch*, because *Punch* was a funny magazine and nothing but, and for me it was fatal to work in a funny context. The only way I can find a point in what the Americans depressingly call 'humor writing' is to be funny in a serious context. I had already formulated this rule after learning in the Cambridge Union that I should never, on any account, accept an invitation to participate in the Humorous Debate. (In the gales of forced laughter generated by an avowedly Humorous Debate, anything genuinely amusing you happen to say will be lost like a fart in a tornado.) But I was so engaged by the company of *Punch*'s then editor, Alan Coren, that I broke my own rule, and suffered the consequences. Come to think of it, Coren might not have been the editor. The editor could have been William Davis, a man with the same Teutonic origins as Wernher von Braun, although not as funny. Either way, Coren was the master spirit. I could check up and make sure of who was nominally in charge, but the whole episode is a patch in my memory that I would rather leave vague. The pieces I choked out for *Punch* are among those I never later reprinted in book form, and even at the time I had the rare experience of wondering why I had written them at all. I record this sad fact in the hope of passing on a useful lesson. If it feels like a mistake before you go in, don't go in. Even when working with a whole heart, you are bound to have the occasional failure, and sometimes the whole heart will be the reason: caring too much can make you try too hard, and what should have sung will merely simper. But to work with half a heart means failure every time, and the results will scream the place down. I got away with the *Punch* misalliance, however; not just because I got out early, but because nobody you were going to meet read *Punch* even under Coren's editorship; the magazine was destined for dentists' waiting rooms, where it played its traditional role of making what happened next seem comparatively amusing. Having got out, though, I never got away from the enigma of Coren's personality. For me he remains the most enigmatic man of his generation, because the sprawling palace of his attainments has so many rooms he has scarcely bothered to look into. He can fly planes, drive fast cars, dance accomplished jive, speak perfect German. But who is he? His writing never tells you, because its humour is a shield. He understood exactly why I could never settle in at *Punch*. With that kind of writing, you keep yourself to yourself. Not my thing at all.

Other outlets were an unequivocal plus. Those who had wanted book reviews from me now wanted features as well, including the *Observer* itself. To conduct their side of the annual salary round for my TV column, three of the *Observer*'s top-echelon corridor-stalkers were waiting for me in a conference room off the main open-plan office. On a glass-topped table, three pairs of Turnbull and Asser cufflinks gleamed in concert. Wearing a new brown corduroy velvet jacket carefully chosen to look as wrong as possible in combination with my chocolate chinos, I shambled into their presence. Usually their faces would have conveyed the strained politeness of Roman senators receiving a Hun plenipotentiary whose army was parked outside the city gates, but I detected a new warmth. Things went well from the start. They would up the fee for the next year's column by a healthy percentage if I agreed to throw in four features during the year for either the paper proper or its new colour magazine. Since I would have thrown them in for free, just for the kudos, this seemed like a good deal. But it got better while it was still being negotiated. The *Observer* now seemed prey to the flattering belief that as the author of a book I must be in demand from other sources. Would I care to suggest an additional figure to ensure exclusivity? A decent response would have been to say that I would be flat out writing just the stuff they had stipulated, with no time left over for a postcard to my mother. But the challenge of picking my own figure for the sweetener ruled out any response at all. I hadn't a clue. This turned out to be an advantage. Being forced to think has the effect of temporarily shutting my mouth, while my tiny eyes are too deep-set to transmit panic, and even, I am told, can make me look quite shrewd, as if weighing the odds instead of looking for the exit. Faced with a Mississippi gambler daunting in his taciturn immobility, the *Observer* suits reached further into the bag. Exclusivity, they explained, meant only that I could not do comparable work for any other Sunday newspaper. (Effectively, this meant the *Sunday Times*, the *Observer*'s only real rival for the liberal audience in those years.) I could write for any periodicals I wanted to. Somewhere about this point they named a figure themselves, at which my mouth began to say 'Wow!' but got no further than the first consonant, for lack of breath. It must have looked as if I were pursing my lips thoughtfully. Far inside my head, my eyes bulged, but the effect was to lower my eyelids and seal them shut. Having finished adjusting the exclusivity downwards, the suits went on adjusting the fee upwards. There was a lesson here: in life as in love, it rarely hurts to say nothing. By the time I summoned up the strength to nod, I was on a stipend that any unattached freelance would have recognized as top whack, and certainly no staff writer would be doing better. The staff writers, of course, had guarantees if they got into trouble, and if they croaked on the job the paper would pay for the funeral. But that was OK, because I was going to live forever. We Mississippi gamblers know how to look after ourselves: that silver derringer isn't just for decoration. I glided away down the corridor, mentally adjusting a black Stetson.

With dependable affluence in prospect – dependable as long as I stayed healthy – I thus passed into the second stage of the freelance writer's life. In the first stage, any job you can get looks good, so there are no choices to be made. In the second stage, you can choose between good and bad. There is a third stage, the really tricky one, where you must choose between good and good, but I hadn't reached that yet. For now, the choices between good and bad were quite tricky enough. I wrote a three-thousand-word piece about the current state of British television for *TV Week*, the American equivalent of *Radio Times*. The piece took several days to write, nobody could read it in Britain, and in America, where it could be read, nobody wanted to. The money was good, but the piece was a dead loss. Ergo, the money was bad. There was a clicking of the tumblers. The door opened on a revelation: earning for the sake of it was a waste of time. At the opposite pole, *Encounter*, an outlet I had once courted in vain, now asked me for a long article about Tom Stoppard. It was hard work, and the magazine paid mainly in prestige, but I could reprint the piece. So there was more than a cheque to show for the effort. Making such decisions was no doddle but they would have been a lot harder without an assured income to back them up. To the feature articles I wrote in this new phase, I brought a determination to get the ebullience under control. The sneer of Ian

Hamilton hovered before me. I could see Terry Kilmartin's blue pencil floating like a dagger in *Macbeth*. Karl Miller *was* Macbeth, and the spirit of Professor Carey was reading over my shoulder, all set to expel a snort of sulphur. The joint was jumping with ghosts, but like all ghosts they were the expressions of a mind in search of equilibrium. As any Grand Prix driver will tell you, the car's straight-line speed is only part of what matters: everything else depends on control. For a writer, the control is tone control. Without that, your force of expression will pull your prose to bits, leaving it wrecked by its own impetus. Writing all day and every day, I got a lot better at keeping the extravagance within bounds.

Eventually this new capacity fed back into my TV column, where I developed a useful trick of undercutting a showy sentence by following it with a plain statement, alternating the inebriation and the sobriety throughout the paragraph, as a man in his cups might stride with heroic certitude for several yards before once again bouncing off a wall. This strategy made it even easier for an enemy to quote me accurately to my detriment – all he had to do was leave out the context – but an ordinary reader, who wasn't looking for ammunition, was able to see that I was throwing in the hoopla only as an illustration to an argument. Each week I varied the pace within the column, sometimes writing four-fifths of it as a straight, serious review of a couple of programmes about, say, WWII, before winding up with a high-speed dissection of the latest failed courtroom drama, or with a miniature quote-fest from the latest verbal accidents of the sports presenters. ('Harry Commentator is your carpenter.') If the main subject brooked no levity even as an appendage – a series on Auschwitz, say, or an interview with Solzhenitsyn – I would sometimes put off the vaudeville stuff altogether until the following column, timing the effects within the month rather than within the week. I was alarmed as well as pleased to discover that there were readers who would object if their favourite routines were absent too long. The mailbag increased to the point where I could no longer deal with it by my usual method of stuffing it all into the bottom drawer of my office desk and hoping that it would go away. I was supplied with a temp secretary to transmit dictated answers. Dictating them, which I did after wavering back to the office after lunch with the Modish London Literary World, often took longer than typing out the column had done in the first place. This was solid evidence that I was earning the money. It still wasn't a fortune, but it felt like one, and all the more so because I had never expected it to happen.

Meanwhile it became steadily clearer that the fortune I had expected wasn't going to show up. Pete had made a couple more albums of our songs. They had been, on the whole, well received, and they had also, on the whole, dropped dead. I could see a lot of reasons why we weren't a commercial hit. One of the reasons was a circumstance I wouldn't have changed anyway. Pete didn't sound in the least American. It was a sad but seldom mentioned truth that most of the British singers who sold in big numbers sang 'yeah, yeah, yeah' instead of 'yes, yes, yes'. Pete did not believe that the opposite of 'no' was 'yeah', or that 'ah' was the way to pronounce 'I'. But the excellent Ray Davis of the Kinks didn't sound like an American either. Although he was an exception to the rule, if there was one exception to the rule then there could have been another. Here a better reason for our continued poverty came in, which I might have pointed out if I had more guts. Though the first album had been made for peanuts, the subsequent albums – *Driving Through Mythical America* and *A King at Nightfall*, to name the two that did best – were recorded on a budget big enough to allow more lavish arrangements and some production time to spare. The big-enough budget was still tiny by the prevailing standards: in the lounging area at Morgan Studios we saw maned and booted groups with names like Yes being provided with plates of mixed sandwiches that would have cost more than what Pete spent on a whole day of recording. But even more than with the first album, I still couldn't dodge the uneasy suspicion that the words were being mixed too far forward. One sign that this might be true was that the demo tapes often sounded better to me than the finished album tracks. The demos, done on a single track, sounded more integrated to my uninstructed ear, and an uninstructed ear is what I shared with the public. After the instructed ears had got through with mixing the multiple tracks of the studio sessions, the words always seemed to get in front of the music. I should have feigned humility, said that my lyrics were of secondary importance, and pleaded stridently for more reticent vocals. But timidity, which is always a force in itself, won out: with so many musical experts on the case, I thought I must be wrong.

There was another reason that Pete and I could agree on. The record companies, whether Philips in our initial phase or the mighty RCA later on, had no idea how to market the stuff. We never had the A&R man who might have exploited the fact that we didn't fit. Actually this was no surprise: the truly imaginative record executives, such as John Hammond and David Geffen, are very few even in a music industry as big as America's. Pete's manager, Simon Crocker, was a naturally wise young man, but he was hampered by lack of power: had he been working within one of the record companies instead of just knocking politely on their bronze doors, things might have been different with the marketing, although I doubt if some of the handicaps I have already outlined could have been overcome, in the absence of a firm hand to take hold of our throats and choke out the hit single on which everything depended.

There was one more factor, however, that outweighed all the others, although I was painfully slow to admit it at the time. The insoluble problem was so close to home that I couldn't see it. It was me. My assumption that popular music could be dragged towards literature was fundamentally wrong-headed. It was a sure-fire formula for creating unpopular music. What we were doing, even if it had been done with large resources, was strictly for a minority. The popular-music business dealt with majorities, a fact with which I never had a quarrel: I would have been glad enough, after all, to take the rewards if they had come. But I was killing us with every clever lyric that I wrote. I was even killing our chance to get cover versions, which had been the whole idea of Pete's making an album in the first place: to attract other artists who might sing our stuff. (Bob Dylan, whose first album sold barely one copy each for every record store in America, made his first money from having his songs performed by other people.) A few cover versions might have at least given us a plastic bucket of small change to start compensating for the big canvas bags of banknotes that never came. But largely through my choice of words, our work was too quirky to be borrowed.

In addition to a few critics who wrote the kind of notices you end up quoting to yourself when the cold night gets in through the cracks around the window, there were fans who loved our stuff, and thirty years later, when our work was rediscovered against all expectation, their children, who had grown up with our music in the house, were to form the core of a whole new audience big enough to make theatre tours by me and Pete viable in both Britain and Australia, and even in Hong Kong. But part of our appeal to that original group of thoughtful loyalists was that our songs made them feel like members of an elite, and elites are death for the popular arts. Indeed elites are death for the arts in general. Everything created should be composed on the assumption that it can be enjoyed by anybody, even if not by everybody. Verdi, my pick for the greatest creative genius of the late nineteenth century, did not compose for a special class of opera lover, and from the moment when composers began to assume that only an instructed few could possibly understand what they were up to, the art they presumed to serve was a gone goose. This aesthetic belief, which is at the head of my political beliefs as they stand today, was in the forefront of my mind from the very start, although it has taken me a lifetime to make it clear even to myself. My early lyrics were an attempt to act on that belief while it was still in the birth canal, heading in the right direction but upside down.

As so often in my life, an interior suspicion that I might be on the wrong course expressed itself by a transference of energy to another area. Gradually I began to write fewer lyrics, and to put that kind of effort into verse letters, nominally written to friends. Actually they were meant to have a bigger audience than that; they were public poetry. Written in what were meant to be strict forms, they were ideal vehicles for all the literary allusions and linguistic razzmatazz that had previously been clogging my lyrics. I wrote the first of them, a letter to Russell Davies, when I was on location in Wales for the second Bazza movie, subtly entitled *Barry McKenzie Holds His Own*, in which I had indeed been given the promised bigger part. Upright and conscious this time, I was cast as Paddy, an aspiring Aussie film critic attached for some reason to Bazza's entourage as he battled Dracula in Transylvania, whose sinister castles were being doubled by the Burges castles of Cardiff, kitsch replicas that had been put up in the nineteenth century like film sets for an industry that did not yet exist. (Today, no visitor to that city should fail to avoid them.) Barry Humphries had no great love for aspiring Aussie film critics and that lack of enthusiasm was expressed in the script. Paddy had few lines and they all conveyed his amiable stupidity. With Bruce's encouragement I tarted the lines up as I went, making Paddy's obtuseness even more salient. Some of these improvements I found quite clever – clever expressions of stupidity, that is – but later on, in the editing room, they all vanished, leaving Paddy not much more articulate than the corpse I had played in the first movie. Little knowing that my featured role was fated for the gurgler, I threw myself into the task.

My first big chance to throw myself was in a fight scene, in which I would be one of a dozen victims of Meiji Suzuki, a karate champion playing the evil oriental cook in Dracula's castle. Dracula was played by Donald Pleasence: my first close look at

an important actor actually at work, instead of just being interviewed. Beyond the standard set by the spray-on cobwebs and
the prop bats, Pleasence had a haunted look, probably having
guessed that this project would not add to his lustre. The humour
of the first film had depended on Bazza's being out of context in
contemporary Britain: a fruitful sociological proposition that led
to all kinds of speculative press coverage in both Britain and
Australia, with learned articles being written about whether the
arrival of Bazza on the big screen signalled, for the perennial
vexed question of Australia's conception of itself, an advance
through self-mockery or a regression through self-abasement.
This time he was merely out of context in a Gothic fantasy. There
would be no point in trying to explain the plot now, because the
script had trouble explaining it then. When the film was released,
even Humphries, who had worked hard on its preparation,
quickly realized that it belonged somewhere in the lower half of
his illustrious CV, although I should hasten to say that it still
made money. But for all concerned, realism came later. For the
moment, enthusiasm ruled. Nobody sets out to make a dud
movie. Humphries, still in the difficult early stages of saying
goodbye to alcohol, had a tendency, when he dressed up as Dame
Edna, to repair to his or her trailer and refuse to come out,
having temporarily forgotten that any putative maltreatment
could only have been at the instigation of a company he entirely
owned. 'Barry, come out!' I once heard Bruce shouting, '*You own
the movie!*' But it wasn't as if Barry didn't care: quite the opposite.
And we were all fired up by the incendiary energy of Bruce, who
reacted as if everything he could see through the eyepiece was
funnier than *Mr Hulot's Holiday*.

Nobody's commitment exceeded mine. According to the sto-
ryboard, Suzuki would sock me in the jaw with his flying foot,
and I had to fly backwards some distance before going over in a
backward roll. Determined to raise my backward roll to Olympic
standard, I practised on the bare earth. Armed with distant
memories of my star performance in the Sydney Technical High

School gymnastics squad that won the coveted Pepsi Cola Shield, I threw myself backwards and carried out the opening phase of a backward roll. It was there, some time later, that the film's stuntman, Alf Joint, found me. Famous in his trade, Alf was tall, handsome, brave, and magnificently athletic, a combination of characteristics that had attracted the attention of Grace Kelly during the filming of *Green Fire* on location in Africa. By day, Alf had doubled for Stewart Granger in the embrace of the killer ape. By night, Alf was in the embrace of Grace Kelly. He didn't boast about it, but the news, propelled by gusts of bitter envy, ran all around the industry. It was hard not to hero-worship such a man. In *Where Eagles Dare*, Alf had been one of the stuntmen fighting on top of the cable-car high above the star-lit valley full of Nazis while Richard Burton and Clint Eastwood sat on the terrace of the hotel far below, sinking drinks as they laid bets on which of their doubles would fall off first. For the most successful ever Cadbury's chocolate commercial ('And all because the lady loves Milk Tray'), Alf had dived a full 180 feet out of a helicopter into the sea off Malta. The camera messed up the first take so he had to do it again. He toppled out of the dive and smashed his spine into a string of broken beads, so he knew exactly what a back injury felt like. Looking up from where I was lying flat, I could see his handsome head outlined against the weak Welsh sunlight. 'Can you move?' he asked.

In the attempt to convince him that my prostration had been planned, I tried leaping to my feet, but succeeded only on rolling onto my side. He probed with a thumb. 'I don't think you've broken anything, but you're going to be feeling the bruise for about ten years.' He was thirty years short in his estimate: I can still feel it now. I can also still remember exactly what he said next. 'Bruce tells me you've got two university degrees. Do you think I'd be doing this stuff if I had two university degrees?' Arising, as so often, out of hubris and humiliation, this was one of the moments that resonated throughout my later life. From then on, I was more willing to let the tennis champions play the tennis and the racing drivers drive the cars. In my daydreams I still believe that I could have done all those wonderful things if I had set my mind to it. But daydreaming is mindless; it works on wishes, not on thoughts; and in my thoughts, prompted by my aching back, I gradually came to accept that my capacity to reflect verbally on the achievements of the danger men was exactly what had ruled out the possibility of my ever being one of them. Since it had also excused me from the danger, there was more reason to be grateful than resentful. 'When we do the number,' Alf said as I hobbled away leaning on his arm, 'for shit's sake do exactly what I say and don't do anything extra.' Much taken with Alf's delightful professional term for the trick, I did 'the number' the next day. Taking Alf's advice, Bruce captured my tiny part of the fight sequence in separate shots. There was a close-up of Meiji's horny naked foot apparently impacting on my jaw just before I exited frame to the left, drawn in that direction by Alf yanking on the back of my pants. There was another shot of me executing the kindergarten version of a backward roll, with my face registering authentic agony. In the editing room, the second shot was cut out, no doubt because it looked too feeble.

Otherwise, most of my time on set was spent waiting. The natural condition of the film actor, at whatever level, is to sit around for hours doing nothing while the practical aspects are arranged for the next few seconds of work. Wasting as much of their lives waiting as they do in sleep, the big stars are compensated with huge amounts of money, but never enough to offset the nagging impression that they are being robbed of life. The only possible cure is to do something else. Dumb stars play practical jokes, conduct love affairs, or complain about the inadequate facilities of their trailer. Some stars meditate, perfect themselves in the mysteries of the Kabbalah, fulfil the daily mental exercises incumbent on members of the Church of Scientology who have attained the status of Transcendental All-Clear Super-Brain Grade Nine, or occupy themselves with some other method of being exclusively concerned with the continuing miracle of their own personalities. Not being a star, and lacking the where-withal for a sustained contemplation of the self, I wrote verse letters. Having wrapped up the one to Russell Davies, I began, when we changed location to Paris, another one for Pete Atkin. In Paris there was even more waiting around to do than there had been in Wales. A two-minute scene on the upper level of the Eiffel Tower took a whole day because the wrong official had signed the permission, or because the right official had signed it at the wrong angle: stuff like that. Apart from a wonderful night-time expedition, led by Barry Humphries, to the Alcazar cabaret – the dizzy standard of the stage effects had a big influence on Dame Edna's later career – there was almost nothing to do but wait. I spent a lot of time sitting in cafes, hunched over my open notebook while I chiselled away at stanzas in ottava rima, rhyme royal, or Spenserian measure. I fancied myself as a meticulous craftsman.

The brutal truth was that I was still measuring lines by eye and fudging the syllable count with the slovenly insouciance of a Soviet plasterer, but at least I was learning to recognize the sweet click a line of verse transmits when all its stresses are in the right spot. What I couldn't yet do was make it happen with every line. At about the same time as we were approaching the end of our shooting schedule, Gough Whitlam, back there in Australia, was approaching the end of his government. (With typical generosity, and perhaps with typical recklessness, he appeared briefly as himself in the final, Australian scene of the movie where Bazza comes home in triumph after the defeat of Dracula.) Whitlam, when a schoolboy, wrote far more accurate formal verse measures than I did in maturity. I wish I had known that at the time, and had been able to ponder the implication, which is that exuber-ance, for that kind of verse, is indispensable, but not enough. Accuracy should be part of the inventiveness. But I was carried away by my flood of ideas, which is always the first desirable condition. Into my stanzaic boxes of tricks I poured all my learned irrelevancies and interdisciplinary gags. It was, I thought, a way of airing my knowledge while heading off the standard accusation, often levelled at my prose, that I was putting everything I had in the shop window. I had never thought that jibe to be fully accurate, but there must have been something to it, because while my verse letters filled up with bricolage, my TV column emptied of it at the same rate.

The TV column was still a pretty flashy number, but I got better at cleaving to a straight argument, gradually learning to trim and guide a rococo tendency to make architecture out of decoration. If my song lyrics were only partly a success in dragging the popular towards the literary, the TV column, if only because the reader response kept growing, could be thought of as making a better fist of dragging the literary towards the popular. Later on, there was a whole new generation of journalists doing the same thing. The new emphasis was given a fancy name: postmodernism. Actually it had been going on for so long that you could trace it back through time all the way to wax tablets. T. S. Eliot wrote about Marie Lloyd and the music hall; Mallarmé edited women's fashion magazines; *Love's Labour's Lost* is a pseudo-pedantic pop concert from start to finish; and Catullus sang a syncopated blues for the dead sparrow of his mistress. But to me this carnival of the qualities felt like a big and complex event, and the symbolic centre of it was the *Edward Pygge Revue*.

12. PYGGE TO THE RESCUE

We left the cast rehearsing in the Pillars of Hercules. The rehearsal facilities were out of scale with the scheduled venue. In keeping with his tendency to think big and worry about the consequences later, Ian had picked the Institute of Contemporary Arts in the Mall for Edward Pygge's one-night stand. Resplendently situated in Carlton House Terrace, the ICA had a huge hall available for performances, brought in from all over the world, of the sort of avant-garde semi-theatrical events that nobody wanted to see in their countries of origin. There was no doubt that Ian's menacing voice on the telephone would get the whole of literary London to fill the auditorium, but would we, we few, we precious few, be able to fill the stage? Stuck in one corner of the Pillars of Hercules, we already felt short of resources. What would it be like on the night? Ian solved the problem by recruiting one of his entourage, a bright and well-connected bluestocking called Amanda Radice, as the show's glamour girl. No longer among the living, Amanda won't mind my saying that she couldn't act for nuts. But she was so beautiful that it scarcely mattered. I wrote little bits for her all over the continuity script, so as to get her on stage as often as possible, thus to cash in on her appeal, and off stage as soon as possible, thus to minimize the effect of her limitations. But the main thrust of the show was the string of parodies, variously presented by Ian, myself (each of us always sounding the same), and Russell Davies, always sounding different.

I should say at this point that Russell Davies had a real first name, Dai, that had been stolen from him by Actors' Equity because they already had a Dai Davies on their books. But everyone who knew him called him Dai in private – they still do – and from that evening literary London rang with his name in whatever version he found it expedient to use. He stole the show, as we all expected him to: but he stole it on the scale of the Brinks Mat bullion robbery. His costume helped. He wore a black suit, black shirt, white tie with a Windsor knot, and a black wide-brimmed fedora. He carried a violin case that looked exactly as if it had a tommy gun inside it. The visual image of ruthless gangsterdom was a key element, but the killer blow was provided by his variety of voices, as if the spirit of Peter Sellers had entered the body of Lucky Luciano. His best bit, and the hit number of the night, was his reading of my three Robert Lowell sonnets. If I can be permitted a cross-reference to myself, these pseudo-Lowell sonnets are still available in my book of collected poems, *The Book of My Enemy*, and I am still proud of the way they capture Lowell's knack of presenting his own personality as the focal point of all human history. But they needed Dai's voice to bring out the full flow of Lowell's self-obsession. There were people in the audience who had real-life experience of the great man's vaulting solipsism and they yelled with recognition. More important, people who had never met him now felt that they had.

I might be getting things a little bit out of chronological order, but perhaps this is a good place to record my general impression of Lowell's impact on London, whither he had already, or would shortly, divert his full attention, on the correct assumption that the worshipping natives would crash to their knees with their bottoms in the air as the ground shook to the weight of his Olympian tread. They weren't entirely wrong. I should say in haste that his early poetry gave him the right to think of himself as a giant. But he was also a nutter, one of the manic-depressive type who, when in a downhill phase, accuse themselves loudly of being Hitler. (They never accuse themselves of being the seventh anonymous stormtrooper from the right at a dedication ceremony for the new blood banner in a provincial town twenty miles from Dortmund: they always accuse themselves of being Hitler, just as the people who had previous lives in ancient Egypt always turn out to have been pharaohs or chief priests, and never night-shift workers on the crew that put up the third tallest obelisk in one of the satellite temples at Karnak.) Eventually I saw Lowell giving a live appearance, as it were, at a memorial evening for John Berryman, held at that very same ICA. Berryman had committed suicide, probably because, as an even bigger egomaniac than Lowell, he was feeling the effects of having a smaller reputation. The memorial evening was organized by Alvarez. Before the event there was a gathering of all those of us who were going to read from Berryman's poetry or deliver short valedictory speeches.

The gathering took place in a pub only a couple of blocks from the ICA. Alvarez explained to us all that there was a strict fifteen-minute limit on how long each of us could speak. Alvarez explained this very carefully, on the correct assumption that some of those present would have trouble understanding it. Lowell's lack of protest at the restriction was taken as a sign of assent. Everyone tiptoed around him as if the mere fact that he had been told there was a time limit might be enough to put him over the edge. I was already finding all this pretty weird, but then the funny stuff really started, when Lowell had to be initiated into the concept that the ICA, although only about two hundred yards away, was not in plain sight, owing to an intervening corner. Though Alvarez and several others volunteered to ensure that Lowell would reach the destination successfully, Lowell made it as clear as he could make anything that he looked on the proposed journey as the equivalent of being asked to cross the Andes on his own, with condors circling above the valley and snakes waiting in the bare rocks to bite the ankles of his mule. On the epic journey through the open air, we surrounded him as if Gandhi were transferring his radiant humility from one village to the next. Blessed to be in his company, we reached the venue to be greeted by the crowd as if our individual status had been raised merely because we had walked with the mahatma.

What happened during the event was so predictable that it was scarcely to be believed. In praise of the departed Berryman, we all did our fifteen minutes each. When Alvarez introduced Lowell in roughly those terms with which John the Baptist might have introduced Christ, I particularly admired the way Lowell didn't reach into the inside pocket of his tweed jacket until Alvarez had finished. Then Lowell produced a fatly folded manuscript that unfolded into something that would clearly take an eternity to read out even if there was only a single sentence on each page. He read the whole thing. It was about the Condition of the Poet in an Age of Nuclear Confrontation. You had to give him credit, though. Berryman was mentioned several times. As Lowell murmured endlessly on, I saw people in the audience fighting sleep as if they were being mugged by it in an alley. Then as now, however, this effect was taken as a sure sign that something truly serious was taking place. Never, at a literary event, have I ever seen even one person rise from the audience and say, 'This is too boring to bear.' The loudest rebellion I have ever heard was from Karl Miller at a *TLS* mass rally somewhere around the year 2000. A heavily laurelled Irish bard – no, not the one you're thinking of: another one, with less talent – was reading a purportedly humorous poem to the usual sporadic titters, and I heard a recognizable Scots voice in the crowd near me growl, 'I don't think that's funny. Why does anyone think that's funny? I don't think that's funny.' I looked across in time to see the people around him looking at the floor, as if the secret name of God had been mentioned and they hoped to stave off a vengeful lightning bolt by pretending that it hadn't. If the cherubic Irish poet could generate that degree of respect, it was no wonder that Lowell, while he still lived and bestrode the Atlantic, was a figure of awe, as if Napoleon, dressed for his coronation, had assumed the proportions of the Colossus of Rhodes.

As I remember it, at the time of the *Edward Pygge Revue*, Lowell was not yet regularly on the scene, but the word was out, so there was an element of recognition. We got some of our biggest laughs, though, from pure fantasy. I had written a version of *The Waste Land* as if London's wartime Indian poetry editor Tambimuttu had written something called *The Wasted Land* under the impression that he was being original. This was an abstruse enough connection but Dai gave it extra life in two ways. He did a terrific Indian accent of which the Indians in the audience were the loudest in their appreciation. The beautiful Gita Mehta was always a good giggler but it was rare to hear Sonny Mehta laugh aloud. I could see him rocking. The piece got practically a laugh a line and I was already seeing a new future of writing poetry for performance by the time Dai got to the punchline, whose effect on the audience would have completed my spasm of self-satisfaction if I had actually written it. Unfortunately (or, rather, fortunately) it was Dai's. He had improvised it during rehearsals in the pub and I had incorporated it into the poem instantly, with a premonition that I would have to go on pointing out for the rest of my life that one of my best lines was borrowed. A writer should always be careful to own up on that point, in my view: on a practical level, he will be known as a plagiarist if he gets rumbled, and on the spiritual level there is a penalty of guilt to be paid even if he gets away with it. Or there should be a penalty. I know several writers who steal anything that is not nailed down, and it doesn't seem to bother them at all. Anyway, at least I had created the pinchbeck crown in which Dai could place his jewel. 'Shantih shantih shantih,' he intoned. Gita was already doubled up. 'It's only a shantih in old shantih town.' He took a bow while she howled. I could only tell by the way her teeth shone. There was too much noise.

The *Edward Pygge Revue* wasn't all as good as that but it sent them home happy, and it sent me home even happier. From that night until this day, I have always worked on the principle that a poem, whether comic or serious, should pay its way as a theatrical event. There are always plenty of poets – Ian was one of them, in fact – who prefer to believe that poetry, when recited, should merely be overheard. They might have a point. (They certainly have a point if they are seriously gifted, but it should be remembered that most poets are writing poetry only because they can't write prose, have no more sense of structure than the director of a porno movie, and will escape being forgotten only in the sense that they have never been remembered.) If a poet writes something sufficiently charged with meaning, it should be enough to be present while he or she reads it out. But the degree of self-effacement required would not suit my temperament. Though I like to think that I would go on writing poetry even if it had nobody to appreciate it beyond the four walls of my cell, the evidence suggests that I can't function without an audience, and that even my periods of solitude – which get longer as I grow older – are always a preparation for the next public appearance. On Pygge's big night, I had made a public appearance in which poetry had been accepted unquestioned as an item of entertainment. It was a sweet moment, and like so many sweet moments it had powers of deception, as the sirens did when they sang. Immediately I began to dream of bigger things. The gift of foresight might have told me that the success of the event had a lot to do with its having been small. But foresight has never been among my attributes, and indeed I wonder if anybody with the necessary capacity to get carried away is ever truly wise before the event. In those years, I was scarcely capable of being wise after the event. Nowadays I am better at assessing the implications of what has already happened, but that's about the extent of the improvement. A depressing thought, and not an appropriate one in relation to how I felt at the time.

I felt on top of the heap. The TV column was going well enough for me to contemplate collecting the best of its first four years into a book. Once again I pasted a manuscript together out of clippings, ruthlessly discarding gags that had gone phut or straight statements that had started to generate the unmistakable odour of the platitude. Rather than rewrite to save an idea, I cut it out to profit from the added speed. There were whole columns begging to be put out of their misery. But there was still plenty of stuff left. This time I took the title from a line by Sir Thomas Browne, 'Dreams out of the ivory gate, and visions before midnight.' I had first read the line while pretending to study in my college library at Cambridge, and had always thought that those last three words would make a good title for a book. Here was a book to fit the title. I was disappointed that Charles Monteith at Faber didn't seem to think that *Visions Before Midnight* was a publishing proposition. Regretfully he assured me that books of collected journalism didn't sell, and that the column's regular audience, of which I was so proud, would not buy the book, for the precise reason that they had already read everything in it. But Tom Maschler at Jonathan Cape heard about the manuscript, asked to see it, and said that it might be worth the chance. It was flattering to think that he might be trying to poach me from Monteith, less flattering to notice that Monteith didn't seem to mind. Though it would take time before Cape brought the book out, for now I could warm myself with the notion that I had two publishers squabbling for my favours. In modern terms, I was in the position of Brad Pitt, torn between the attractions of Jennifer Aniston and Angelina Jolie: maybe the one with tattoos knew something that the other one didn't. My agent Christine told me to give my conscience a rest: since Cape, with the famously penny-pinching Maschler at the controls, were even more unforthcoming with money up front than Faber, there was no danger of getting a reputation for pulling a fast one. Later on, if there was a hit book in prospect, I would have to choose, but for now I might as well play both ends against the middle. It sounded rather daring.

But what really thrilled me was the prospect of taking the poetry-revue enterprise to another level. It should be said in fairness that the idea of a performance-poetry show was in the air at the time. Such imported Americans as Allen Ginsberg would go on at the Albert Hall under the sponsorship of the British 'youth culture' impresario Michael Horovitz, with loud proclamations, in the preliminary press barrage, that the new poetry was now, the now poetry was new, and that poetry, to fit the historical moment, had to be experimental. Though Horovitz's own way of proving that poetry was for the moment was to write not a line that anyone could remember for five minutes, he had an undoubted gift for herding the more obstreperous poets together and turning the occasion into a news item. Either under his leadership or in emulation of it, performance-poetry events were everywhere. I could not help noticing, however, when it came to the lighter moments of the evening, that scarcely anyone involved was actually funny, unless they were trying to be serious. In the poetry world, as in the literary world taken as a whole, the notion always lingers that the only thing you have to do in order to be amusing is to lighten your tone. The notion is hard to kill because the audience itself, committed to a night out but already desperate with boredom, is ready to go along with any attempt at lightness. At any literary event, most of the people buying the tickets have no more idea of how comedy works than most of the people on stage. There is a big difference, though, between the laughter that an audience will politely grant to some dullard feebly signalling that he considers himself funny and the laughter that is forcibly wrenched from them when someone else actually is. You can't miss it: it is the difference between a genteel, effortful titter and an involuntary paroxysm. This second kind of laughter is the headiest wine a performer can drink, and now I saw a chance to drink it by the gallon. What about a long poem in rhyming couplets that would take an hour to read out by a bunch of carefully chosen reciters, would incorporate all the parodies I could dream up, and would go for real laughs instead of the tolerant smile and the well-bred snort? I even had a name for the hero: Peregrine Prykke. And I had already invented his area of operations: the London Literary World. To cash in on the Augustan flashback, and to convey the proposed scale of epic grandeur, I would call the poem *Peregrine Prykke's Pilgrimage Through the London Literary World.*

By that time the London Literary World's Friday lunch had moved from Mother Bunch's to the Bursa Kebab House, an obscure bistro near the new centre of the action. From the literary viewpoint, the *New Statesman*, still occupying its insanely valuable piece of real estate in Holborn, was in its most glorious period. You could be indifferent, or even hostile, to the opinions expressed in 'the front end', but 'the back end' had an authority not to be ignored, entirely because the standard of its editing was so high. At one time or another, Anthony Thwaite, Francis Hope, John Gross, Claire Tomalin, Martin Amis, and Julian Barnes were all active at the command level of the magazine's cultural pages, with a direct line to all the best critics in the country. Contributors flocked and flourished. Christopher Hitchens and James Fenton came to write and stayed to lunch. Mark Boxer started turning up regularly. An erudite student of the dandy tradition, he proved by his mere presence that this was a fashionable event in the rarest sense: but his fastidiousness also had the salutary effect of discouraging the anecdote as a form – he wanted the flash of wit. James Fenton was also quick to spot the threat of boring self-indulgence and curl his lip at exactly the right angle to frighten it into silence. Nobody was allowed to take his time except Terry Kilmartin, who, applauded for every 'um' and 'ah', knew that he was being guyed and had the charm to make it funny.

The conversational results turned the Bursa Kebab House into a stock exchange for literary quotations. I have never heard better talk about the arts and don't expect to again, but I think all who participated would agree that the thing really took off when traditional fact gave way to current fantasy. Already becoming famous but still retaining enough anonymity to move among other people without their putting on an act, Martin Amis, in conversation, could translate the circumstances of ordinary life into the kind of phantasmagoria that didn't show up in his novels until later. When he got going, he was like one of those jazz stars, relaxing after hours, who are egged on by the other musicians into chorus after chorus. He had a favourite riff about the number of thieves in his area. (As I remember it, he was living in Notting Hill at the time, but it could just as well have been Belgravia: in his imagination, all of London turned into a single country, which I think I was the first to call Martinique.) On one occasion the riff developed into a symphony. According to him, he was one of the few non-thieves allowed to live in his district. The thieves did not emerge from their lairs until evening. Then you started seeing them on the skyline, moving, to the beat of tom-toms, in stooped silhouette across the rooftops, on their way to a previously determined destination. During the night, every residence of a non-thief would be visited, even if the non-thief was at home and awake. 'A pair of white eyeballs at the window,' Martin would explain, 'reluctantly absorbing the evidence that the place is inhabited. I look back casually, trying to convey with my lazy sprawl that I would only with reluctance reach for the .357 magnum in my desk drawer. I keep typing away at my article about Henry James. The eyeballs blink.' By this time the whole table would be helpless, and Martin would be ready for his final evocation of the stooped thieves marching nose to tail along the skyline, ending up in each other's places, and taking the stuff that had already been stolen from someone else, perhaps even from them.

The key to Martin's style of talk, apart from his protean range of pinpoint mimicry, was the economical stroke of the whip that did just enough to keep the top spinning. Granted time to think by the massed laughter, he could make the next bit up. (It took him a while to get that good on the page, and there are great talkers who never make the jump, perhaps because they are too modest to be their own delighted audience when they sit alone.) Hitchens, on the other hand, did the reverse of economy, or seemed to. At that time his world fame as a political and cultural essayist still lay in the future, as it was bound to, because his style of conversation – the key to his penetrating sarcasm – was too extravagant to be absorbed into a normal paragraph of prose. If he had been leading the conversation, he could have done a ten-minute version of the chicken crossing the road. ('Blind drunk ... drunk as only a chicken with no head for alcohol can be ... headless chicken ... sobbing, *clucking* drunk ... not shedding the occasional feather as chickens are wont to do ... every feather *glued to its body* by wine-flavoured perspiration ... out of El Vino's with hanging beak ... the busy, roaring road looming before it ... the broad thoroughfare as an unbridgeable chasm, if I may quote Edith Wharton ... doomed from the egg onwards ... a fish out of water ... standing up to be counted ... helplessly victimized in a chicken-hostile environment...') But he hardly ever led. His decorations and interruptions were applied not to his own monologue, but to someone else's. Thus, if someone was being straightforward he could make them funny, and if they were being funny he could make them funnier. Since the cause of wit in other men is always popular with the other men, his knack of saying the unforgivable thing was invariably forgiven. To ostracize him would have meant staying away, and nobody wanted to be absent when Martin and the Hitch were head to head.

Trying to keep up with either of those two, when they were flying, was the mark of a beginner. It was better to wait and let things die down. In similar circumstances, Oliver Goldsmith used to go home annoyed if he could not, as Boswell put it, 'get in and shine'. But to listen was sufficiently pleasant, and a lot of us looked forward to Friday as the best day of the week. I think Jonathan Raban, flying back from an assignment abroad, was the first participant ever to re-book his flight so that he would be in time for lunch, but later on a lot of us did the same. It was a very competitive scene, though, and therefore very male, and nowadays it would probably be against the law. Doubtless there were a few women in town who could have done what Dorothy Parker did at the Algonquin before World War II, but they would have had to be ready to fail at it. Nor was it enough to be a good speaker. You had to be a good listener, which is a surprisingly rare quality, and one that I could have used a bit more of. Julian Barnes is still getting a lot of mileage out of my ability to turn the conversation back to my own concerns. Still, they used to accuse Scott Fitzgerald of the same thing. If the assembled company rags you for a failing, you can usually play up to it for comic effect: it's the failing they don't mention that you have to watch out for.

Exaggerated stories about my childhood, I noticed, went down well. On the other hand, my liberal democratic political opinions – situated in what Ian McEwan nowadays usefully calls the radical centre – were regarded with barely disguised impatience by almost all those present, and with open contempt and disbelief by both Fenton and Hitchens, who were still basing their positions on the belief that the Russian revolution, even if it had been betrayed, had started off as a good thing. Later on I would have been able to defend my views better, but at the time I was content to be steamrollered. When Kingsley Amis and Robert Conquest started showing up, the steamrollers rolled from the other direction as well, and there were some resonant collisions, especially between Conquest and Hitchens. The Hitch had the snappy rhetoric but Conkers had the right quotations in the original Russian. It isn't true, however, that they became fast friends later on. They always were. The spectacle of people with radically opposing views still managing to amuse each other is something that makes London different from New York, and very different from Sydney. Amusement was treated as a value – which, of course, as long as it doesn't attempt to erode sincerity, it is. If it does attempt to do that, it soon ceases to be valuable, and not much later it ceases even to be amusing. There are a lot of people who talk well enough but forfeit a hearing when it becomes clear that they will say anything for effect.

The Friday lunch was too enjoyable to waste. When I realized that I was wasting at least half of it through getting smashed too quickly, I finally resolved to temper my drinking by the only method that I knew would be effective: i.e., to quit altogether. To my later remorse, I could have gone on bearing the shame of passing out on the train while bringing a hangover home to my family. Also I had managed to live with the knowledge that I had been cruelly rude to a keen young Indian who had seen my face on television and concluded that this feat of recognition entitled him to occupy my chair at the table in Mother Bunch's while I was away in the toilet dealing with the overflow of a largely liquid lunch – one of the last before the move to the Kebab House. Luckily I was the last one left of the assembly that day, so there was nobody there except my voluble victim to see me in action when I came back from the bog and told him to take off. He was out of line, but I would have been more polite had I been less drunk. I might even have engaged him in conversation – or at any rate joined the conversation in which he was already engaged – and thereby learned something. As things were, I gained only the memory of having been arrogant. The young man's fallen face got into my dreams, haunting me as the imperialist police-man Merrick in *The Jewel in the Crown* might have been haunted if he had had a conscience. Congratulating myself on having one of those, I foresaw many an internal struggle when drunken idiocy would have to be paid for with mental anguish. Well, I could live with that, too. In other words, I could bear the prospect of carrying on as before. But I couldn't bear the thought of speaking with a furred tongue in eloquent company. So it was for the sake of ego that I gave up drink, and not out of virtue. These are sorry confessions to make and I feel doubly sorry that I feel bound to make them, but a book about growing wiser would be dangerously untrue if it suggested that there is always something charming about the attainment of self-knowledge. Sometimes it is exactly like meeting the wrong stranger in a dark alley.

Perhaps encouraged by recent theatrical success, I arranged the trappings of a show-business event for the occasion when I would forever abjure the demon rum. It never occurred to me that the best way to quit would be to quit sober. I was intent on going out with the receding wave of one last party. On the big Friday, I told everyone that the drinks were on me. Two hours later, quite a lot of them were. My sweater was soaked. After an initial half-hour during which I had the impression that I was talking brilliantly, I had to be warned against shouting. Well, another glass of wine would be a quick cure for that. But I kept on missing my mouth. Tipping a bottle over had always been an early sign that I was losing the plot, but trying to drink through my chin, instead of my mouth, was sure evidence that locomotia ataxia was setting in. I explained this to the few people left to listen. The trip to the toilet turned into a more epic search each time, until finally I came back and found that only Terry and Peter Porter were left. They were talking about Proust. I joined in, although for a while they did not realize it, because I seemed to be talking about someone called Bruce. Then Peter went off to do a broadcast, leaving only Terry, who kindly reminded me that I had to get back to the *Observer* and read proofs. ('Broofs,' I said knowingly.) Even more kindly, he let me share his cab, which must have been like offering house-room to someone wired up with a time bomb who sincerely wants to abandon his mission but has forgotten the code to cancel the explosion. With a wealth of experience from his own roaring days – which he had spent blessed with a far stronger stomach than mine – he was all too aware of what must eventually happen. That it didn't happen in the cab was a stroke of luck, especially since it had the sort of driver who didn't hesitate to announce that if the geezer with the green face had not yet started vomiting – instead of, as Terry claimed, having already finished – there would be a fee to have the upholstery washed, or, if necessary, replaced. Terry exerted his natural authority and kept the driver driving. After that he kept me walking, all the way to the most out-of-the-way of the *Observer*'s staff toilets.

He waited outside, an exercise of tact for which I was grateful, because a man doesn't want other men to see him supporting himself at the urinal by leaning his forehead on the wall while he attempts to shuffle backwards far enough to keep his shoes away from the erratic effusion of his bladder. (Shuffle back too far, and your forehead starts sliding downward, pulling the face upright until the upper lip comes in contact with the wall, by which time the momentum is hard to arrest as you go down sneering. Very few women know about any of this.) When I emerged, Terry saw me to my desk. 'Are you, um, going to be, ah, all right?' Not daring to speak, I nodded. Seeing that a word was called for, I searched for one, but could not find it. So I nodded again, as carefully as I could.

Thus reassured, he retired to his office and could not have seen me leaving for the toilet again. Once more I placed my forehead against the wall, but partly, this time, because the wall was cool, and I felt very hot. I had not felt quite so hot since the night of the killer joint. It might be a good idea to go into a cubicle. Not that I really wanted to vomit. I never do want to. Once again I was struck by that familiar fear, a fear bred not so much by the actual thing, as by the accumulated memories of the apprehension leading up to it. This reflex attempt to keep it in probably multiplies the force when it comes out. It certainly did in this case. First leaning over the bowl and then kneeling in front of it as if it were an altar, I repeatedly yelled repentance for a misspent life. Mixed liquids and insufficiently pureed solids gushed past my teeth. I heard the noise of an early post-war Italian two-stroke motorcycle giving birth. Things really got noisy when there was nothing in my stomach left to chuck. Through a throat already restricted by the intensity of its efforts, I went on vainly trying to hurl my personality – a hedgehog the size of a badger. When Terry came for me, I was lying on the floor of the cubicle, my body wrapped tightly around the pedestal of the bowl, as if the porcelain were my last source of warmth.

13. THE NAME'S PRYKKE:
PEREGRINE PRYKKE

By the time I was well again, the story was all over London. Humiliation was complete, but it had one big advantage. It was very hard to go back on such a public promise, although even I would have been surprised to have been told that I would never touch alcohol again for another thirteen years. Not long afterwards, I quit smoking as well, and for just as long. Terry, who had a front-row seat for my transformation, said an interesting thing. Minus its ums and ahs, it went like this: 'You've always managed to get quite a lot done, but what are you going to be like now?' I was naive enough to take this as an unmixed compliment, but there might have been an element of apprehension in it. Although his regard for Proust suggested otherwise, Terry didn't much approve of anyone who missed out on life through being too assiduous in pursuit of its honours. He had seen too many promising young men deprived of its pleasures. There is something to that view, and I try to respect it, although from holding it I am debarred by nature.

No longer required as a receptacle for sixty cigarette butts a day, my Bedford hubcap was thrown into the skip parked in front of our house in Cambridge. The skip otherwise held the debris emerging from our new knock-through. We were expanding. I was slow to admit that cutting out the booze and fags had improved the financial position, because the admission would have suggested that I had been robbing my own household since the day of its foundation. I preferred to think that several ships

were coming in at once. There was something to that interpretation. Donald Trelford, who had now taken over from David
Astor in the editor's chair at the *Observer*, looked with favour on
my work. Too much favour, initially. When the paper came up
for a redesign, I was only just in time to stop the design team
doubling the size of my photo at the top of my column and
adding a bold subheading that promised yet another weekly dose
of hilarity fit to cure all ills among the living and bring the dead
up dancing out of their tombs. Never one to be hobbled by
modesty, I nevertheless have a horror of being overbilled. Above
all I can't stand being introduced as some sort of cheery fellow in
a floppy cap and long, pointed shoes. The error wasn't Trelford's
but he had let the designers get too far along the road to setting
it irrevocably in lead.

On the other hand, it was Trelford who had the excellent idea
of sending me off all over the world to write feature articles
about foreign cities. Although I always prepared as thoroughly
as possible for these assignments I couldn't hope to equal the
knowledge of the *Observer*'s man on the spot: whether staff
appointee or local stringer, he was likely to be jealous of his turf
for a good reason – that he knew every inch of it. What was I to
gain by dropping out of the sky for a few days of room service?
Trelford was clever enough to spot the plus. I wouldn't be writing
the informed letter of the man in residence, I would be recording
the uninhibited first impressions of the flying visitor, which
would be of value to the reader precisely because the man who
lived there no longer thought them worth noting. It would suit
my style. It was also Trelford who thought of the generic name
for the pieces: Postcards. Thus one of my standby formats was
born. Eventually I was to write enough Postcard pieces to furnish,
in 1981, a book called *Flying Visits*, and in the next decade I
transferred the idea to television, in which medium my Postcard
programmes were always my main claim, if not to fame, then at
least to work painstakingly done. The whole project, whose legs
turned out to be a full twenty-five years long, arose out of a

single conversation. I got a lot of glory out of it in the long run, so I owe it to Trelford to acknowledge his imaginative encouragement. He had to think like that on everybody's behalf every day of the week, with nobody noticing except when things went wrong. But that's what editors do. Thank God I was never one of them.

One of my first Postcard assignments was a two-part piece about my home town. It was my first trip back to Sydney in fifteen years. (I hadn't stayed away on principle: I just never had enough money for the flight.) Though the street where I was born and raised had barely altered, Kogarah's dinky little railway station had been buried under a massive reinforced-concrete bunker of the kind once built by the Organization Todt to guard the coast of Normandy. Todt, however, had never equipped his hulking masterpieces with restaurants and a shopping mall. There was even more culture shock available in the city's downtown area, which had gone scraping skyward like a miniature Manhattan. It even had a new name: CBD, for Central Business District. (Despite all the evidence to the contrary, Australian journalists have always been convinced that plenty of initials and acronyms make their prose more readable instead of less: 'NRMA officials against the GST quoted CSIRO statistics at their AGM in the CBD this morning...') But there was a much bigger change going on than that. Post-war immigration had civilized the place. I wasn't yet quite civilized enough myself to take in all the implications: I didn't quite realize that the new standards of eating and drinking weren't just good, but the best on Earth. But I got some of the story into my notebooks, and wrote it up on the plane back to England. I couldn't help, however, thinking of it as the plane home. That was the real subject, but I wasn't ready for it, and probably I'm still not. Though nowadays I am back and forth to Australia half a dozen times a year, I still don't know where I live. But I tried to address the serious issues along with the other stuff, so I was miffed to discover, from the proof pages, that the *Observer*'s illustrator had decked me out as a comedian. I made a quick and correct decision to lay down the law. My stuff, I told everyone concerned and several bystanders who weren't, depended on being presented as a serious argument. If it picked up any laughs along the way, that would be a plus. But if it was presented as vaudeville, anything serious it contained would count as a minus. So nix the funny hats. One of the artists got a bit shirty but the message went home. Trelford backed me up, although it couldn't have been easy. The artist really had put in a lot of work. But that's an argument you always have to be wary of: we've put all this effort into doing the wrong thing for you, so you have to use it. Sympathize with that viewpoint often enough and you'll find yourself being crowded into oblivion, helped in that direction by people whose undoubted pride in their own craft is unaccompanied by any insight into yours.

Another early Postcard trip was to Moscow. I had already been teaching myself Russian for a couple of years and it paid off in a big way, because I could actually read the resolutions of the XXVI Party Congress mounted hugely on every building. LET US IMPROVE THE QUALITY OF CONSUMER GOODS. It was all too apparent, however, that resolutions wouldn't work the trick. Anybody who might have been able to improve the quality of consumer goods had been murdered long ago. My wife, who was along for the ride, was amazed by the range of soaps and oils that were not available for our bathroom in the Metropole Hotel. Still equipped with its original chandeliers and a sub-Benny Goodman quintet noodling assiduously in the dining room, the Metropole had once been the NKVD's favoured point of concentration for those refugee officials of foreign Communist Parties who would need to be dealt with. All too aware that there had been a time when some of the previous occupants of our room had been called to the door at two o'clock in the morning, I was less amazed but even more depressed. I had thought things might have come on a bit, but they hadn't. Our key moment of revelation, which I put in my article, was a window display mounted by the GUM department store in Red Square. There was nothing in the window except a chipped and rusting chromium stand draped with a pair of tights proudly billed as coming from East Berlin. That was the pitiable condition that the resolutions were resolving to transform: a cultural hegemony in which East Berlin was regarded as a fashion centre. My wife looked at the pair of tights for a long time. Inside the store, in the women's department, she sat down at the standard-issue, one-size-fits-all makeup table – a super-luxury item – and duly noted that it was impossible to get the knees in underneath it. She didn't need to be told by me that her hard-working and dedicated life in the West would have been heartbreakingly worse here, where even the things you had to save up for weren't worth having. At our first dinner in the Metropole she enjoyed the blinis but spotted before I did that our plain but sweet Intourist guide was putting any blinis we didn't eat into her purse. At an evening of folk-dancing held at the Palace of Congresses in the Kremlin we were three-quarters of the way through the interminable bill – the flirtatious peasant girl with the knee-length knickers was once again pretending to run away from the boy with the big shoulders and small head, although this time he was dressed as a factory worker rather than a tank commander – when my wife conceded that I might be allowed to regard these assignments as work rather than a family outing. Paris and Rome might be another thing, but no more folk-dancing. Please.

On future voyages I overcame my guilt for going it alone by setting myself a crowded schedule, throwing in a lot of stuff that nobody I was trying to keep happy would conceivably have wanted to see. Already, when I came back from Moscow, I was faced with the proof that to write a solid piece, with a factual basis for every paragraph, you needed a notebook with enough detailed entries to write a book from. From then on, I kept that rule: come back with enough notes for a book and you could get a decent piece. Get enough decent pieces and you might eventually make a book. But don't try to take a short cut just by stating

what you fancied to be your common-sense view and tarting it up with local colour. A few loose observations linked by opinions wouldn't do, whether the opinions were standard, so as to flatter the reader's store of ordinary wisdom, or perverse, so as to stir protest. The concrete detail not only told the story, it gave the interpretation. When I saw our Intourist guide quietly snaffling the blinis, I was seeing the ineradicable truth about how the requirements of life were distributed in the Soviet Union. The reason why she had hopes of being allowed to join the Communist Party was that she would be allowed access to the special stores and so wouldn't have to steal. At the very dinner in the Metropole when she made the blinis disappear, one of our party, a sociology lecturer from the LSE, was explaining to the assembled company that the discrepancies in standard of living between the well-off and the poor in the Soviet Union were not so marked as in the West. Even as our guide was saying, 'Of course,' in her excellent English, the blinis were on their way into her purse.

I couldn't write that part of the story because it might have got her into trouble. When she took us to what was meant to be a performance of classical ballet, she broke down in tears when it turned out that the performance had been cancelled and replaced by a new allegorical ballet about the triumph of Communism over Fascism. Trying not to be delighted by the extra opportunity for sarcasm, I reported faithfully what happened on stage – the dancer representing Fascism had a particularly threatening bottom – but I left out her tears, which she dabbed at in the darkness under the pretence that she had a cold. She had so wanted us to see her beloved country's heritage at its beautiful best. Had I mentioned that, however, she might have ended up somewhere in the Gulag system, whose psychiatric correctional facilities, under Brezhnev, were still fully functional. And lest you think that I overrate my importance, let me tell you that the Soviet authorities read my piece with great care when it was published. A page and a half in the *Observer* earned two and a half columns in the *Literaturnaya Gazeta*, whose resident satirist cleverly identified me as an agent of Western propaganda. But I wasn't. I was an agent of all the Intourist guides who were dreaming of a pair of tights that could simply be bought without being worshipped, of a makeup table that you could fit your legs under instead of sitting sideways like the Queen at the Trooping the Colour, of not having to pretend that bad art was more bearable because it carried the correct message, and above all of not having to steal food from tourists. Her tears, her tears. I can mention her name now. It was Valentina. I wonder how she is. There has been a new, unofficial, and therefore even less predictable kind of gangsterism in Russia since the Soviet Union collapsed, and no doubt her life has not been easy. She certainly didn't seem to have the makings of a crook, and her fundamental honesty has probably not helped her. But I can remember when the country she loved was breaking her heart a little bit every day.

When our sociology lecturer asked Valentina whether she had a place of her own, she said, 'Of course: everybody has.' It didn't seem very likely. It had never seemed very likely to me that I might one day have my name on two places of my own, but suddenly I did. Rivalling the splendour of the new knock-through in Cambridge, there was now a London apartment, situated below podium level in the Barbican, down beside the famous artificial lake around which, on the brick patio, ducks gathered from all over the world for their annual shitting competition, for which the qualifying rounds took most of the year. I was no longer sharing my London base with the rest of the boys. I was sharing my London base with my family. Since no member of my family except my wife was there very often, this in effect gave me an opportunity to produce the ideal conditions for the essential requirement of a writer's life: the freedom to do nothing. At last I was free of any distractions that might dissuade me from my course of sweating with frustrated effort and feeling guilty because nothing had been achieved. From then on, with each move, upgrading of property, and extra acquisition, I merely elaborated the surroundings in which this essential condition could be achieved. Today my redoubt is somewhere south of the Thames and only I have the keys. A planned retreat from extremophile media notoriety has not yet entirely rid me of the sort of snoops who would dearly like to know what goes on behind my closed doors, but on the whole, apart from the occasional visit by the chorus line of the Crazy Horse Saloon, the answer would bore them to death if they could see in. They would have to watch a man shambling from desk to couch; pointlessly alternating coffee with tea throughout the morning until the time comes for the choice between the sardines and the over-boiled eggs for lunch; having an early afternoon sleep; writing half a sentence in longhand and crossing it out; having a supplementary, later afternoon sleep; and then finally, as dusk fills the study window, deciding that it has been a day of *getting ready* to write.

Just so was my average day alone after I moved into the Barbican. There I would sit in the felt-covered sponge-rubber-filled couch-cum-chair beside the giant window looking out onto the lake. The bottom of the window was an inverted semicircle designed so that it could not be equipped with a sill. Like every object in the Barbican, big or small, it had been designed so that something normal could not happen. The walls were designed so that you couldn't hang a picture without borrowing a heavy-duty drill with a diamond-tipped bit so as to sink the shallow hole in which to place the blasting powder. The wiring was placed deep within the bomb-proof walls along with the plumbing, so that an electrical failure would interact with a broken pipe to produce an effect that could not be corrected until after the flood put out the fire. There was a garbage-disposal system that connected your sink with every other sink in the building, so that a blockage a mile away sent its gas to you along the complete network of pipes before it came up reeking into your face while you tried vainly to deal with the empty milk carton caught in the jaws of the gunge-plunger. The garbage-disposal system was thus designed so that garbage could not readily be disposed of. But nothing epitomized the whole Le Corbusier-style grandiloquence of the Barbican – its truly monumental combination of misguided social engineering and vaulting incompetence – like the lake. The lake, lined with bricks and floored with concrete, had been precisely calculated so that it was too shallow to keep fish alive and just deep enough to drown a child. The mere presence of the lake meant that the original dream of village family life in the heart of the city could never be fulfilled. Any family that let its children out to play alone would have had to be crazy. One of the side effects was a heavy traffic of prams pushed by au-pair girls, emanating from the flats big enough to have a spare room. The traffic ceased at nightfall and I could look through the window without any guilt except about another working day that had come to nothing. To underline this conclusion, a duck ambling languidly on the bricks would turn its behind towards me and fart a plug of lime-tinged *panna cotta*.

But after an evening spent drinking orange juice while watching television, and a night spent dreaming my standard dreams of being unable to get something done – in most of my dreams of failure, there is a document that needs to be prepared but I can't write it, or else I need to learn it but I can't remember it – I would wake next morning feeling enough remorse to bring results. Wherein lies the whole rationale of making sure you are undisturbed while you do nothing: so as to build up the anguish that will make you do something. Not that there was all that much spare time to be thus squandered on the luxury of waiting for sentences to form. Quite often something had to be written no matter what. There were still deadlines to hit. The Postcard pieces went down with the readers well enough for the *Observer* to want more of them than the four features a year stipulated in the contract. So I was often away, and, when at home, had to work at writing up the results. And a published book, I now found, could have a demanding life of its own, like a baby. *Visions Before Midnight* came out and did surprisingly well. The glamorous young women in charge of Cape's marketing department wanted me to spend time discussing how I might promote it. This seemed time well spent, but the actual fag of trotting around the radio studios was less thrilling. As the years went by I learned not to begrudge that necessary effort, but early on I would easily get into a panic if my do-nothing time was eaten away. It was the wrong attitude. The trick, with the chores, is to turn them into events. Do your best every time you go out, and never go on radio or television without bringing something to the party. The best way to deal with a bad question is with a good answer.

One of the chores relating to *Visions Before Midnight* was all my idea, so I couldn't complain. It occurred to me that if any *Observer* readers were going to defy expectation and buy the book they might like to buy it direct from the paper, signed by the author. There was a recently formed *Observer* promotions department that liked the idea. A little notice was put at the foot of my column saying that a signed copy could be sent postage-free. Enough people responded to help propel the book briefly onto the bestseller list; and even after it fell off, it stayed gratifyingly high among the also-rans. I had to do quite a lot of signing, a process made more demanding – as it still is today – by my ineradicable, grandstanding urge to make my signature look like an actual name. Apart from being a clear invitation to cheque-forgers, this habit is a gluttonous consumer of energy. The signature to have is one like Pavarotti's, that starts with a tiny squiggle and then turns into a straight line about three inches long. The full story of Pavarotti's glorious ego will have to wait for the next volume, when we move firmly into television heaven and fame hell. At the time we are talking about, I hadn't met him, and it didn't occur to me that I ever would. Sufficient to say now that if he hadn't developed his instantaneous signature he would have lost an arm. Even as things were, when his ghosted autobiography came out he risked carpal-tunnel syndrome just from the number of times he had to draw his little line sideways. People forgave him, as they forgave him everything. In the signing queue, after he made his mark, they would examine the results and always express their gratitude, instead of hitting him over the head with the book. If he had been less fat, of course, they would have loved him less, because he would have been too close to looking the way he sounded. People don't love the darlings of the gods.

There were also my first American reviewing commissions, from *Commentary* and the *New York Review of Books*. It's a useful rule of thumb that anything the Americans ask you to do takes twice as long, because they want everything explained. (Quite often they are right, but it can be very wearing.) Also, when I arrived in New York to make personal contact with my two new editors, I had no clue as to the implications of their having been political enemies for years. In London they could have still been friends. In New York each looked at me with deep suspicion for having breathed the same air as the other. Pussyfooting around their respective sensitivities took tact, tact took time, and there was no email in those days to speed up the process of transmitting copy across the Atlantic. But there was still enough waiting time left over for some good, long, solid sessions of doing nothing. This time the thing I was waiting for while I did nothing was the next bit of *Peregrine Prykke's Pilgrimage*. The big advantage of a project cast in rhyming couplets is that if you get one decent couplet a day, it counts as a day's work, and it will give you a good idea of how to add to it tomorrow. Hemingway, who typed standing up, always kept the rule of quitting for the day when he knew where the narrative was going next. Having written the sentence about the charging rhino, and being fairly sure that next day he would write the sentence in which the hero shot it, he would finally sit down and give his current wife the signal to bring in a daiquiri the size of a bird-bath. The rule is good in the sense that to do the opposite almost always results in barrenness next morning. But I had a fair idea of where the clueless Peregrine was going anyway. A good, simple lad, he would seek literary success. He would find it. It would destroy him. Along the path

to destruction he would meet everybody. I had a list drawn up,
and I could always work on an individual character if I got
jammed on the narrative. Thus Seamus Feamus was born, and
F. R. Looseleaf, Ian Hammerhead, Stephen Spindle, and Doc
Stein. Partly assembled out of components already machined and
polished, the thing pieced itself together at almost alarming speed,
but I won't say that it did so with ease. It's never wise to say that
something which sounds effortless actually was, and anyway, this
one really was hard work. I would wake up at night when I had
an idea, and dawn would find me sitting beside the picture
window, still drafting, crossing out, drawing arrows, and looking up only occasionally to be faced with a duck's arse poised
to dump. Although the first, unimproved version of the poem
looks embarrassingly clumsy to me now, I fancied at the time
that I was performing technical miracles, much of the evidence
for this dizzy level of competence being provided by clenched
teeth, cold sweat, chronic sleeplessness, and voodoo mutterings
as I tested rhymes while walking along. Baudelaire once claimed
he could tell that Victor Hugo was composing couplets in his
head by the way he walked. I probably looked as if I was failing
to compose them. Often I failed to walk. I would have to get out
my notebook, sit down suddenly, and write. Eventually the poem
was in a condition where I could hand it to Dai, who agreed to
play all the parts except two. I would be the narrator. The role of
Peregrine Prykke himself I offered to Martin Amis.

How I persuaded Martin to say yes to this proposition remains
a mystery to me and, I dare say, to him. In the normal course of
events, Martin, rather than step into the spotlight, would prefer
to die in an unarmed attack on the power station supplying its
electric current. His genuine modesty is the main reason for the
fateful discrepancy between him and the journalistic literary
sexton beetles who make copy out of him: they would like to
receive the degree of attention that he would like to avoid, and
the clearer it becomes that he would like to avoid it, the more
they resent him for failing to appreciate their generosity. But he

said yes to being cast as my doomed young hero. I can only
conclude that he saw truth in the role, although Perry's odyssey,
like the personal history of any character in anything I have ever
written, is drawn almost exclusively from my own experience.
(Whence my thanks to fate that I went travelling so much in the
next twenty years: otherwise I would have written endlessly about
a man staring through a window at a lake dotted with the white
floating bellies of dead carp.) Warning me that he must not be
expected to do any acting, Martin settled down to study the part.
I assured him, truthfully, that most of the acting would be done
by Dai.

 And so it happened. The literati packed into the hall at the
ICA heard their own voices coming back at them out of Dai's
mouth. There was no scenery, just the three of us with a lectern
and a microphone each, but one of the microphones was a
cornucopia. Characters in the poem who weren't present to hear
themselves speak heard about it soon enough. (It was on the
evidence of the reception for Bob Lull's featured role in *Peregrine
Prykke's Pilgrimage,* and not the attention given to Edward
Pygge's *Three Sonnets by Robert Lowell,* that Elizabeth Hardwick
was able to inform her ex-husband, 'They're laughing at you in
London, Cal.') Martin had no trouble indicating the diffidence of
the young Perry taking his first steps on the path to glory. As the
hubristic, slightly less young Perry on the road to perdition he
was less convincing, but he got away with it. More amazingly, in
the face of Dai's virtuosity, I got away with it. The audience was
riveted even when not howling. Nobody went to sleep except
Charles Monteith of Faber, and a few days later he sent me a
note pleading jet lag. What might have seemed like a colonial's
act of retributive arrogance was saved by the laughs and by a
central truth: the destruction of Perry's innocence was bound to
happen, because destroying innocence is what literature does.
Since any group feels flattered when told that it lives by jungle
law, the audience afterwards queued to pat my head. Most of
the compliments felt genuine, although there was one from

Michael Frayn that bothered me momentarily. 'It was the *scale* of the thing that amazed me.' Since he could equally have meant the scale of the disaster, this noncommittal encomium can be recommended for use among all the other anodyne stand-by effusions for when you 'go around' after the performance. 'What can I say?' 'Well, you did it again!' 'Only you could have given us an evening like that.' And: 'It was the *scale* of the thing that amazed me.'

But paranoia soon proved to be inappropriate. Apart from the gratifying hubbub on the night, there were a couple of immediate reactions next day that would have yielded a double thrill if they had not so neatly cancelled each other out. Ian Hamilton, who obviously hadn't at all minded being renamed Ian Hammerhead, asked me for the whole 1,400-line text so that he could print it as a limited-edition booklet in soft covers, and then, in full, in the *New Review*. I was so chuffed at his reacting with unequivocal approval to one of my poems that I said yes before realizing other editors might have similar ideas. Anthony Thwaite, then the literary editor of the globe-girdling *Encounter*, asked if he could print the whole thing. If *Encounter* had carried the poem, I would have been unarguably established as a poet from that day forth, no ifs, no buts. There were excellent reasons for double-crossing Ian. But they didn't seem quite as excellent as the reasons for keeping my word. And as Dai put it, over a pint at the Pillars, *Encounter* would have paid me folding money, and we couldn't have that.

Cape paid folding money up front to both of us when it commissioned a booklet of the Improved Version of the poem illustrated throughout by the omnicompetent Dai, whose graphic constructions were as inventive as his verbal ones. To jump forward a bit, I undertook an Improved Version when I realized that the versification of the original was intolerably clumsy. James Fenton helped me realize it. Never hesitant with criticism, he told me that I had glaringly failed to count my syllables. I didn't like him for saying so, but when I started counting I could see that he was right. So I rewrote the whole thing. There is always a danger, when you start watching your technique too closely, that you will develop the kind of *manière aigre* that crippled Renoir after Degas scared him back to school. But a form like rhyming couplets – like, indeed, all the set verse forms – gets a lot of its propulsion from its precision. So I think I sped the poem up, and I'm sure I sped up the companion piece that followed it. The following year's epic was *The Fate of Felicity Fark in the Land of the Media*, with illustrations by Mark Boxer, who hated the title. More than twenty years later I decided he had been right, and I scrapped the poem along with two more mock epics that followed in the same track. For the second poem, the modest perform-ance in the ICA had once more gone well, and this time a long extract from the text was run by the *Sunday Times*, much to the *Observer*'s disapproval. Another year on, the next epic venture, *Britannia Bright's Bewilderment in the Wilderness of Westminster*, once again with drawings by 'Marc', was front-paged by the *Observer* in retaliation. Or I might have got those two serializa-tions in reverse: it doesn't matter now. But it all mattered like mad to me then. Though personally I still feel that my four mock epics got technically and dramatically more adroit as they suc-ceeded one another, there might have been something to the prevalent critical idea that *Peregrine Prykke's Pilgrimage* was the best of them because the literary world was the ambience I knew most about. It was an idea I resisted might and main, because I was having too much fun to quit. If I couldn't have a reputation as a serious poet, this alternative means of expressing myself in verse made a much bigger splash. The poems were written to real contracts, were performed like plays, were showcased on the front of the review sections: more buzz than the average British movie. Even better, they spoke directly to the audience, without inter-mediaries. 'At least I can tell, with your stuff,' John Cleese once told me, 'why it's written that way. With most poetry I can't do that.' Such off-trail encouragement wasn't the same as official endorsement, but maybe different was better. And anyway, how much attention could I ask for? My life in the literary world looked more stable than poor Perry's. I had the column, the commissions for features, some solid reviewing connections, I was the author of a couple of books of bits and pieces, and now, running alongside, there was this mini-industry of the mock epic. I didn't see how anything could stop me.

14. TYNAN STEPS IN

The regular critics tried to when Faber brought out a collection of my verse letters under the title *Fan-Mail*. The hyphen was my mistake and so was the book, which was reviewed like the plague. People scarcely capable of writing a sentence that could be read were accusing me of being unable to write a stanza that could be scanned. For a long time I agreed with the reviewers, although the fact that those poems still appear among my collected verse in *The Book of My Enemy* (2003) is an indication that my opinion has reverted to what it was when I was writing them, in a trance of concentration every time. (The letter to Michael Frayn, composed in Pushkin's cruelly demanding *Onegin* stanza, and the letter to Tom Stoppard, composed in the almost equally tricky Burnsian measure, both sent me to the brink of oxygen starvation: I would forget to breathe as I pieced the phrases into the intricate set schemes.) The verse letter as a genre, however, I now saw as only a small part in my total global output of comic verse. Everything for the stage, for instance, should be in comic verse. If only Shakespeare had followed Chaucer's example! Kenneth Tynan pulled a face when I explained this to him, but by that time he looked as if he was pulling a face anyway: his habits were catching up with him, there had never been much flesh between skin and skull, and now he looked like a skeleton trying to escape. Tynan had called me to his house in Thurloe Square to discuss a project. It was our second meeting. The first had been at a Garrick Club reception not long after I joined the *Observer*. Tynan had been wearing a tailored green shantung Dr No jacket and I had worn one of my usual polyester paisley ensembles from the Nightmare Alley boutique on the Planet of the Drapes. Much to Terry Kilmartin's amusement, David Astor looked at me as if I were a German paratrooper. Tynan, however, chose to address me, grandly telling me how I wrote TV criticism with such verve that I should consider 'moving up' into drama criticism. Our subsequent exchange is no less true for my having told the tale a thousand times. When I asked him if he could really, truly, still stand the theatre, he said, 'I get a thrill every time the curtain goes up.' And I said: 'I get a thrill every time it goes down.'

Or something like that. In reality, dialogue is never as crisp. But theatre isn't reality and I didn't want it to be: I wanted it to be verbally electrifying. Most theatre, in my experience, was the opposite. One of the reasons I admired Stoppard so much – later on I admired Michael Frayn and Peter Nichols for the same reason – was that his plays, despite the room they made for an exalted level of visual hoopla, were so full of lines begging to be spoken. Tynan pointed out that even Stoppard had needed help in pulling *Jumpers* together. Since the help, in that case, had been provided by him, Tynan was speaking with authority. When we met again in Thurloe Square, however, he soon found me more opinionated than ever. In his capacity as the dramaturge who had beaten back sexual constrictions by giving the world the designedly scurrilous revue *O, Calcutta*, Tynan now wanted to make a similarly liberating play out of a book by the prankster, brothel-keeper, and strolling philosopher Willy Donaldson. Tynan wanted me to write the script, which being done, he would take over and supply all the other requirements. After reading the book I suggested that the play should be done in verse.

Tynan had looked pretty ill at the previous meeting, but at this meeting, when he heard my suggestion, his face moved even nearer death. Actually, that aspect was no joke. Tynan had emphysema, and it would eventually do for him, but at that stage he could still tell himself that he only had to quit smoking. There were a lot of people who loved him and wanted to believe the same thing. I was one of them: if only for his gift of phrase, I admired Tynan to the point of worship. I just didn't think that he made any sense politically. He was one of the British theatre's permanent supply of licensed radicals – Harold Pinter and David Hare are other prominent examples – who are allowed, and even encouraged, to rain scorn on the beliefs of the very people who come to see their plays. How this reciprocating system of *gauchiste* rhetoric subsidized by bourgeois self-flagellation actually works is a subject for sociological analysis that need not detain us here. Sufficient to say that Tynan was far too nice ever to realize that the sincerity of his Brechtian revolutionary principles would have stunned Brecht, who had manufactured them to please a state-sponsored market and had banked his foreign royalties in Switzerland. But at least Brecht, whose didactic plays had bored the world for decades, was safely out of the picture. Unfortunately Tynan thought that Willy Donaldson was yet another social revolutionary: perhaps not precisely of the Brechtian stamp, but promising a usefully subversive libertarian critique of the institutionalized inhibitions of Western society.

I went to meet Willy off-campus, as it were, and we soon had each other sized up. His dim little flat in Chelsea was clearly the model for the exciting brothel in the book. All he had done was build up its crumbling face with a few layers of pancake makeup. The same could be said for his girlfriend, whose patterns of speech and behaviour soon revealed themselves to have been souped up and distributed between all the exotic houris, demimondaines and grisettes that populated his story. Willy had the knack for the prose that floods mundane reality with a radiance it could never generate by itself. In his pages, the hypnotic hookers came swaying towards you in couture underwear, drunk on the perfume of their own armpits, their eyes alight with your reflected dreams, hungry to blend their burning need with yours. The money didn't really matter to them. They were driven by desire. In reality, Willy's girlfriend had a sour face painted on the surface of a veteran grapefruit, and the Band-Aids on the back of her calves where the last shave had gone wrong were curling at the edges. Her bloodshot eyes, never very large, were focused on something bad happening a few inches in front of them, perhaps the tiny pall of heat coming up from the cigarette she smoked no hands. Tynan had told me that Willy, once a tycoon of up-market sexual commerce, had fallen on hard times. I hadn't talked to him for half an hour before I realized that there had never been any soft times. This was it. He had been making everything up since the days when the *Beyond the Fringe* boys – he was their first impresario – had twigged that he was a bull artist and eased him out. He and I talked the same language. He was a fabulist. It takes one to know one.

I wrote the play anyway, and I wrote it the way Tynan wanted it: in prose. The manuscript must be somewhere among my junk. It never got any further than script stage, thank God. My main problem with the material, as they say in Hollywood, was that I have never been able to believe in self-fulfilment through sexual liberation. I believe in sexual desire as a transfigurative force all right, but I don't think that it contributes to intelligence any more than salmonella contributes to digestion. Even now, on the threshold of the departure lounge, I still fall in love instantly with every beautiful and brilliant woman I meet; and I am still likely, if the woman is sufficiently beautiful, to think that she must be brilliant anyway, even as the evidence to the contrary becomes mountainous. I could write a book on the subject of sex, and one day, if there is a sufficient pause after it's all over, I probably will. The book's principal conclusion, I imagine, will be that a man whose romantic folly is infinite had better try to find himself the kind of woman who values the realism in him and knows how to bring it out, or he will end up dead, or bankrupt, or surrounded, like Willy, by the kind of faded decor into which the flannel dressing gown decorated with cigarette burns blends like camouflage. If he finds more than one woman like that then he will still be in trouble, but at least he will know what kind of trouble he is in. The idea that the rules for controlling a force could be derived from the force itself was one that only a man like Tynan could sincerely believe. Willy didn't believe it any more than I did. He hoped the project would dig him out of a hole. I was truly sorry I couldn't help. (Later on I was glad when he had a money-spinning hit with his 'Henry Root' caper.) I liked him. He forgave me for being as square as a brick under my air of exuberance, and I forgave him for peddling fake petrol. We had to forgive each other because we both pulled our cons using the same device: the spellbinder sentence, that little castle in the air.

Tynan was probably relieved when I pulled out of the project without needing to be pushed. I told him the truth: that the kind of theatre I wanted to do was a lot smaller, more like a cabaret; that it was almost all talk; and that it was mainly mine, so that I couldn't screw anybody else up. I didn't need to tell him that I wasn't sure yet of how to do it. My mock epics ran for only one night and nobody could pursue a show-business venture on that basis. (The answer to that one is to go touring, but for that you need fame, either your own or borrowed: thus the British touring circuit is replete with acts calling themselves the Platters, the Drifters, Elvis Presley, and Buddy Holly – itinerant bodysnatchers who sign their real names only on the contract.) So I just looked vague on the subject. It was an expression Tynan was used to, having worked with so many actors; and he let me go without rancour. Several years would go by before I saw him again, and for the last time. (I jump forward to the scene now, out of sequence, because his greatness has been wilfully neglected and no signs of enthusiasm should be held back that might help to restore its lustre.) It was in Los Angeles. On an afternoon off from an *Observer* assignment I went out by cab to see him in the house he and Kathleen had taken in one of the canyons. Coldwater Canyon, I think; or maybe Stone Canyon; anyway, one of those names out of Raymond Chandler. If I had the biography here I could check up, but I hated the biography, even though Kathleen wrote it, and with a loving, forgiving hand. The biography, and the letters, helped to sink what was left of his reputation, so that now, when he is out of print, he is patronized, without a blush, by the sort of people he could write rings around. But he was the stylist of his time: the true star critic. One of the things that made him so, apart from his turn of phrase, was what he called his limitless capacity for admiration. When I said that Hemingway's style had fallen apart in the end, Tynan read aloud from that marvellous passage where Hemingway, towards the close of his life, talked about the Gulf Stream's ability to take in any amount of junk and still run clean again after a few miles. I could tell that Tynan was talking about his lungs; and Hemingway was wrong, of course; but the prose sounded like holy writ in Tynan's strained voice as the hot sunlight inexorably ate its way into the absurdly green lawn. Tynan was giving me a final lesson in what lasts: the style impelled by the rhythm of the soul, breadth of feeling with a narrow focus. Any youngster who wants to get into this business should find a copy of Tynan's first book, *He That Plays the King*, and do what I did – sit down and read it aloud, paragraph by paragraph. It will soon be seen that his sometimes pedestrian radical opinions were far outstripped by his perceptions, which moved like lightning to energize almost every sentence. Tynan had drama in his prose: drama far beyond anything he could do as a dramaturge. It was only fitting that his death should be a drama too. It was a fight between him and the oxygen machine. He looked at it with hatred because he knew that when he sucked on it, it would taste nothing like a cigarette.

But when he showed me out of his elegant front door in Thurloe Square he wasn't dead yet: he just looked like it. Back in the Barbican I once more had enough spare time to wonder what my writing life would be like if I had all the time in the world. The column still provided a must-do for the end of every week. In answer to the must-do, phrases popped into my head. Would they still do that if there were no compulsion? Phrase-making is something I don't much like to talk about because I don't know how it happens. When I build a stanza in ottava rima, I know exactly how it works; how the fifth and sixth lines move at a different speed from the first four, how a pre-echo in the middle of the sixth line will multiply the clinching effect of the final couplet; and though there will always be surprise discoveries while I build it, the surprises will always be recognizable. But I don't know how a phrase works in terms of its origin: I just know how to neaten it up when it arrives, how to make sure that its order of events doesn't injure its internal economy. Somewhere about then – to put this argument on a suitably elevated plane – I described Arnold Schwarzenegger as a brown condom full of walnuts. The idea must have been a registration of his bulges and skin texture, but I still don't know how the visual perception translated itself into a verbal creation. As far as I can tell, looking inwards from within, the gift of phrase is the semantic equivalent of something mathematical, but I don't know whether the mechanism is clever, like the chess master's ability to see the whole board with all its possible combinations, or stupid, like the idiot savant's capacity for following the line of prime numbers all the way to eternity. All I know for sure is that the knack is in my life's blood, and that if it ever failed me it would be time to turn my face to the wall.

The Schwarzenegger phrase (which wasn't in my TV column: it must have been in an article) was an immediate hit, especially with other journalists. They didn't try to steal it, but they often quoted it, with a generous attribution. Nearly always it was a misquote (the most common mistake was to leave out the word 'brown', thereby fatally depleting the visual information), but I learned, over time, to take the acknowledged echo of a phrase, even in maimed form, as a kind of sideways compliment, even if the context was hostile. The compliment became too sideways to be borne only when a journalist would attribute to me something I had never said. Some hack pasting together a profile of Kenny Everett ventured to describe him as I might have done. 'As Clive James might say, Everett looks like a drowned rat peering through a loo brush.' Or some such lazy mish-mash. Somehow this uninspired comparison got itself attached to my name, and

I found it cropping up in unofficial profiles about me for years ahead, particularly when the author of the profile was the kind of journeyman who found it usefully contemptuous to call me by my first name and who thought that 'Antipodean' was a long, hard, funny word. ('The portly Clive, the same Antipodean who called Arnold Schwarzenegger a walnut in a condom and Kenny Everett a rat hiding behind a loo brush, is sensitive about his own personal appearance . . .') In the course of time, but not in that decade or even in the one after, I learned to be grateful for any quotation of any kind, however distorted. The journalist was, after all, boosting the value of my stock in trade. On the evidence of the TV column's buzz-making prominence from week to week, my putative knack for saying smart things was undoubtedly the motor of what I did for a living, even if I found it hard to smother the conviction that there must be something more to life. With due allowance for the difference in stature and earning power, Björn Borg, forever smacking the ball with the sweet spot of the racket, probably felt the same nagging doubt every day, until finally he rediscovered himself as the master spirit of a line of designer sporting apparel, and got married in a pink tracksuit to demonstrate artistic abilities too long suppressed.

And so, with most of the hard initial work already done, the second half of that decade played itself out: writing in the ascendant, television never quite going away, and the urge to tread the boards hard to quell. This last urge got yet another small chance to flourish when I went out on tour with Pete to help him preside over the demise of our first career as songwriters. As things have turned out, there was to be a second career, but we didn't know that at the time. We were looking total defeat right in the face. Nevertheless the fans turned out to fill the halls at most of the dates. In places like Macclesfield, people wanted us to sign their copies of *The Road of Silk* and *Secret Drinker*. At Hull, where we went on in the Students' Union, Philip Larkin turned up at the back of the audience. He was stone deaf by then but he said later that he wanted to see what we were up to, even if he couldn't hear it. The people in the auditoriums were notably civilized and unfailingly attentive. It wasn't a bad result for some pretty uncompromising writing. But it had nothing to do with a viable result in the music business. We were all too aware that the total of all these audiences was only a tiny fraction of the number of album buyers we would have needed to keep going. The last album, a patchy collection of spoofs and parodies called *Live Libel* (I sang one of the numbers on it: it was as dodgy as that), was half meant as a deal-breaker and fully did the job. Its cover illustration by the greatly gifted Trog was one of the best things that ever happened to us, but in the popular arts you need a mass audience, not classy trophies. Prescience would have told me that the stage routine we worked out for the tour – a song from Pete alternating with a reading or a short autobiographical extravaganza from me – would come in handy about a quarter of a century down the line, but prescience I didn't have, and still don't. If you know where they sell it, tell me.

Nervously convinced that I had been instrumental in leading Pete down the garden path for the last ten years, I felt guilty that things hadn't worked out, as I always feel guilty after the collapse of a group venture – even, strangely, when I am not in it. Once again, we are less likely to be talking about humility here than about a kind of all-embracing conceit. Deep down, I am always convinced that everything depends on me. I feel the same way about the United Nations. What might I have done to help Kofi Annan this week? Cut up his son's credit card, for example? And how did I ever let Africa get into such a mess? My credentials as an economist are at least as good as Bono's, yet I have done almost nothing about sub-Saharan debt relief. But perhaps nothing is the thing to do. When it comes to a group enterprise in show business, nothing is almost always the thing to do. The surest way of dealing with an oncoming collective catastrophe is to opt out in advance. You can't take anyone down with you if you don't let the project happen in the first place. When the handsome, voluble, original, and erratic Tony Wilson kindly asked me to contribute a two-minute spot to each episode of his new show for Granada, I could accept without a qualm because nothing depended on me and I could go as easily as I came. I wouldn't have had time to hold myself guilty anyway, because the whole show was clearly headed down the drain from its first night on the air.

Tony Wilson was brilliant. Unfortunately there was no other word for him. Much loved and admired on the Manchester club scene, which he pretty well invented, he was a local hero who would have been made a national figure by television if the mass audience had been as clever and well informed as he was. But it couldn't be; and if it had been, he wouldn't have been remarkable. Tony Wilson's whole persona depended on his being perceived as more brilliant than anybody else; and brilliance, like virtuosity, has only a limited appeal for the audience, which doesn't want to admire what is beyond its imagination; it wants to admire what it already has within its imagination, but doesn't know how to do. When it comes to words, it wants to hear recognizable opinions originally expressed. If it wanted to hear undiluted originality, it would sit at home reading Mallarmé aloud. Tony Wilson was continuously astonishing, but a viewing public that wanted continuous astonishment would have a season ticket to Chinese opera. The same stricture would later haunt *24 Hour Party People*, the film based on Wilson's memoirs. The brilliant Steve Coogan brilliantly incarnated the brilliant Wilson, and the film was a hit with an audience of the brilliant: roughly enough people to fill the first two rows of the average cinema anywhere except Manchester, where everyone turned up along with their pets. It was the least the Mancunians could do for him, because Wilson's other mental aberration, apart from the one by which he thought that the punters would cry out with delighted recognition at quotations from W. B. Yeats, was his faith in the romantic magic of Manchester. I don't think his faith has ever died. Not long ago we bumped into each other one night in Paris, and while we were both talking simultaneously about

how much we loved the Left Bank I floated the subversive contention that there were probably very few people born in the area
who felt the same way about Manchester. I don't think he got it,
and when I ventured to translate 'I love the Bull Ring' into French
his smile definitely died. Perhaps I got the grammar wrong.

I suppose he might have seemed right about Manchester if
you lived there. Off and on, I was there a lot in those years, but I
always put the return half of my train ticket just behind the
banknotes in my wallet, where I could find it by feel in the dark.
As well as for Tony's show – which lasted only for a short season
before the network chiefs declared that they couldn't understand
even the bits they didn't hate – I would come to Manchester to
do *What the Papers Say* fairly regularly. A taxing format, it
provided invaluable practice at getting the words in exactly the
right spot, so it was no wonder that very few journalists – Richard
Ingrams and Russell Davies were always a long way ahead of the
pack – could get it right. I also did the odd film-clip special when
someone like Alfred Hitchcock rolled over dead. But I never
became a Granada stand-by. Bill Grundy had been one of those
for too long. Granada's veteran star front-man and resident
drunk, Grundy had one of those faces where the bags under the
eyes acquire bags under the bags, until finally you are looking at
the terraced paddy fields of a Chinese hillside. Gravel-voiced and
ready to quarrel even with inanimate objects, he had an indis-
criminate hostility that must have cried out to be avoided even
before alcohol let it loose. We only ever had one conversation.
On a train trip south to London, during one of the rare periods
when he had not been banned from the bar car, he approached
me, teetered for a while in what looked like a summoning of
strength, and fell towards me while shouting, 'Fuck off!' The first
word occurred in front of my face and the second behind my
back. Miraculously, he did not hit the floor, but swung back into
the vertical position, from which he continued to fix me with a
glare made incandescent by hate and blame. But he was sober on
the famous day at the studios in Manchester when he hosted the

Sex Pistols for their very first television show. The Sex Pistols had been dug out from under a wet rock by Tony Wilson. Grundy, along with the rest of the world, had no idea of who they were.

Grundy's encounter with this new cultural phenomenon became instantly famous, on the assumption that an uptight tradition had come face to face with a new anarchy. The fact that Grundy, in his lifetime, had done far more damage to his body with chemicals than even Sid Vicious would achieve before his early death was not apparent on screen, where Grundy continued to look like a model of established poise even as the Sex Pistols demonstrated their prototype version of the collective psychosis which, while it may well have given a salutary jolt to popular music, also did so much to make Britain a nastier, uglier, and more unsettling place. All I can add now is that their behaviour on screen was nothing to what they got up to backstage. The little shits were genuine, you could say that for them: they weren't putting it on. Cooling my heels while waiting for a gig of my own, I was in the green room before they went on. I was there while they were digesting the information that Lord Bernstein would not let them on the air unless their girl mascot discarded her swastika armband.

Though it was obvious that the boys had little idea of who the Nazis had been, and equally obvious that the girl had no ideas at all about anything, nevertheless there could be no doubt that the whole bunch fully understood the moral choice before them. Either they must accede to this irrational demand from the ruling toff or else they must forgo their television appearance. As rebels, they resented the coercion. But as professional rebels, they wanted the telly exposure. A band of revolutionaries who blamed the authorities for their own compromises (they were exactly like the previous generation of dissenting young thinkers in that respect) they had, in their anger at being forced to submit, no way of reasserting themselves except to attack something. Luckily they must have decided that I was even less interesting than the furniture. So they attacked themselves. The one calling himself

Johnny Rotten snarled at one of his lieutenants – I think it was Ken Putrid – and informed him that he was a wanker and a tosser. Ken Putrid told the girl Nazi that she was a slag and a cow. Sid Vicious spat vengefully into the biscuit bowl. They jabbed their bunched knuckles towards each other's mouths, head-butted the air between them, lashed out in all directions with improbably large boots. 'What are you looking at?' Sid Vicious asked me, his lips flecked with foam. It was the first time I had ever heard this deliberately terrifying question, and I didn't have an answer ready. (The only advisable course of action, I have since found, is never to have an answer ready. Replies such as 'I thought I was looking at the model for Michelangelo's *David*, but it turns out that I was mistaken' are not to be recommended.) The volume of their acrimony was ear-splitting, the monotonous filth of their language soul-destroying, the intensity of their randomized galvanic aggression all the more unnerving because they directed it at themselves. But they all went slouching into the studio when their moment came. And later on I was told that they had merely been discussing the matter. Apparently they were always like that. Well, at least they had each other.

15. ALL DAY SUNDAY

Being a solo act was lonely but there was a lot of aggro that it got you out of. It was as a solo act that I joined the line-up of a BBC2 no-budget late-night show called *Up Sunday*. A few journalists I knew said with an *Observer* column before lunch and a TV show after dinner I was there all day like the Archbishop of Canterbury, but only media people ever take in the whole of the media: the public never noticed. One of the nice things about the show was that hardly anybody watched it, so it wasn't really like being on television at all. *New Faces*, a much bigger show mounted by ATV in Birmingham, had been too much like being on television. I was invited to do the first two of the three pilot programmes and I had a big in-house success as the hard critic telling the pitiless truth to the hopeless aspirants who wanted to be stars. One of the acts I had seen before: he was a bloke who blew up a hot-water bottle until it burst and then sang 'Mule Train' while hitting himself on the head with a tin tray. The studio audience, which included the mandatory number of women in knitted hats, appreciated my saying, while he was being carried out, that I hoped the following contestants would be able to match the standard he had set. Laughs along those lines were not difficult to obtain. In the hospitality room afterwards, the ATV executives painted pictures of big things to come, mentioned improbably large sums of money, and promised to introduce me to Noele Gordon, star of *Crossroads*, an epically tedious soap opera which rated on such a scale that it kept ATV afloat, and thus conferred on Miss Gordon the same status as a queen termite.

I, too, quite liked myself in the hard critic's role. It consisted mainly of thinking up smart lines during the hapless punter's number and then delivering them when it was over: an easy gig. But I didn't like the role itself. If I took the job, I would have endless opportunities to crack wise, but I would also have endless opportunities to look like a witch-finder personally operating the joystick of a ducking stool. I thought the aspirants were touching even when untalented, and if they were talented then they had a better right to hog the screen than the judges. (When the show finally went to air with somebody else sitting in the hanging judge's seat, Victoria Wood turned up as one of the contestants, won in a walk, and went on to help revolutionize light entertainment so that such a format, though it would never cease to flourish, would also have to live with a general awareness that the real joke figures were the judges.) I also didn't like a clear suggestion from the second in command of the studio that we, the judges, might like to consider the handsome young male tenor among our slate of contestants as the only possible winner. The handsome young male tenor was contracted to Lew Grade's agency, and Lew Grade owned the studio. Not that Lew Grade could be accused of a conflict of interest. As he would have been the first to point out, he just liked it when his interests as an impresario, agent, and broadcaster all coincided: no conflict there. In my first year as a TV critic I had received a bottle of champagne from Lew Grade and I sent it back to him without acknowledgment. When I met him after the first *New Faces* pilot he was ready to forgive my rudeness, although not until after he had mentioned it. I could see that the forgiveness would continue on a large scale if I stuck around. I can't deny that I had visions of a white Rolls-Royce convertible with a blonde in the passenger seat, like the one driven by the show's producer, who charmingly referred to the audience as 'the nellies', and to the genre of spectacle into which *New Faces* fell as 'nelly-vision'. But I was already heading for the door before my departure was accelerated by the promised encounter with Noele Gordon, fresh from recording the latest episode of *Crossroads* and on her way, apparently, to tea at Sandringham, if not to cocktails with the Shah of Persia. It was clear that the Queen, if she indeed proved to be the target, would be outpointed for grooming and hauteur. Employees of ATV moved just ahead of their greatest star, removing obstacles from her path, waxing the woodwork, and repapering the walls. Burt Lancaster would have found the scene familiar. He and Noele were rather similar personalities, actually, although Burt was perhaps a touch more feminine in his manner: he snarled, but he didn't bark. Not that Noele didn't possess a certain glacial beauty, but so does a Norwegian fjord anywhere north of Trondheim between October and early March.

Getting typecast as a heavy who beat up the helpless punters would have been a mistake, and the scale of the publicity would have made my position at the *Observer* untenable. There was neither typecasting nor publicity to be feared from *Up Sunday*. That was the whole idea. It was an off-trail variety show run by Will Wyatt, then an up-and-coming producer, and always my pick for the budding executive who would one day run the whole BBC. If only that prediction had come true. As things happened, he went all the way to second spot, which meant that he had the responsibility of carrying out every demented notion the latest bad-choice big-wig had, but never enough power to straighten out the madhouse. But all that lay in the far future. *Up Sunday* involved only a very small part of the corporation's resources. Indeed it was put together in Television Centre's very smallest studio, Presentation B, which was about the size of a squash court. On a single day of rehearsing and taping, the contributors did their various things while watching each other from the control gallery, because there was no space left to stand around in the studio: three cameras left barely enough room for the performer. Such *Private Eye* stalwarts as John Wells and William Rushton appeared in various personae while they bashed away at the Establishment of which they were transparently vintage products. The veteran journalist James Cameron held in

his false teeth with his lips while he irascibly pitched the line that
nowadays would be associated with John Pilger or Robert Fisk. It
was subversive stuff from all concerned, but it was still all very
British. My contribution to the supposedly iconoclastic concept
was a series of impersonations, of which I suppose the best was
my Henry Kissinger, and the worst my Lord Litchfield. (I could
get Kissinger just by changing a few consonants, but to get
Litchfield I would have had to change my entire past, repopulat-
ing it with pheasants, fallow deer, and Joanna Lumley, with
whom Litchfield was at that time friendly: a sufficient motive for
revenge.) It didn't make much difference what I did, because
whether on form or off I was hugely outclassed by Viv Stanshall,
an alumnus of the Bonzo Dog Doo-Dah Band who did stuff that
was from another planet. Clad in tie-dyed overalls a couple of
sizes too short, wearing pop-eyed joke glasses that proved, on
closer examination, to be his actual eyes, Stanshall, I suspected,
was the kind of next-century anomaly that Will was really after.
Living at his rate, Stanshall could last only so long, and I think
that he eventually vanished in a sheet of flame after his breath
caught fire while he was meditating in the lotus position, or it
could have been when he was meditating in a Lotus sports car:
I'm a bit hazy about the details, and so, I think was he. But I
learned a lot from watching him. He did a thing where he
misinterpreted bits of film. Most of the film was weird, so that he
was only making something weird more weird; but it occurred to
me that there might be some mileage in misinterpreting ordinary
news footage. Over the next twenty-five years I would do a lot of
that. Nowadays everybody does it, but I can honestly put my
hand up and say that if I didn't invent the idea, I was the first to
steal it, and that I stole it from Viv Stanshall. That was the great
thing about *Up Sunday*. You could stand around and watch the
workings of each other's box of tricks. And finally everyone
watched Spike Milligan.

Spike didn't do the show very often, but he left everybody
breathless when he did. As a manic depressive, he came through

with the goods only when he was up, but when he was up he was never off, so some of his best stuff happened in rehearsal, and I often moaned aloud if the tape wasn't running to catch it. (In those days nobody could afford to run the tape all the time.) I remember him pretending to be a hotel reception desk in Scotland, complete with ringing bell. The number got started when he found the bell left over from somebody else's sketch. By the time it finished he was the whole hotel. In the control gallery we were falling about to the full extent that space permitted. When the tape rolled Will asked him to do the number again but he had forgotten it. That was the way he was. You have to imagine an illuminated manuscript propagating itself at the speed of a ticker tape. You could hear the ideas bumping into each other, blending, rebounding, starting a new comic universe. Though he thought me timid, square, and uptight compared to himself – he was right on all counts – Spike took a shine to me and asked me out to dinner in South Kensington.

His Australian wife told me, on the way into the deeply fashionable restaurant, that Spike was currently on a plane of psychological equilibrium, held there by various carefully matched antidepressant pills. She thought she could promise me a relatively uneventful evening. 'Just tell him your stories about Australia. He loves that.' So I did my numbers about the snakes and spiders, and the great man did indeed seem to enjoy himself, effortlessly topping my yarns with his vivid memories of Woy Woy. But he tempered his laughter to the dignified ambience of the restaurant, and when he told stories of his own they were accompanied by only a small range of gesture, even when he was evoking a Messerschmitt 109 that had strafed him in North Africa. ('Today, that pilot is one of Germany's leading surrealist comedians.') He drank water and made no fuss. Only the famous Italian actress, surrounded by her protective retinue at a corner table, needed to be told who he was. Everyone else including the Foreign Secretary knew that a giant was present, and behaving beautifully. It was only during the coffee that the subject of conversation turned to jazz. In answer to his question about who was my favourite trumpeter, I was in the middle of explaining why Bix Beiderbecke's lyricism moved me whereas Dizzy Gillespie's virtuosity did not. 'Finally,' I said, 'feeling comes first.' 'Yes,' said Spike intensely, 'but there must be excitement first and foremost.' And at that point he reached into a hold-all under the table, produced a trumpet, and began to play an ear-splitting chorus of 'A Night in Tunisia'. The noise was shattering, and, it gradually emerged, continuous. People looked first worried, then indignant, then desperate. In the corner, the Italian actress clutched her pearls to her throat. Spike's wife was talking into his ear but I don't think he could hear a word.

He calmed down after a long while, put the trumpet away, and didn't mention it again. Not for the first time, I wondered if I was making enough demands on the world. My family would probably have said that I was quite unreasonable enough, but even they would have had to admit that I was responsive to the opinion of others, even cravenly so. It mattered to me how I went over. When it seemed not to matter, it was only because I had made a mistake. Even my poetry is predicated, even at its most hermetic, on pleasing an audience of some kind. I have never been able just to pick a course of action and keep going with it whatever people think. This might be the secret of sanity but I feel it as a loss. My night out with Spike Milligan was a daunting reminder of my fundamental predictability. I began to be depressed about not being quite depressed enough. Melancholy was a useful thing to have, but mania, obviously an even more desirable condition, seemed tantalizingly out of reach. Still, there was obviously latitude available for bad behaviour from anyone who could be relied on to write the words coming out of his mouth while he was looking plausible on screen. What he did off-screen was likely to be forgiven, as long as it didn't frighten any under-age horses.

I tried out some of that latitude when *Up Sunday* finally folded and noises were made about giving me a show of my own.

Will Wyatt having moved up a notch, the project was deputed to a second team of producers whose judgement I didn't trust. For one thing, they laughed at anything – always a fatal sign in a comedy producer. Also they had trouble getting organized, and the job of a producer is to organize people with that very characteristic. I had been here before: a bunch of people was assembling on the assumption that I would know where to lead them. How had I let that happen? We spent a lot of time having meetings to discuss when the next meeting would be, rather like the French Resistance cell that counted Jean-Paul Sartre and Simone de Beauvoir among its members, and which never had time to do any resisting, because it was too busy having meetings. One of my proposed fellow cast members was the young actress Madeline Smith. Previously I had thought that the word 'orchidaceous' had been invented for orchids. Now I realized that it had been invented for Madeline. She was so beautiful that men otherwise ebullient would, after they had seen her, go away, lean against something, and look sad. But she was still an unknown. The show was thought to need a female headliner. Marianne Faithfull was supposed to be the one, but dithering months went by without them being able to get her signed. Eventually I remembered that they had not signed me either. So I walked away. There was no contract. But I was walking away from a verbal agreement, and although Sam Goldwyn's classic formulation has its validity ('A verbal agreement isn't worth the paper it's printed on'), there is such a thing as honour, which I had violated. I felt bad about that, and when *Private Eye* got the story I was invited to feel even worse. But what really tore me up, after I had learned a lot more about the harsh realities of show business, was how I had helped to waste several precious months of the saintly Madeline's time. The beautiful young actresses measure their careers against the lifespan of a butterfly, and to keep one of them waiting is the act of a vandal. Eventually the world was saved from yet another underpowered variety show, but I should have been more decisive at the start, and from then on I always tried to be, if only by being more careful to make clear that the word 'maybe' meant what it said. I can offer that as a valid general tip: be very careful that your hesitations are not construed by hopeful people as a licence to proceed. Among the clever young performers in the generation after mine, the one who got himself and others into most trouble was the cleverest of them all: but he kept saying 'yes' just to make people go away, so they went away to prepare some huge event for which he would fail to show up. Thus his brilliance and his sensitivity were at war, a paradox arising from that deadly characteristic I described earlier, by which one lacks the moral courage to tell people early enough what they don't want to hear.

Up Sunday didn't pay big money. No white Rolls-Royce with inbuilt blonde was in prospect. By that time my family was working its way through a succession of small cars that all shared the gift of breaking down on the way to Italy. Since I had no licence, they weren't my concern and the white Roller wouldn't have been either, although I suppose I could have sat beside the blonde while she drove it. But the show paid something, and we were now enjoying what it would be hypocritical not to call prosperity. The children were taken on a trip to Australia so that their grandmothers could go crazy about them in the open air. Their mother had already gone crazy on the flight, after they used up their colouring books before the aircraft had reached cruising altitude. In those days there was almost no entertainment available in economy class except to watch the break-dancing displays put on by people who had made the mistake of waiting until they wanted to go to the toilet before they started queuing for it. For those sitting down, there was scarcely room to have thrombosis. It was like the First Fleet in there. After that, it was held more feasible to take vacations less far-flung. Italy being short of the kind of beach life that doesn't leave children crying because there isn't enough sand to dig a hole, the choice fell on Biarritz, where our friend Michael Blakemore had a house. Though it rained often, a sunny day on the Côte des Basques could be lyrical, especially towards evening, when the water turned a soft silver to match the sheen of gold dust on the tamarisks that clothed the cliffs. Enviously watching Blakemore – a magnificent surfer – catching the last wave of the day from about half a mile out, I tried to copy his knack of putting aside the insanely complex problems of his professional life while he soaked up the shimmer of the sweet surroundings. I almost relaxed. Among the rocks when the tide was out, I built driftwood houses for the children. Typically I overdid it, so that the results could have been published in *Architectural Digest*. The point is still sore, so I won't pursue it. Sufficient to say that when the rain released me from the obligation to lie idle I would sit at my favourite cafe with its instantly memorable Basque name – the Bar du Huahuahu, next to the Café Xerox – and I would start writing a new book. One of the new books I started writing was an autobiography.

The only general idea I had for an autobiography was that it would be the story of someone who hadn't really done anything yet. There was truth to that. I had such a knack for avoiding the big time that it was starting to look wilful. In New York I wrote an *Observer* Postcard at the same time as the serial killer Son of Sam was on the loose. As far as I know I never met him, but I had an encounter in the same league for being hard on the nerves. William Shawn of the *New Yorker* had been reading my stuff and sent a message that he hoped I could spare him some time. I didn't need telling that he rarely had to make such a formal request. He could safely assume that most people read his thoughts. Since I was staying at the Algonquin, there was no problem about a meeting place. All he had to do was cross the street from his office and occupy his regular table. The intermediary who told me this – I think it was the deputy editor's deputy assistant secretary's deputy – told me that Mr Shawn would be waiting for me after he had finished his lunch. Everybody I knew in New York told me that Shawn was so shy and polite that it would be impossible to tell when the meeting was over, so the best thing to do would be to assume, as with royalty, that an exit could not be made too early. Plead a heart attack if necessary, but leave. I was also told by everyone that Shawn would never raise the subject he wanted to talk about, so I should go on raising subjects myself until the one came up that he wanted to pursue. This last bit proved not to be true. Everything else was: he was so quiet and self-effacing that he was hard to detect against the red-plush banquette even though he was wearing a black suit. He was also quite small, so that he tended to disappear behind a salt cellar if you shifted position. He himself never moved. But after we had both quoted to each other our favourite bits from S. J. Perelman, Shawn raised the subject almost straight away. Or rather, he raised two subjects. Could American television be thought of as a fruitful object of criticism? And had I ever thought of coming to write regularly in New York for, say, a weekly magazine? Tentatively but inexorably, the two subjects grew closer together, until finally they were joined by an arc of light whose blinding significance not even I could miss. He was asking me if I would like to become the *New Yorker*'s TV critic. If I had said yes, my life would have changed right there. But I said no without having to think about it. My wife's work was in Cambridge and London, my heart was with the old Empire, and America appealed too much to my sweet tooth.

Like the first, this last factor would have been decisive even without the others. In America I was too much at home. As Milos Forman once said, there are only two places in the world where we are truly at home: home, and in America. In Los Angeles, I had only to lie down beside the hotel pool and in half an hour I was dreaming of a screenplay. In Biarritz, a Hollywood producer called David Giler (the first *Alien* movie was among his credits) turned up to ask me if I would adapt Michael Frayn's play *Clouds* into a screenplay for Twentieth Century Fox. Frayn's play was set in Cuba, but the plot entirely depended, for its wit and point, on Cuba's being represented theatrically by a few chairs and a table. Giler, a suave and knowledgeable Ivy League type, said quietly that Fox had secured permission for location shooting in the actual Cuba. This coup had removed the play's raison d'être at a stroke, but I said yes because Giler had Camilla Sparv on his arm. In *Downhill Racer* her silk, suede, and cashmere appearance had induced in me the terrible suspicion that if America could take over the class and gloss of a Euro beauty like her then it would take over the world. I saw myself in Hollywood, growing young twice as fast as I grew old while I rescued troubled movies with a quick dialogue polish at a million dollars a pop. For a blessing, the *Clouds* screenplay got no further than the first draft before Sherry Lansing took over the studio and cancelled the project, leaving me with (a) a lot more money than I had ever earned in such a short time, and (b) a lasting realization that the merest taste of that way of life would turn my brains to blancmange. Nor was all the nonsense confined to Los Angeles. New York was different but not different enough. In America, there would still be no way out of the life measured by success. I had, and still have, the instincts of someone born for that life. But I could never lead it any better than it would lead me. America would suck me in so thoroughly there would be nothing left to spit out. By the second week, I would have the third wife and the fourth car. Hear that whining sound? My Gulfstream IV, waiting on the tarmac. See you in Aspen.

Shawn gradually absorbed the evidence that his offer was being turned down. It probably hadn't happened to him since WWII, but he was a polite man, and ready to whisper of other things. Remembering all the advice I had received as to the desirability of an early exit, I made noises about leaving, but Shawn made noises – very quiet ones, as of a mouse on the rack – about how it would pain him if I deprived him of my company so soon. Thus it went on until the air out there in 44th Street grew dark. For years ahead I went on being astonished by how much time Shawn had lavished on me, but it could have been that Lillian Ross, his great secret love, was out of town for the day and had left him with an afternoon to fill. Or he might have just been hungry for a conversation that didn't matter. He was a powerful man, but perhaps he had been lonely. Almost everybody you have ever heard of spends a lot of time being that. Finally he left to meet J. D. Salinger or Mary McCarthy or John Updike, or whoever was first on his evening roster. I sat there alone, faced with the long task of finding reasons for what I had done by instinct. Even today the best reason I can think of is that I didn't want to exchange my life for an illusion that so exactly fitted my desires. Reality was meant to feel like the conquest of the self, not of the world.

So there was my subject: an ordinary life. I was quite aware that I could do things only a few people can do. But I was equally aware that in most aspects of character I scarcely attained the average of the common run: I was a very ordinary person. That was the principle I stuck to while I was writing the first volume of my autobiography, and I have stuck to it ever since, as the project stretches into this fourth volume and now looks like heading towards a fifth. The self-deprecation is still sincerely meant. Back at the beginning, it seemed like the least I could do, so as to start paying back the luck that had given me the means to earn a living when I had no other qualifications. By then, my first agent, Christine, had left the literary business to go into television, a move that I myself still regarded as drastic. My new agent was the equally glamorous Pat Kavanagh, who was quite accustomed to being admired by her male clients. Blessed with a direct manner, she made it clear that she didn't necessarily salute the idea of my writing an autobiography. 'You haven't *done* anything.' That, I tried to explain, was the point. The very idea was ridiculous, and therefore automatically comic: as long as I could make my memories of an Australian childhood and adolescence amusing in themselves, the book would stand a chance through being the opposite of serious. She looked dubious but thought that Tom Maschler of Cape might go for it. To Charles Monteith of Faber, he who had gone to sleep during *Peregrine Prykke's Pilgrimage*, it would probably sound like the boy from the bush pulling another fast one. As things happened, Monteith

wasn't asked for his opinion. The project got no further than
Maschler, who called me in and did a routine by which he
proved, with statistics, that publishing such a book would be, for
him, the same as throwing money on the fire, but he would do
so because occasionally a man has to risk all in the defence of his
integrity. The print run would be small, he warned me, and the
advance would be small to match. I said with some confidence
that Pat Kavanagh would be interested to hear all this. Nothing
daunted, Maschler went on to say that I would be risking my
future but he would be risking everything. His spiel practically
had soundtrack music by Elmer Bernstein. It was him and me
against the world. He would clear the path ahead, placate the
board of directors, drug the sales representatives. But this unique
idea of an autobiography by someone who had done nothing
must go through. All I had to do was write the thing. He even
offered me a free cup of coffee – a spendthrift gesture he usually
made only for John Fowles. But it was his enthusiasm that
clinched the deal. Between author and publisher, the relationship
works awfully like sex: there is no substitute for being keen on
each other. There was also a biscuit.

After a build-up like that I expected that the actual writing
process would be agonizing, but it came easily when I could find
the time. Some of the time found itself. My television appear-
ances, dotted irregularly through the decade, had attracted the
attention of one of the smartest executives at LWT, Barry Cox. If
he had been less smart he might have ended up running a TV
channel, but like Will Wyatt he was doomed by his sanity and
competence to making sense of the chaos created by managerial
zanies. I owe him a lot. In fact – it just occurred to me – I owe
him a thousand quid. The year before last I bumped into him on
Waterloo Bridge and he made the mistake of asking me what I
had been up to since my retirement. I told him that my new idea
for a multimedia personal web site was going to revolutionize
television. No doubt sick of hearing about new concepts that
would revolutionize television, he handed over a grand to help

www.clivejames.com stay on the air for a few more days so that
it could burn his money along with mine. He's that kind of man,
although, since hardly any men are that kind of man, you might
not recognize him when I say so. At the time, I had met very few
people like him. The show he was cooking up for LWT at its new
citadel on the South Bank was called *Saturday Night People*. It
would feature Russell Harty, Janet Street-Porter, and one other in
yet another survey of the week, but this time based on solid
journalism. Harty, whose life was to be cut sadly short, was a
very sophisticated man with a knack for looking shocked on air.
Since Janet Street-Porter specialized in the outrageous, they
worked naturally as a double act, although off screen Janet
privately, but sometimes very audibly, denounced Harty as a
patronizing git. There was something to it: gay men, still fighting
their own battles, weren't yet very attuned to feminism.

But once the cameras were on those two, they were the ideal
couple. Harty looked and sounded like an aesthete who knew
Alan Bennett quite well, and Janet looked and sounded like a
cockney female assassin who had been trained to kill with her
voice, which was not only raucous but seemed permanently
surprised, like a macaw taking off repeatedly from a steam
catapult. They were the two sides of the class war, temporarily
seated behind dodgem-shaped desks. The question was about
who would occupy the third desk. How would the Third Person
fit in? Barry's rationale for picking me was that I didn't fit in at
all. The more that I played the visiting Aussie with the unexpec-
tedly confident perspective on disintegrating Britain, the better
he liked it. All three front-persons were fed with proper news
stories. These had been put together by a team of journalists
commanded by Peter Hillmore, an able young editor whose
career was to be cut short by illness. But he was still going full
blast when we started off, so we weren't short of material. The
question was how to comment on it. Each in his or her own way,
all three of us worked it out. There was plenty of time because
the show was only local in its first season. At first I was the

slowest to get going. I took the stories handed to me by Hillmore's research team, switched the words just enough so that I
could read them out, and saved my comment for the end. Things
were a bit dull. Then I learned to interlace my commentary all
the way through, and things brightened up. Finally, with Barry's
encouragement, I learned to get outdoors, find a suitably gro-
tesque showbiz story, and bring it back for dissection.

By an accident that helped to change the course of my career,
I found myself sitting through the first screening of a movie
called *The Swarm*, starring Michael Caine as a scientist saving the
world from the killer bees. In the dark of the Leicester Square
Odeon, as the killer bees swarmed all over Richard Chamberlain
and reduced Olivia de Havilland to a hive, I wrote down Michael
Caine's dialogue in my notebook. 'Everyone inside! The killer
bees are coming!' (Tip for writing in the dark: write big. The
worst you can do is waste paper, whereas if you can't read what
you wrote you will have wasted the whole assignment.) In the
next edition of the show I gave an account of the movie's plot,
with a recital of Michael Caine's best lines. Since everybody can
do Michael Caine's voice – the only question is whether he can –
my deficient powers of mimicry were no handicap. As I evoked
the splendours of the screenplay – while being careful not to
underrate the threat to civilization posed by killer bees – I could
feel my story going over with the studio audience. There was a
lady in a knitted hat who could take no more. Better than that,
there was evidence next day that it had gone over with the
audience at home. People came up to me in the street and talked
about killer bees. Some of them imitated killer bees. On the other
side of the street, people would wave their arms rapidly and do a
buzzing thing with their mouths. It was my first experience of
starting a craze on TV and I could feel it working exactly the
same way as the first drink I ever had. I tried to remember the
effect of my last drink, and how the first drink had led to it by
an inexorable process. But there seemed just as great a danger
of getting addicted to Puritanism. Here, surely, was a harmless

pleasure. The following week I spoke again of *The Swarm*, and found that the audience couldn't hear enough about it. For the last show of the season, the studio crew, in cahoots with the art department, rigged up a huge killer bee so that it could be lowered to attack me at the appropriate moment. Usually surprises don't work in studio, but I managed to keep my head as I struggled, summoning my Michael Caine voice to cry: 'Everyone outside! The killer bees are attacking the franchise!' Janet hit the bee with a rolled-up script. Or something like that. There is no tape to say any different.

Saturday Night People was off to the races, but it never raced on the network. Lew Grade would not have Russell Harty on the air in the ATV area, which was too large a chunk of the network for the other stations to ignore. If Lew Grade's prejudice against Harty was based, as seemed likely, on Harty's homosexuality, then we were out of business until such time as the victim could prove he had gone straight, perhaps by marrying Janet. Otherwise there was nothing we could do about it. Luckily for me, there was nothing LWT could do about it either. The show was too expensive to keep running without a network slot. On the other hand, we had contracts that had to be honoured. So we all got paid top whack for a whole season of not making a television programme for LWT. Since the contract said that we couldn't make television programmes for anyone else either, there was time to burn.

16. BEYOND THE ATTACK
OF THE KILLER BEES

I burned it writing my autobiography. In Cambridge I would sit in the Copper Kettle, writing down my memories of being a failure at high-school mathematics while Stephen Hawking hummed past outside with equations for the birth of the universe spinning in his head. In the Barbican I would sit in the sill-free window and conjure the kookaburras of childhood while ducks came in to land on the lake for the next round of their world crapping championship. It would have been slower work if I had delved deeper into my psychological condition, but a cautionary instinct, which might well have been part of the condition, kept me safely on the surface. Nevertheless I could spot the occasional stain of grief soaking through. Quickly I would cover it with the moon-dust of tall stories, some of which I had been telling for years. Veterans of the Footlights club room or the Kebab House literary lunch would have been able to recite some of them along with me. It was not the first outing for my routines about Australia's deadly snakes and spiders. But it was the first time they had been put to paper, and it was soon clear to me that the structure of the narrative had benefited from long rehearsal. There was an episode about billycarts which had once actually been written down, when I was doing my year as a junior literary editor on the *Sydney Morning Herald* in the late 1950s. On that first flight, the episode had been called 'They Fell Among Flowers'. This time it was incorporated seamlessly into a larger narrative, but there could be no doubt that the hurtling, booming, disastrously crashing billycarts had set the tone for the book long before the book occurred.

The book was an animated cartoon. Although I liked to think that the story being told was roughly in line with the emotional facts – all the confessions about awkwardness and inadequacy were untrue only in the sense of being understated – it couldn't be denied that some of the details sounded a bit exaggerated. As when I spoke, these embellishments, when I was writing, tended to arrive out of the blue. Suddenly they were there, and too good to leave out. The secret (as always, it was a matter of tone control) was to trim and time the extravagance of an embellishment so that it would be congruent to its setting, lest the readers withdraw their consent to being had. But being had they unquestionably were. It seemed best to come clean that I knew this was happening. So I called the book *Unreliable Memoirs*. Since this initiative was tantamount to calling my own sworn testimony a pack of lies, there was no automatic professional acceptance for the finished manuscript. Pat Kavanagh, still wary about the idea of someone who had done nothing writing a book about how he had prepared himself for not doing it, now had another reason for suggesting that I shelve the manuscript for ten years. Tom Maschler ominously assured me that the small print run he had envisaged could be made smaller yet: five thousand copies should be plenty. But I noticed that they had both laughed, even against their better judgement. There is no more precious laughter than that, and even today I am still out to write the kind of book I most like to read: the book I despise myself for being unable to stop reading.

So I wasn't completely devastated, only almost, when Penelope Mortimer jumped the gun by about a month and posted an early review denouncing *Unreliable Memoirs* as a crime against humanity. She didn't precisely dance on my grave, but she did march up and down on it while declaring herself insulted by my self-proclaimed satisfaction at excusing conscious falsehood with would-be drollery. The insult, apparently, was not to her alone, but to all serious writers. It was an insult to literature itself. Whether literature itself was an activity that Penelope Mortimer could plausibly be thought of as representing was open to question. (As an admirer of her novel *The Pumpkin Eater* I rather thought she could.) But the month that followed would have felt like a year if the unofficial buzz had not been building up. The publicity lovelies at Cape told me that the pre-production copies had all been stolen instantly. Apparently this was a good sign. Then the broadsheet reviews started to come out, and most of the reviewers quoted so much of my stuff that there was scarcely room for theirs: an even better sign. John Carey, who had once buried *The Metropolitan Critic*, hailed *Unreliable Memoirs* as the written equivalent of sliced bread. Instantly I revised my opinion of his critical prowess upwards. To my delight – for once I managed to enjoy the moment – the book went straight into the bestseller list and took only three weeks to reach the top spot. But what kept it there for months on end was undoubtedly a guest appearance on *Parkinson*.

Parky, at whose expense I had made far too many unreasonable remarks in my TV column when I was starting off, would have had ample reason, after I sat down opposite him on the set, to pull the lever that dropped me through the trapdoor to the waiting crocodiles. But he took Chinese revenge. He told me, and the watching millions, that my book had made him laugh. He said he particularly liked the episode about the dunnyman. Visited by my guardian angel, I suddenly acquired the sense not just to agree that it was a nifty stretch of writing but also to quote a few bits from memory, climaxing the act with the bit about the dunnyman tripping over my bicycle and engulfing himself with the contents of the full pan. In the studio audience, the ladies in the knitted hats had the choice between dying of shock or howling in approbation. They did the latter, and out there, in millions of living rooms I couldn't see, other people were doing the same. I could hear them. They made my feet vibrate. On television, a successful gag doesn't just click, it thumps. From that moment, I was made. In future years, the irony did not escape me that the delicate little boat of my literary fortunes had been launched on a wave of liquid shit.

The commercial success of *Unreliable Memoirs* ensured that those future years could never become financially desperate, although it was never true that I could have lived on the royalties of that book alone, or of all my books put together. You have to sell on the scale of Jeffrey Archer or J. K. Rowling to get rich as a writer. I try not to tell journalists what *Unreliable Memoirs* sold because they would be unimpressed by the figure. People assume that any book they have heard of sells a million. In cold fact, it is a lucky book that sells a thousand, and I know of one literary memoir – in my review of it I called it a classic, and still think I was right – that sold fifteen copies. *Unreliable Memoirs* did eventually sell a million copies, but it took about twenty years to do so. The nice thing is that it is still going, as if it doesn't know how to switch itself off: it's like a broken washing machine that goes on with its spin cycle until the house falls down. Why it should have attained such longevity is a nice question. My own guess is that the British readers simply like to hear stories about a warm country, but the book is a steady seller in Australia too, where evocations of sunlight are like coal to Newcastle. Perhaps I succeeded in one of the things I consciously tried to do: evoke what it was like to be young in the free countries after World War II, when all the adults could still remember their lesson in the value of liberty. It was a story of simplicity, and as time goes by there is nostalgia for that simplicity, so the hankering for a clear account of it doesn't fade. Counting the initial hardbacks along with the later paperbacks, there have been about a hundred printings so far, but that word 'printing' is the tip-off. All those books were never anywhere all at once, not even at the warehouse. Supplies get renewed according to demand, and over time the figure alters upward to denote a quantity that nobody has ever actually seen. You can just count yourself lucky that the number advances. It would have

advanced more quickly if Sonny Mehta, who was chief editor at
Pan Macmillan's highbrow label Picador when the Cape hard-
back took off, had not persuaded me that the paperback should
be in the Picador 'B' format rather than the Pan pocket-book
size. A pocket-book would go on the rack and sell faster. A
Picador would go in the spinner and sell more slowly; but it
would, he assured me, sell forever. So far he has been right. The
number continues to advance. Sometimes I visualize it going in
the other direction as people start to hand their books back.
They can, if they wish, but I can't return the money. It all got
spent. Only in television did I make enough to keep something.
I suppose I could have gone on with regular journalism and
kept raising my price, but there might have been a limit to what
the market would stand, and would certainly have been a limit
to my satisfaction. Much as I respected journalism as a form, I
was starting to fancy myself as an Author. Not even I, however,
was conceited enough to believe that I could always expect a hit.
After all, I hadn't expected this one.

On the television front, the prospects were now looking good
enough to raise the question of whether I could plausibly continue to be a TV critic much longer, lest I be faced with the
awkward likelihood of having to review my own programmes.
For LWT, Barry Cox asked me to write and present a documentary about Sydney. I didn't do my part of it all that well. There
was a lot of clunky walking around my childhood haunts while I
droned on about the past. A sequence set in Luna Park had me
pointing out that it was a funfair while the camera was showing
it to be a funfair. I said that it was falling apart while the camera
closed in to show that it was falling apart. But I quickly saw that
I could have done better if I had talked about something else
while the pictures were talking about themselves. Unfortunately
Barry, when we got back to London with the footage, made the
mistake of telling me that he thought me hopeless when talking
to camera. I thought I was just bad, which is not quite the
same thing. Another LWT executive producer, Richard Drewett,

thought I was even worse than Barry said. But Drewett also
thought that ways could be found to ensure that I would improve.
I should hasten to say that Barry had probably taken the more
responsible view. It is an expensive business, pouring in the
resources while someone improves on air: a company can bankrupt itself while it waits for a few new presenters to come good.
But Drewett was running an outfit called Special Programmes
that was actually briefed to do the irresponsible thing. He had
been given the job because he was a miracle man with the
practicalities and a reliable inventor of high-yield formats: the
first Parkinson series and the *Audience With* specials had both
been his idea. If the unpredictable was required, he was the man
to call on. A racing-car nut who had been put out of competition
by a smashed foot, Drewett now slaked his craving for danger by
building programmes around me. I sometimes had to be hosed
out of the studio when things went sideways, but he got me into
the salutary habit of sitting down with him after the programme
and analysing exactly what had gone right or wrong. For quite a
while the wrong outweighed the right. A meticulous producer
called Nick Barratt was assigned to me for a short series of little
clip-shows about television. I almost drove him nuts with my
new and purely nervous habit of stopping dead in rehearsal when
I fluffed a word. I chewed up time as if I was paying for it myself.
In my defence I can say that the set might have been designed to
make me as nervous as a trainee human cannonball. I had an
egg-cup plastic chair into which I fitted like Humpty Dumpty, an
impression added to by my excessive weight and the new, tailored
three-piece suit that had been chosen to suit the set rather than
my figure. But the show got better despite these drawbacks, and
there was talk of a future one-hour version of the format, perhaps
to be called *Clive James on Television*. I liked the sound of that.

Even in its short version, though, the show about television
did something to offset the debacle of a series called *A Question
of Sex*, which I fronted with Anna Raeburn, Fleet Street's all-time
most-presentable agony aunt. The two of us sat around – or,

even worse, stood around, or, even worse than that, walked around – pontificating about the differences between the sexes, as established by various scientists, some of whom came walking on in white coats, threading their way along complicated paths between large styrofoam models of chromosomes marked X and Y. Various animals were wheeled on in cages, supposedly to demonstrate their different approaches, according to gender, to such tasks as ramming their heads against a rubber button in order to earn the peanut. Unfortunately some of the animals were apes and the only task they had in mind was screwing each other. Denied the opportunity to do this, they retired to the back corners of their cages and would not come forward even when threatened. Anna and I coped stoically, I thought, especially when compared with the senior executive, whose name I have finally succeeded in forgetting after years of hypnosis. He went berserk, shouting into the floor manager's earphones and finally appearing in the studio so that he could shout at everybody. He did everything that the apes were supposed to do when excited. Finally the studio crew declined to go on. Since the apes had decided the same thing already, there was nothing left to do except wrap up the episode. Eventually, after much editing, a truncated version of the series got to air, where it was universally ignored. But I actually learned a lot from it. Apart from gaining confirmation for the basic principle of never working with a senior executive who has a more volatile artistic temperament than you, I started getting the measure of how to be an asset on studio day, rather than a liability. The show had a studio audience, and during the frequent pauses while the apes were being unsuccessfully persuaded out of their corners, or the scientists were being taught to walk and talk simultaneously without knocking the chromosomes over, or the senior executive was being put under sedation, I had an opportunity, indeed an obligation, to keep the people in the bleachers happy. In the course of time I got good enough at doing it to dispense with the services of a warm-up man. Although I hadn't formulated it as a rule yet, here was an example of the importance of turning a disaster into a training ground. It's only a variation of the Czech philosopher Martina Navratilova's great central maxim that applies to all creative activities and not just to her own sport: What matters is not how well you play when you're playing well, it's how well you play when you're playing badly. With those early shows for LWT, I got my average up.

The television shows were only in an embryo stage but they had the useful effect of getting me away from the *Observer* often enough so that I didn't get bored with what was becoming, after ten years, a predictable weekly task. Perhaps the effect was deleterious: with fewer distractions I might have faced facts sooner. As things were, the nimbus granted me by *Unreliable Memoirs* made it easier to follow up any prospect that took my fancy, thus conferring a feeling of invulnerability which was potentially dangerous, had I but known it. Exactly the same feeling led Napoleon to invade Russia. He was pursuing one of his own sound principles – the army that never leaves its defences is bound to be defeated – but he pursued it too far. I was still well short of doing anything conspicuously crazy, but the descent to hell is easy. Not that it felt like hell when I teamed up with David Bailey to produce a series of illustrated profiles for *Ritz* magazine. *Ritz* proved to be short lived, partly because its owner and editor was a Willy Donaldson type who was always moving on, and who is now probably somewhere in the Andes, running an export agency for condor eggs. But the magazine's quick demise was a pity, because it was the most convincing British example ever of a glossy magazine on newsprint – a form that otherwise only the French have ever mastered. Newsprint makes female glamour look more human and therefore, to my mind, even more glamorous. Bailey understood that – he is a very sharp character, behind his thuggish persona – and did some of his best photo shoots. One of them was of the young Meryl Streep, then in the early stage of her career.

Having spotted her on her way up and persuaded her to sit

for her portrait, I ushered her into Bailey's house in Chalk Farm and he asked, well within her hearing, 'Ooze iss?' Usually he could be depended on to be kidding when he said stuff like that but this time he wasn't. Luckily she loved the idea of posing for someone who had never heard of her. The following week she received me for lunch at Claridge's so that she could fulfil the written part of the portrait. For any actress, no matter how intelligent – and they don't come any smarter than Meryl Streep – the pictures are always more important than the words. The last thing any actress needs is some hack speculating about her inner life. But this actress couldn't have been more gracious. Highly literate as well as funny, she talked easily of modern English and Irish poets as well as of American ones. Well aware that I was dippy about her, she told lots of stories about her wonderful husband after she had ordered the sole, asking for it to be boned. Forever green about the finer points of life, I thought 'boned' meant with the bones left in, so I neglected to ask for the same thing, because I wanted them taken out. Still determined to play an indispensable part in the life of this angelically lovely and lyrically gifted person, I began an anecdote designed to illustrate my poetically sensitive nature, an aesthetic responsiveness enhanced, rather than injured, by my easy famil-iarity with the literary world. By then I had discovered the bones in the sole, but I was operating on the assumption that I would be able to tease out enough of the flesh between them to provide a few bone-free mouthfuls so that I could talk safely while I ate. 'And then,' I said, 'Lowell hauled this enormous manuscript out of his pocket and began to *ark*! Ark! Ngggh!' A trident of needle-hard small bones had gone vertically into my palate. I had to reach in and pull them out individually. The next twenty minutes were agony until she insisted that I order something else and quit trying to be suave. I liked the way she did that.

I liked her too much, of course. As ever, the combination of beauty and talent reduced me to an idiot. Bailey, who was surrounded by celestially lovely women at all times, used to get a big bang out of seeing me bite the back of my hand. One evening I walked into Langan's Brasserie for a business dinner and without warning I was confronted by the spectacle of Bailey lolling on a velvet banquette with Catherine Deneuve on one side of him and Marie Helvin on the other. It was such an assault on elementary justice that I closed my eyes with the pain. When I opened them again, Bailey was laughing his head off, a rusticated cherub with a bad shave. But it was another cockney photographer, Terence Donovan, who dug deeper into my psychology. Donovan was physically very big: six feet plus of judo-trained muscle packed into a Dougie Hayward grey suit, he made his drop-head dark-blue Rolls-Royce Corniche look like a pedal car. It was his delight to take me for rides around London while he wised me up on the realities of life in the spotlight. 'Them upmarket birds are going to go on doing your head in,' he announced, 'until you realize that they're just human. I mean, they do a poo every morning, don't they? What you need is Paris.' Donovan, a married man himself, was by no means impervious to the allure of a bright female. Not all of the models were dumb. There were several famous ones who were as bright as he was, and Donovan, though he had quit school early, was fully as clever as Bailey. But Donovan clearly had life in perspective, otherwise he would have turned into King Kong's dangerous younger brother the first time he saw Tatiana Patitz with her clothes off. So I respected his opinion.

Donovan had directed a movie in Japan that had crashed in flames. Now he was eager to get started again by directing a television documentary. Drewett thought it would be a good idea if I should make a programme about the Paris cat-walk shows, because the material would be so attractive that I could spend most of my time in voice over, with no need of the dreaded 'piece to camera', a clumsy technique that he and I were agreed should be avoided by anyone, let alone me. Drewett took a punt when he assigned me to the job, but he took an even bigger punt when he hired Donovan to direct. Donovan had the entrée into the Paris fashion world, but he was easily bored, which is a dangerous characteristic in a film director, because there is a lot of humdrum detail that can't be skimped. For the *Clive James Paris Fashion Show*, the first mainstream television programme ever devoted to the subject, Donovan invented a new kind of shot by which the camera was positioned at the end of the catwalk and the models were filmed walking towards a long lens. A long lens slows things down, so the models appear to float. The shot later became a staple and is now seen in every film or TV show about the catwalk ever made anywhere in the world, but I was there on the day Donovan thought of it. He was that original. Unfortunately he was also very impatient, and didn't want to do the standard bread-and-butter shots of me arriving at the shows and leaving, or ringing the doorbell of Sonya Rykiel's apartment and walking away afterwards, or, as he put it, 'any of that'. In other words, he was out to make a film that couldn't be edited. I was still too green to realize the importance of what Donovan was leaving out. But when Drewett heard about it he was on the next plane to Paris, where he revealed an unsuspected but impressive command of French. He needed only English, however, to tell Donovan what was what. I saw straight away that Drewett could do what I couldn't. His hands were trembling; he didn't actually enjoy speaking uncomfortable truths; but he did it. I decided right then that he was the man for me, and I hope it is not giving too much away if I say that he was the executive producer on every television programme I did for the next twenty years.

Donovan took his knackering well. He grumbled a bit but he got on with the business of doubling back to secure the dull stuff we couldn't do without. And he was still unbeatable on the exciting stuff: the backstage sequence at the Lagerfeld show (now a legend in the television industry, because it was never allowed to happen again) was made possible by Donovan's physical strength. He held off the security men while I sat there being filmed as the models went skidding by half naked. But Donovan still never managed to get a clapperboard on anything, so the van-load of unsynchronized film and audio tape that we sent back to London took about a year to sort out, leading directly to a senior editor's death from a heart attack. I persisted, however, in thinking of Donovan as the model of sanity and good will. A few quirks aside, he walked and talked as if he had the secret of happiness. The day would come when he would take his own life, and I still can't believe he did it. Dear man, he was so funny: one of the funniest talkers I have ever heard. And like all genuinely funny people, he was funny because he was perceptive. He had seen the look of longing in my eyes and he was right about the cure. In Paris I was bombarded by so much beauty that I finally learned to listen. Gradually it became apparent, from the flow of prattle, that a young woman of heavenly appearance was not necessarily Mary Cassatt or Berthe Morrisot just because she could paint her nails successfully. The great beauties are certainly works of art, but that doesn't make them artists. The lovelier the woman, the less likely it is that she created herself: the genius belongs to nature, not to her. But it was still very satisfying when Donovan and I, taking a casual break for lunch between the chaos at Yves Saint Laurent and the riot at Thierry Mugler, strolled into the Coupole and sat down at the best table in the place: satisfactory because we had walked in arm in arm with Marie Helvin and Jerry Hall. There were a couple of British male gossip columnists at the next table and I saw one of them die. His body still ate, drank, talked, and eventually walked, but his soul was gone. I knew just how he felt, but I was over it. Well, almost.

While the Paris programme was in its long agony of being made ready for editing, I had so much going on that I might have forgotten it existed. But when all the miles of film and tape were finally synched up, a process began that I couldn't, once I had tasted it, get enough of. Richard encouraged my presence in the editing room, which was still no more advanced than the one I had grown familiar with in my days at Granada. Younger readers will find it hard to realize that the footage could not be digitized and edited electronically. All the film and sound still had to be cut and spliced physically. But this time it wasn't bits and pieces of a Hollywood movie: it was our movie, in its raw form. With alternative takes for almost every shot, there was an infinity of choice at war with a paucity of means. So it took hours in the editing room to put even the shortest sequence together. 'If we can get that shot of me shambling down the boulevard to echo that shot of Jerry swaying down the catwalk at the Kenzo show, the audience might like the contrast.' 'Then we'll have to get out of her shot a few frames earlier, before she starts to turn.' Today, you could try the effect in thirty seconds. Then, you had to place the order and come back tomorrow. But when every tweak took so long to do, it had to be thought about hard. It was like the difference between handwriting and a word processor: there was more initial resistance from the medium, so you had to be definite. I got a lot of free tuition in the business of choosing which frame of film should go where and when. Thus I knew every foot of the rough cut when the time came to record the first draft of a commentary. It was a long, intricate, and enthralling business and it should have kept me sufficiently busy. Perhaps fatefully, however, there was enough time left over for another project.

The news media had been banging on for a year about the pending royal marriage. Most of the coverage was absurd but I was sufficiently in favour of constitutional monarchy as a political institution to contemplate a fourth mock epic, which would express, I hoped lightly, my views on the subject, while exploiting the comic potential as people lined up to bow, scrape, cluck and sniff. Still far too fond of giving my mock epics alliterative titles, I called the project *Charles Charming's Challenges on the Pathway to the Throne*. I had, of course, no idea that the marriage itself would be one of the challenges. The piece seemed harmless enough as it grew, but it rapidly began growing too fast, like a pet baby crocodile. With illustrations once again by Mark Boxer,

the poem became a newspaper serial, a book in Britain, a book
in America, and then – the step into the unknown – a West End
stage show. If the show had been on the small scale of the
Pygge and Prykke pantomimes, danger might have been averted.
Though radical acquaintances such as Christopher Hitchens
would have given me the bird, the bird would have flown inside
a charmed circle. But a team of impresarios moved in, and several
backers, among them the erratically generous Naim Attalah, put
up the money for a month's run in a proper Shaftesbury Avenue
theatre. The West End! Here was something to write home about.
When I did write home about it, I assured my mother that her
little boy still had his head screwed on. I had, but if I had shaken
it I might have heard a rattle where the screw was working loose.

Once again, I was the narrator, and Dai kindly stepped
forward to play all the male parts including the Prince of Wales,
for which role he developed a tone so strangled that he put his
vocal cords in jeopardy: he would practise whole speeches with
his teeth locked together, the words emerging only from his
sinuses. So far, so normal. The innovation lay in asking Pamela
Stephenson to join the cast. Pamela had become famous for
the improbable combination of elfin prettiness and comic skill
she brought to the BBC TV show *Not the Nine O'Clock News*.
She liked my script, and from the minute she came on stage
at the first dress rehearsal in her Bruce Oldfield silver dress,
everyone involved on the finance side liked her. It was one huge
love affair all round right into the previews, which were smash
hits. The audience howled and raved every night. I started
regretting not having invested a few grand. Say, ten. Maybe
twenty? I gave cocky interviews, in which I counted chickens by
the squadron. Australian correspondents interviewed me in my
black tie on the afternoon of opening night. Television cameras,
after they had finished circling around Pamela like sharks, waited
for me down corridors. Out in the street, they pointed their
lenses upwards to capture my name. It was up there on the front
of the theatre: my name in lights.

Well, you guessed it, but you can't possibly guess the details. As Count Ugolino tells Dante in the *Divine Comedy*, yes, my death was terrible, but let me tell you how terrible it was. The preview audiences had been a cross-section of the general public, and their manifest delight had led me to believe that the press-night audience would react in the same way. But the press-night audience was a cross-section of the press, plus a cross-section of the backers' families and friends. Naim Attalah, in particular, seemed to know almost nobody except platoons of well-bred English young ladies who said 'Oh, really?' as a sign of enthusiasm. The relatives of other backers seemed to consist mainly of people whose command of English had been only recently acquired. From the moment we started to recite, you could hear a discreet rattle of knuckles cracking from the number of people sitting on their hands. Lines that had earned a gale of laughter on the preview nights now were lucky to get a titter. The first time that I paused for a laugh that didn't come, a violent attack of flop sweat came instead. Under my jacket, the sides of my white shirt were suddenly soaked, and by the end of the first half even my shoes were full of water. During the interval I needed a complete change of kit, and I was already thinking that I might need a complete change of address, not to mention of personality. How had I got myself into this, and other people along with me? It wasn't as if I hadn't learned this lesson long ago. But I had lulled myself into forgetting it, and now, suddenly, there was an even harder lesson to be learned. Pamela and Dai taught it to me. They gave me a lesson in keeping my nerve, and on the whole we got through the evening with a show of confidence. Indeed I thought we had done better than get away with it. There was solid applause at the end, and people 'came around' afterwards to say they thought it was something new under the sun. Rowan Atkinson said that he had been roped in by the impresarios and hadn't expected to enjoy it at all, but he really had. Alas, none of these people were writing the reviews. The press were writing them instead, and the press killed me. The worst review came from James Fenton, who said it was the most embarrassing evening he had ever spent in his life. What made it the worst review was that it was also the best written. I tried to believe that I would have put it more kindly had I been reviewing him, but I had signed up to take my chances in a theatrical event, not group therapy.

The press decided the matter. The word of mouth from the previews was good enough to keep the thing going, but from the second night the audiences started getting smaller. It was a big theatre, so if you had watched a speeded-up film of the auditorium from night to night you would have seen an increasing emptiness seeping down from the gallery to the back of the stalls, and then rolling forward until finally, on the last few nights, only a few of the front rows were occupied. Every night of the run my two brave cast members, when they took up their beginners' positions, would find me looking through the peephole in the front curtain as I counted the house like the quartermaster at Rorke's Drift counting cartridges. To keep the thing running for the promised number of nights, I had started putting my own money into it, chasing bad money with good in the full knowledge I was doing so – and in the full knowledge, also, that the money belonged to my family. Dai was uncomplaining as always, and Pamela was saintly. At the shining start of her career, the last thing she needed was to be imprisoned in a flop. But she went on every night and gave me a continuous lesson in how to lavish everything you have on the people who attend, and to forget those who don't. After all, the fewer tickets you sell, the smaller the number of people who know or care that anything has gone wrong. Among those who did attend were some very intelligent people who told me afterwards, either personally or by letter, that they thought the venture original. These paragons, however, were just a few voices in a mighty show of indifference.

The catastrophe would have been complete if it had not also been the making of me. Had it happened sooner in my life, I would almost certainly have cut and run. But I stayed with it, all the way to the end, even though I accepted quite quickly that the critics had been right. Mark Boxer had warned me even during the triumphant previews that the show was too big to be attractively small but too small to be big: for a ticket costing that much, the West End audience wants to see something that fills the stage. Words alone, no matter how cleverly written, won't do the business. Those critics who had found my political opinions absurd I still thought narrow-minded, but their objections would have been only incidental if I had swept them off their feet. I hadn't done so, and now I was off my own feet – flat on my back, in fact. I retired to Cambridge and made myself useful around the house: always a tacit confession that I was severely wounded. Those in residence did their best not to look accusingly at the man who had robbed them.

Luckily I had other irons in the fire. By their combined glow I could dimly see the way ahead. When the *Paris Fashion Show* went to air, it was watched by an audience that would have packed my West End theatre every night of the week for fifty years. Drewett said we could do a lot more stuff like that, but it would be a full-time job. William Shawn wrote asking me to review Robert Hughes's new book *The Fatal Shore* for the *New Yorker*. If I myself need convincing – and for a while I did – here was evidence that there were things I knew how to do. Surely people would not be asking me to do these splendid things if I really was as incompetent as I felt. Even more encouraging, for the long run, was the growing evidence that there were things I knew how to avoid. The impresario Michael White wanted me to write a screenplay based on *Unreliable Memoirs*. I said I would if I could direct the film. Such a degree of hubris was not unfamiliar to him, but he agreed, and there was a token fee of five thousand pounds to seal the deal. Educated by my West End fiasco, however, I thought again about a project that I wasn't sure I could deliver on, and I gave the money back. White told me that it was the first time anyone had given him back the money. That felt like progress.

But I still felt that the time had come for more demanding pursuits than regular journalism, even if they were less certain. Helping to cut film in the editing room had given me the taste for composition on a larger scale, in more than one dimension. My TV column had got to the point where I was feeling the lack of room when a serious subject came up. When I wrote about the much-derided American series *Holocaust*, and predicted – correctly, as it happened – that its soap-opera qualities might be the very element that would ensure its beneficial effect in Germany, Conor Cruise O'Brien kindly said that I should be writing that kind of thing more often. The implication was that I wasn't writing that kind of thing often enough. Journalism had me trapped with its money. Each year Harry Evans of the *Sunday Times* called a meeting to make a bid for my television column. With rare acumen I always got him to stage the meeting over lunch at the Garrick Club, a notorious stock exchange for Fleet Street gossip. The news that Harry was talking to me was back in Donald Trelford's office before we had finished our dessert. Only after that did I enter into a new salary round with the *Observer*'s corridor-stalkers. I could still convince myself that I was worth what they paid me, but surely the day would come when I would give short weight. My time in Fleet Street reached an unmistakable peak with a brace of Postcard essays I sent back from China. I joined the press corps for Margaret Thatcher's visit to Beijing, where she talked with the Chinese leaders about the upcoming handover of Hong Kong. The two Postcard pieces, one written in Beijing and the other on the flight back to England from Hong Kong, were, from the technical angle, the most taxing efforts I ever pulled off as a journalist. The first one, in its entirety, I phoned back to the *Observer* from the Beijing post office, which had equipment with Alexander Graham Bell's name still on it. Perhaps benefiting from the pressure, the two pieces, which collectively carried the title 'Mrs T in China', were the best writing I could do. I knew as I wrote them that I would never do better in the genre. On the RAF VC-10 from Kai Tak to

Heathrow, I put the draft of the second piece aside for half an hour to write a little play about the tour. Mrs Thatcher and the Downing Street personnel were riding at the front of the aircraft, with the press in the zoo section at the back. The Downing Street people, the Prime Minister included, came back to watch the play. Anne Robinson, in those days still a mere journalist, played Mrs Thatcher. It was a stunning performance, although perhaps not quite as amazing as her current imitation, on *The Weakest Link*, of a woman nothing like as nice as her real self – and, let it be said, more than a touch younger. As Anne's talented voice made the lines I had written swoop, howl, and whine through an authentically Thatcherite *tessitura*, I knew that I would always go back to the theatre, but also that I would never again forget to keep it small, like this: like a cabaret. You have to get the expectations down, not up. Then the words become a plus, a wealthy return on a cheap ticket, and nobody notices that nothing has been spent on costumes and sets. Mrs Thatcher quite enjoyed being sent up, incidentally. She was already at forty thousand feet, and anyway she never minded satire, as long as it was accompanied by abject worship and total agreement.

But the thing about the China trip that would eventually have the most drastic effect on my life was working too deep inside my soul for its implications to be considered yet. The mainland schedule had been crushing, and in Hong Kong we were granted a couple of days to recover the use of our credit cards. ('We're back on plastic,' said one of the female journalists. I wish I could remember her name: she was a poet.) While the tireless Mrs Thatcher bustled around visiting military bases and reassuring the locals that the Communists would behave when they took over or else she would get her friends the Americans to drop atomic bombs on them, we of the press caught up with our real lives. It was my first time in Hong Kong, and after an hour in a foam bath at the Hilton there could be no doubt about what had to be my first destination. I caught a cab out to the Australian Military Cemetery at Sai Wan Bay and visited my father's grave.

I have visited that quiet place many times since then, and after
my mother died two years ago I have even felt able to write about
it, but the memory of that first visit is still clear in my mind.
Down the hill between the terraces of headstones, the long lawn
that tilts down to the sea, I walked to find his name and number.
When I did, I fell to my knees and cried. I cried to heaven, which
never listens, but has the excuse that it never causes anything
either. There is only chance. I cried as I had never cried since
I was very young. It was the dates that did it. Already I was
ten years older than he had been when he was killed. Time to get
something done.

17. NICE BIKE, CAPTAIN STARLIGHT

You will have noticed, during the preceding book, that I was more than once jolted by harsh reality into the feeling that I had not yet achieved anything substantial. But that doesn't mean I skimped what I previously did. I have done my best to give this book a beginning, middle, and end, and now here are a few paragraphs by way of a coda. Clearly another volume will be necessary: more than half my working life was still ahead of me, and it would turn out to be full of stories about the stars, whom I met in great profusion, and not always when they were at their best. If I can't keep the reader interested while I tell stories like those, I won't need anyone else to turn me off at the wall: I'll pull the plugs myself. But the previous chapters contain the story that matters most about the author. These were the years in which I really learned my stuff. Later on I just got a bit better at avoiding the big mistakes. But, as I have tried to show, without those big mistakes I would never have learned anything in the first place. The graph of your increasing profit from your own errors is the only authentic measure of progress.

Everything else is just time passing on the way to death, which has since overtaken quite a lot of people mentioned in this book. Some of them I met only briefly: Lord Bernstein, Lew Grade, Maurice Richardson, Edward Crankshaw, John Weightman, Conor Cruise O'Brien, Bill Grundy, Noele Gordon, Johnny Mercer, William Shawn, Burt Lancaster, Robert Mitchum, Peter Sellers, Richard Burton. Some I worked beside long enough to know their character, and almost always to be grateful for it: Russell Harty, Ken Tynan, Donald Pleasence, Barry Took, Willy

Donaldson, Richard Findlater, Helen Dawson, Charles Monteith, John Wells, William Rushton, Viv Stanshall, Spike Milligan. Others were close to my heart: Jonathan James-Moore, Alan Sizer, Kingsley Amis, Philip Larkin, Terry Kilmartin, Ian Hamilton, Amanda Radice, Mark Boxer, Terence Donovan. In all categories and in every case, I was surprised that any of them should leave without my permission, but I rarely railed at fate. Although I was so annoyed with Donovan that I boycotted his funeral, I still thought that he had had a fair spin. Unless they die young, I hardly notice. Probably I just got too used, too early on, to the idea that living a reasonable span was a luxury, and that the thing to do, as Montaigne once insisted, was to live every day as if you would die tomorrow. I grew up with the Grim Reaper as a house guest. Every night he sat down with us to dinner in the glassed-in back veranda, the stave of his scythe bumping against the plasterboard ceiling. He stank a bit, but he was part of the furniture. I felt old when I was young, and feel young now I am old. I have never had a very well-developed sense of chronology. I just know that the dice roll and the river flows. I didn't know, while the period recorded in this book was going by, that some of the best things in it were already on their way out, never to return.

In Fleet Street, the age of hot metal was coming to an end. I loved the old technology, but there was never any doubt that the new technology would take over, although it took a futurologist to predict that a newspaper office, of all places, would become as silent as an aquarium. Since the spanking new equipment was not only a lot quieter than the clattering junk it superseded but also much lighter and far less demanding of total space, here was a neat example of how an economy, as it expands, actually gets smaller. When the print unions tried to keep the change under their control, Rupert Murdoch saw his chance. He broke the unions and saved the diversity of the newspaper business. If he hadn't done so, London would now be essentially a one-paper town, like New York. But when he broke the unions he broke

Fleet Street as well. Freed from their shackles to the obsolete investment in the Linotype machines and the heavy presses, the newspapers took their offices wherever the rent was cheap, and within a year Fleet Street was no longer a real place. By now it is just a memory.

Roughly the same thing happened to my other great romance, the Modish London Literary World. The hard-core personnel of the Friday lunch became first busy, then successful, then celebrated, then world famous. Just as the venue had moved uptown from Mother Bunch's to the Bursa Kebab House, it moved upmarket from the Kebab House to Bertorelli's in Charlotte Street, and finally it moved from Bertorelli's into limbo, and from there into legend. Like a star that grows more brilliant in its dying days, the Friday lunch had gone nova. Some of the remnants still get together once a year, to make promises, never fulfilled, about meeting more often. But it should be said that the centrifugal forces that eventually pulled the thing apart had nothing to do with ill will. It was lack of spare time that did the trick. Quarrels were always repaired, and still are. The intelligent and the talented always look like a mafia for the simple reason that they value each other's friendship. That was the point that the bunch who came up next had trouble grasping. The *Modern Review* crew thought that our lot had smoothed the way for each other. It was never true. We cared too much about our own integrity, and I, for one, could always count on receiving my fiercest criticism from among my friends. (After he read a serialized instalment of my royal epic, Christopher Hitchens was actually being quite restrained when he said, 'You don't really *believe* all this shit, do you?') In time, the new guard learned that the only road to the top was the one on which the goods are delivered. We could have told them, but they weren't listening. Youth rarely does listen, although the most gifted among the young are invariably those who have the capacity to take a lesson in when it hits them over the head. I suppose this book is meant to prove that I was once like that. I must have had something, or why would I have so often been brought whimpering to my knees?

There is a false equation there, of course. Not everyone who gets knocked out comes back, and some who fail deserve to. But for those who learn in the hardest way that they are not cut out to do the thing they love, there is always the opportunity to do it some service. And for those who can do the thing they love, but who encounter a disheartening setback, there is the chance to rediscover the solid discipline that should always underlie bravura, and which is sometimes eroded by the photon stream of the spotlight. Success can weaken anyone if it goes too long uninterrupted. The muscles go, like an astronaut's in space. The experienced practitioner knows this, and gets more interested in both himself and his craft when the going gets rough. A big crash is just a concentrated version of what is happening all the time as he learns his business. He learns by falling short, and finding out why. Anyone who can write can write better. But he can do so only if he realizes his mistakes. The most common and most destructive mistake is to neglect the simple for the sake of the spectacular. Some of my favourite works of art are stunning for the wealth of their technique. In the garden of the Nymphenburg Palace, the dwarf architect Cuvilliés built a little pavilion called the Amalienburg that is almost too beautiful to look at even in the detail of its decoration, and in its totality almost makes you believe in the inherent virtue of the human race. But the first thing it was designed to do was to keep out the rain. When the writer is licking his wounds after a public disaster, he has been given time to remember what he was put on earth to do. He might one day make history and might even make a million pounds, but the first thing he must do is make sense. Sometimes it helps to write nothing at all for a while, rather than even one more sentence that tries too hard to impress. Let the field lie fallow. After my defeat in the West End, I drifted around the house in Cambridge looking exactly like a zombie. For a while my dead eyes saved me from being asked to carry heavy objects upstairs: what wife wants her new chest of drawers covered with scraps of decaying flesh? But somewhere in the throbbing haematoma that had once been my brain, calculations were being made. It was at this time that I had the first glimmer of the plan, finally carried out twenty years later, to include my own enthusiasm among potential threats to the family finances, and to build in a protection barrier so that I could not get at my own money when hit with yet another idea that would duplicate the effects of the Italian Renaissance while helping to save the baby seals in the rain forest. This train of thought had the merit of putting the family first: a reliable way of getting the emphasis away from myself, and thus partly nullifying the characteristic that had got me into trouble in the first place. People who dress up as Superman don't always jump off buildings under the impression that they can fly, but the costume and the air of superiority are powerful hints that they might. The advantage of having a couple of children scooting around the place is the reminder they offer that you used to be one of them. You used to be a lot closer to your instinct. Whatever creativity you might have developed since, your instinct was where it came from.

The little people in the pixie caps were big enough to have bicycles by that stage. The bikes were second hand and needed a coat of paint. I did the painting. I gave each bike a basic colour – one shade of red for the larger and another shade for the smaller – and then started to embellish this basic coat with little painted stars of silver and gold. There were four-pointed stars, six-pointed stars, and the very rare eight-pointed stars with the peripheral dots. I couldn't stop adding stars until each bike was a candy constellation prettier than a wizard's wagon and the owner was crying with impatience to get on it and ride away. But the owners brought their friends home with more bikes for me to paint. As I kept painting compulsively onward, frosting the spokes with silver and making the seat-post a barber's pole for leprechauns, the anguish of defeat melted. A wrecked project can hurt worse than heartbreak, so it is no wonder that some people give up altogether, even though their talents would have merited another chance. Noel Coward was right when he said that the secret of success is the capacity to survive failure. The failure can hurt so much. But unlike heartbreak, which really is a dead loss, failure has a function. It asks you whether you really want to go on making things. And I wanted to go on making beautiful bicycles. Finally I had made enough of them, and knew it from the moment when, applying silver dots to the perimeter of an eight-pointed gold star, I found myself thinking: I'll write about this one day.